FOR THE SOUL OF THE FAMILY

THE STORY OF THE APPARITIONS OF THE VIRGIN MARY TO ESTELA RUIZ AND HOW ONE FAMILY CAME BACK TO GOD

BY: THOMAS W. PETRISKO

Author of *The Sorrow, The Sacrifice, and The Triumph, Call of the Ages* and *The Last Crusade*

Queenship

PUBLISHING COMPANY
P.O Box 42028 Santa Barbara, CA 93140-2028
(800) 647-9882 • (805) 957-4893 • Fax: (805) 957-1631

CONSECRATION AND DEDICATION

This book is consecrated to the Holy Spirit. May He use it to restore the family.

It is dedicated to my wife Emily's family, the Sanchez family of Philidelphia, especially her mother and father, Martha and Tomas Sanchez and her brothers and sisters; Marcia, Aurea, Toni, Mercedes, Andrew, Gilbert, William Carlos, Gapito, Angel and Thomas Sanchez.

Cover Artist: Gerry Simboli, Simboli Design

©1996 Queenship Publishing

Library of Congress Number # 96-71244

Published by:
    Queenship Publishing
    P.O. Box 42028
    Santa Barbara, CA 93140-2028
    (800) 647-9882 • (805) 957-4893 • Fax: (805) 957-1631

Printed in the United States of America

ISBN: 1-882972-90-2

ACKNOWLEDGMENTS

I am indebted to many people. It is impossible to thank them all. Most significantly, I thank Estela and Reyes Ruiz and their entire family. This is their story, but their humility was truly inspiring. I also want to thank some who were especially helpful with this work: Joe and Bridgette Hooker (editing - Come Alive Communications), Therese Swango, Dr. Frank Novasack, Jr., Robert and Kim Petrisko, Father John Koza, Joan Smith, Sister Agnes McCormick, Carole McElwain, Karen Seisek, Bud McFarlane, Stan and Marge Karminski, Father Luke Zimmer, Father Richard Foley, Michael Brown and Ted and Maureen Flynn. A special thank you to Bob Schaefer and Queenship Publishing for their tremendous support.

I am grateful to many others who helped me by their encouragement and support, especially Father Robert Herrmann, Father John O'Shea, Jan and Ed Connell, Patty and George Pietripola, Georgette Faniel, John Haffert, Rosalie Turton, Joan Ulicny, Anatol Kaszczuk, Tom Collins, Dan Lynch, Denis Nolan, Bernard and Sue Ellis, Father Edward O'Connor, Eleanor Wetzel, Janet Petrisko, Carol Brown, Sister Isabel Bettwy, Tom Rutkowski, Drew Mariani, John and Barbara Marion, Charles Gaffney, George Malouf, Eduardo Esparza, the staff at Family Chiropractic Center, the Pittsburgh Center for Peace prayer group and the Ambridge Holy Trinity prayer group, Amanda Ree, Jim Petrilena, Linda and Audrey Santos, Dominic and Joan Laitteri, Charlie Nole, Josyp Terelya, Carols Pontja, and Joe and Gerry Simboli (cover design).

A big thank you to my mom and dad, Mary and Andrew Petrisko and my uncle Sam. Last but not least to my precious wife, Emily, and my children Maria, Sarah, Joshua and someone new expected in seven months.

ABOUT THE AUTHOR

Dr. Thomas W. Petrisko is the President of the Pittsburgh Center for Peace. From 1990 to 1996, he served as editor of the Center's three Special Edition newspapers, which featured the apparitions and revelation of the Virgin Mary and were published in many millions throughout the world. He is the author of *The Fatima Prophecies —At the Doorstep of the World, For the Soul of the Family – the Story of the Apparitions of the Virgin Mary to Estela Ruiz, The Sorrow, the Sacrifice and the Triumph – the Visions, Apparitions and Prophecies of Christina Gallagher, Call of the Ages* and *The Last Crusade.*

Along with his wife Emily, they have two daughters, Maria and Sarah, a son, Joshua and expect their fourth child in May 1997.

If you wish to have Dr. Petrisko or someone from his staff speak at your church or organization, you may write to:

St. Andrews Productions
6111 Steubenville Pike
McKees Rocks, PA 15136
(412) 787-9735

CONTENTS

Acknowledgments. v
Author's Preface. ix
Foreword. xi
Prologue. xiii
Introduction. xvii
1 - "Medjugorje was Supposed to Take Place". 1
2 - "Little Rey" 9
3 - Dancing with the Devil 15
4 - God, Mary and Family. 21
5 - Two Sides to the Same Coin 31
6 - America: Good, Bad and Very Ugly 35
7 - Power and Prestige. 45
8 - "Let it Convert all the Americas". 53
9 - "Good Morning, Daughter" 67
10 - From Blood to Roses 75
11 - The Woman Clothed with the Sun 81
12 - A Decisive Battle 91
13 - Our Lady of the Americas 99
14 - A Woman Molded to Perfection. 107
15 - "I Want You to Learn to Love Each Other" 115
16 - The Diagnosis 123
17 - Our Lady of Conversion 133
18 - "Like John the Baptist" 147
19 - A Gold Mine of Revelation 155
20 - Pearl Hunting 171
21 - Abortion and the Return of Quetzalcoatl 189
22 - For the Soul of the Family 197
23 - Armando and Fernando Come Home. 211
24 - Tonali 221
25 - Signs of the Triumph 229
26 - The Greatness of God 243

27 - Preparing Hearts............................... 261
28 - A Celebration of Family........................ 271
29 - From Evangelization to Sainthood............... 275
30 - The Top of the Mountain 289
    Epilogue –To the Workers in the Vineyard 301
    Notes... 305
    Selected Bibliography......................... 311

AUTHOR'S PREFACE

This book is not a scholarly attempt to present the history of the apparitions of the Blessed Virgin Mary to Estela Ruiz. I am not qualified to do so. Nor have I ever discerned God's desire for me to attempt to do so. That work remains to be done.

Rather, this book is meant to be a vehicle of conversion. With the Holy Spirit firmly in command, I submit its contents to His desires for each soul that may read it. I make no claim to convert anyone, but pray God will bless this work in a special way so souls, like the Ruizs', will find and know God's love for them.

I am, however, not without bias, for I believe history will show that during this epic period, the apparitions of the Virgin Mary to Estela Ruiz were the primary apparitions of Our Lady in America.

Indeed, I also believe time will show the apparitions in S. Phoenix, Arizona will achieve the same status as some of the great apparitions in church history.

Reyes Ruiz, Emiliy Petrisko, Estela Ruiz and Tom Petrisko.

FOR THE SOUL OF THE FAMILY

This is a true story. I made no attempt to embellish it with any contestable information or exaggeration.

While there are those who will criticize the style it is written in as being not suitable for such serious content, I can only, once again, submit that in my own heart this is what the Holy Spirit desired of me.

Who, more than God, knows how and what this world needs and when. He who knows all sometimes leads us in ways that are mysterious. God bless you dear reader, for after you read this story, I pray you will know exactly what I mean.

Thomas W. Petrisko
November 1, 1996

FOREWORD
by
Richard Foley, S.J.

Estela Ruiz is certainly the most impressive visionary I have so far been privileged to meet. To begin with, she has abundant human charm; this is a natural gift which divine grace, as is always the case, enhances in a most appealing way.

Estela has a grown-up family and is a former career woman with two university degrees. But, besides being cultivated and worldly-wise, she is now, as a result of her mid-life vocation to be Mary's messenger to the Americas and the world, totally dedicated to God's kingdom of holiness and apostolate.

Yet even more impressive than Estela the messenger are the messages she conveys from Our Lady. They are profound, practical, and always lucidly worded. Above all, they are in every detail prefectly in sync with Catholic doctrine. Indeed, I challenge even the most lynx-eyed of critics (as might be expected, these are not lacking) to find any theological inaccuracy, let alone error, in anything coming from this source.

We see in the history of apparitions how the Queen of Prophets unfailingly picks apt human instruments for whatever specific tasks she wants done on earth. Thus, Estela's background fits her ideally for the role of Mary's messenger to both the Americas, since she speaks English and Spanish equally well besides being fully bicultural. Also her computer skills enable her to deal professionally with what might be called her secretarial function of registering and transmitting the words she receives from heaven.

Dr. Petrisko is doing us a great service by bringing Estela and her message to our notice. She is undoubtedly a major prophet for this benighted generation of ours. Nobody could possibly fail to realise that the Americas and the entire world desperately need the precious values and good things of the Kingdom of God. These are here dealt with by our heavenly Mother in messages after message. They focus on such items as prayer, God's universal call to holiness, the all-important status and role of the family, the primacy of brotherly love, God's golden gift of the Eucharist, the key role played by priests and our duty of praying for them.

Fr. Richard Foley
London, England
October 13, 1996

PROLOGUE

NOW IS THE TIME FOR HEROIC SANCTITIY

by Bud MacFarlane

No family can avoid the spiritual and moral challenges of these dark and strangely exciting times. This book will provide spiritual solutions for your family, and if you respond to Our Lady's call, to the families of your friends and relatives.

For the Soul of the Family is the story of the miraculous conversion of the Ruiz family through the apparitions and messages of *Our Lady of the Americas* to Estela Ruiz in South Phoenix, Arizona. I believe this book will be one of the most important ever written about private revelation—if people respond to the call within its pages.

Like our author, Dr. Thomas Petrisko, and like so many other unlikely individuals in recent years, I have been constantly studying and praying for discernment. I have been speaking publicly for over fourteen years about Marian Apparitions as they have occured throughout the history of the Church and especially in this century.

All over the world, the overwhelming evidence of signs and wonders, as well as the frequent and urgent messages of Jesus and Mary (and even God the Father) tell us in no uncertain terms that we are living in those times described in the Holy Scriptures as the End Times. This is the final battle: the Woman of both Genesis 3:15 and Revelations 12 will destroy her adversary, Satan. Our Lady has been re-evangelizing the Church throughout the world by assembling and mobilizing her mighty remnant army of priests, religious, laity. She has even obtained from God her hand-picked

Pope John Paul II, to lead her Son's Mystical Body, the Church, through the Tribulations. She has said he is the Pope about whom she spoke in the Third Secret of Fatima.

As we now live through the final years of this century of sin and the satanic destruction of society, the Prince of Darkness has intensified his attack on the priesthood and the family. This is the evil one's last, desperate effort to fulfill his boast to Jesus that he would destroy the Chruch—a boast which he made in the presence of Pope Leo XIII in 1884.

My wife Pat and I have eleven children. We have educated them in the Faith and have tried our best to fortify and protect each one by our prayers and fasting; yet we have experienced Satan's constant and continuing attempts to destroy our family's faith, unity, love, and peace. In the same way, the families of every single one of our brothers and sisters, friends, and acquaintances have been severely wounded by Satan and also experience constant attacks. For many families, it seems hopeless and they feel helpless in this supernatural battle against the Evil One.

The Ruiz family of South Phoenix was typical of the decline in faith and the inevitable results of the godless, materialistic lifestyle which has ever so gradually enslaved most American families from the 1960's to out present time. Reyes's and Estela were married in 1955 and consecrated all seven of their children to the Immaculate Heart of Mary. Despite Reye's life of total consecration, daily mass and rosary, fasting, and mortification, his children drifted from their faith and even his good wife Estela became obsessed with her teaching career and growing public esteem. She became a nominal, indifferent Catholic who regarded her husband as a boring religious lunatic. Not a fanatic, but a lunatic, because she literally believed that Reyes was insane. Reyes, despite the great suffering his family's loss of faith caused him, and despite the constant ridicule he received from Estela and the children, persevered in his prayer and fasting. He trusted in God and never lost hope. Upon hearing about the reports of apparitions in Medjugorje, Yugoslavia, he made arrangements to go there on pilgrimage for Our Lady's birthday, September 8, 1988.

While there he was inspired to consecrate his family, Phoenix, and America to the Immaculate Heart of Mary. He then implored

Our Blessed Mother to not only convert his wife and children, but also to make them into Saints! His tremendous faith and his entire life of prayer, fasting, and holiness shook heaven as he looked up for help from that mountain top in Medjugorje. God the Father answered his prayers and sent Mary as *Our Lady of the Americas* to quickly convert Estela and all seven children. Then she commissioned Estela as her messenger to all the families in America to be an instrument of God's Divine Mercy. Through Estela, Our Lady brings the good news of how personal holiness and evangelization will save our families and save our country and save our world from the otherwise certain destruction which Satan has planned for us.

Mercifully, our loving Father answered the lifelong prayers of Reyes Ruiz, *"Hail Holy Queen, Mother of Mercy, our life, our sweetness, and our hope. To thee we'cry, poor, banished children of Eve; to thee do we send up our sighs, mourning and weeping in this valley of tears..."* Their miraculous transformation was the sure sign Our Lady's messages to Estela would in similar fashion be capable of converting and bringing peace to every family, and thus to our whole country. Then, potentially, the whole world will follow.

Since 1988, Estela, Reyes and their children have evangelized this good news from Our Lady of the Americas through their travels and the limited distribution of Our Lady's monthly messages.

In order to ensure the rapid and broad distribution of the full story of the Ruiz family's extraordinary conversion, and more importantly, heaven's key messages for all families, God inspired Dr. Thomas Petrisko to write *For the Soul of the Family*. This book is a great gift of the Holy Spirit, a ringing bell of hope and revelation, a brilliant rising sun which will enable us to expel the dark night of the soul of American families, which now lie so close to death.

Thomas Petrisko has captured the essence of Our Lady's foolproof plan for family holiness and peace when he refers to the detailed messages as *"pearls of wisdom"* and a *"veritable gold mine of revelation and truth."* Our Lady of the Americas defines the problems and prescribes effective heavenly solutions. Reyes and Estela are portrayed as ideal role models, not so much because of the great graces they received, but rather because of their courageous response to God's call to holiness and evangelization. Reyes, blessed with great faith, never gave up on his family and never gave up his trust in God's Divine Providence, no matter how hopeless it seemed. Estela readily gave up the career and the fame she had worked so long and so hard to achieve; she responded with great trust and faith in abandoning herself totally to the Will of the Father.

The mission and messages of Our Lady of the Americas are truly on-going Divine Mercy, similar in spiritual richness and revelation to those of Medjugorje. They re-emphasize the Catholic Church's constant teaching that personal holiness, total consecration, loyalty to the Holy Father, and evangelization are the vital and essential means and mission of every member of the Mystical Body of Christ.

You, the reader, are called to this heroic sanctity.

It will be my constant prayer that you will read, study, and quickly distribute *For The Soul of the Family* to every Catholic family in the United States. Let us all be instruments of Divine Mercy and confidently ask God for the opportunity and means to bring about this message of hope and peace to the Catholic Church, to America, and to the world!

Bud McFarlane
July 13, 1996

INTRODUCTION

What has happened to the family? In just a little over thirty years, we can trace a pattern of destruction that has literally left the family, the building block of civilization, in ruin.

Divorce, separation, role - reversal, abortion, contraception and a litany of other factors has caused society to reexamine the family unit.

On one side, there are those who move to accept what has occurred. They call for a redefinition of what constitutes a family and dismiss any fatalistic conclusions.

But on the other side, it is recognized that only in reestablishing the traditional family can the world reverse the staggering social and moral collapse it is now experiencing. Indeed, the fate of civilization is seen to hang in the balance. And no governmental "bandaid" solutions are going to help in the long run.

In early America, our Judeo-Christian heritage formed the basis of the constitution of a new government in a new land. The federal government, along with state governments, moved to solidify the nation by also passing legislation that cemented the family unit in place. Once again, they firmly relied on Christian laws and customs surrounding everything from divorce to homosexuality.

As these laws, and the heritage surrounding them, are now cleverly being replaced and rewritten, it seems the only hope people have is to believe that God's laws still hold precedent. That truly what was believed to be right before was divine in origin. And that no re-legislating of morality can stop God fearing people from believing that in order to save the world from its present course of destruction, we must first move to save the family from its present course of destruction.

The Blessed Virgin Mary comes to the world with this very message. Throughout the world, she is now appearing and calling her children to come back to God, to His laws and to His love.

At Fatima on October 13, 1917, as 70,000 people witnessed the sun plunge from the sky towards the earth in what many felt was the end of the world, the three shepherd visionaries never saw this at all. Instead, they witnessed a series of visions of the Holy Family and the Virgin Mary. Jesus, Our Lady and Saint Joseph all were seen by the three children to be blessing the people while, simultaneously, the crowd awaited destruction.

Today, Fatima experts say that the plunging sun was not just a foretold sign in confirmation of Mary's apparitions. Rather, it symbolically represented the danger the world was moving toward with the coming of the atomic age. It is also believed that the two simultaneous visions symbolized that a choice was available for mankind. A choice between the consequences of sin, which are fire and death eternal (and perhaps in this life too) or life which can be enjoyed, renewed and sustained through the family as blessed by God.

Therefore, the vision of the Holy Family was a message God was giving to the visionaries to accompany what the people were experiencing. The family was to be the answer to the woes that would beset the future of the world.

This book is about what God was warning of at Fatima. One family, the Ruiz's of South Phoenix, Arizona, is held up for us all to see in their anguish and in their destruction. They are an American family that since the 1960's has experienced it all. From drugs to abortion, their sins were destroying them; one by one and as a whole. Yet God, in His infinite love moved to save them.

Through the Virgin Mary's call, the Ruiz's rejected death and came back to life. Their story is a story of hope and faith, of persistence, patience and perseverance. Most of all, it is the story of how one family is to perhaps become an example of how all families can come back to God. Afterwards, not just families, but towns, cities, states and nations are invited to follow suit.

From Our Lady's words, we see that Mary is now especially emphasizing the resurrection of the family in order to restore the world. Not just in her words to Estela Ruiz, but also to her other "chosen ones."

In a message to Father Stefano Gobbi on December 31, 1995, that was granted an Imprimatur by Cardinal Bernardino Echeverria Ruiz, OFM of Ecuador, Our Lady declared,

> *"Above all, spread the family cenacles which I am requesting as a means of saving the Christan family from the great dangers which threaten it. I am the Mother of Life. I am the Queen of the Family."*

Likewise, following as usual in line with Mary's words, *Inside the Vatican* reported in its August - September 1996 edition that the Holy Father is adding a new title to the Litany of Loretto, *"Queen of the Family, pray for us."*

Thus, the necessity of the salvation of the traditional family is not just a political opinion. Rather, the Virgin Mary says it is God's plan for His people. A plan that will help the forces of good combat the forces of evil. And at Fatima, Mary promised that *"in the end My Immaculate Heart will Triumph."*

FOR THE SOUL OF THE FAMILY

CHAPTER ONE

"MEDJUGORJE WAS SUPPOSED TO TAKE PLACE"

The babushka-clad grandmothers who shuffle along the dirt roads and stony paths of Medjugorje seem impervious to the thousands of pilgrims invading their lives. While seldom failing to acknowledge the many strangers with a smile or a wave, the Bubbas scurry along their busy way, usually to and from Saint James' Church for morning or evening Mass. Their daily schedules are fixed between these dutiful visits to Saint James', as the apparitions of the Virgin Mary quickly produced this devotion in the already pious and humble village.

Living century-old lifestyles that provide income and food, the people of this shepherding town tend to their cows, sheep, chickens and goats during the day. Most have little stucco homes with a stable attached and some land for the animals to graze. Some tend to fields of tobacco and grapes, others to prosperous little gardens, while many simply tend to their homes. On summer days, they can be seen resting, as siesta is still a tradition.

While the village of Medjugorje is comprised of several hundred families, it is joined by four other villages that seem to blend into one medium-size town. For hundreds of years, the Church and the faith have been the center of their lives, along with one of their holiest sites of devotion, Mount Krizevac.

This heavily foliaged mountain stands at the rear of the villages and towers thirteen hundred meters high. In 1933, the villagers erected a huge cement cross on its summit in honor of the 1900th anniversary of Christ's death, and it has since become known as "Cross Mountain" (i.e., Mt. Krizevac). Long before the apparitions, Krizevac was a focal point for prayer. This is especially evident by the tablets displaying the Stations of the Cross that are fixed along the steep, rocky path up the mountain. It's a climb that usually takes at least a half-hour to complete.

Once atop the summit of Mt. Krizevac, the view is breathtaking. Though the land is poor and undeveloped, one easily recognizes the Creator's involvement, as waves of colored fields and hills poetically intertwine for miles in every direction. In the distance, mountain ranges with snow-capped peaks are reminiscent of giant natural sentinels, fashioned to protect and surround the priceless terrain. Indeed, it is a spectacle of incredible contrast.

Many travel to this rural hideaway from the ancient Adriatic port city of Dubrovnik. This journey helps to clarify Krizevac's breathtaking view: a collage of limestone alps alternating with intervals of hills, trees and shrub-laden wilderness. With a slight knowledge of history and geography, it is obvious that this terrain is classically Mediterranean. Rich in red soil, oak and maple trees, and an assortment of berry vines, the area has been the same for centuries.

While the terrain surrounding this southwestern village of Bosnia-Herzegovina is certainly captivating, the faces of the people leave the deepest impression. Like the work of a sculptor who carefully accentuates key features, the tanned and deeply-lined countenances of the people consistently prove to be the area's most striking, and most memorable, characteristic.

As if in harmony with the sharply diverse terrain of valleys, hills and mountains, these faces, too, reflect a clear contrast. As most of the older women wear no makeup, their time-chiseled facial lines are deep and numerous. Around their eyes, hundreds of little spider-webbed cracks have been permanently baked in by the sun. Indeed, when these Croatian Bubbas smile, these cracks and crevices seem to unfold like a blossoming rose, somehow revealing their souls. Likewise their teeth, often partly missing, become exposed in grins of joy that stretch into huge smiles of love and compassion.

Their faces reveal the history of the land. While Roman and Greek culture once filled this region, the people are somewhat trapped in a time warp. Their lives reflect centuries of ox-driven carts and little stone homes, while their four official languages (Croatian, Serbian, Macedonian and Slovenian) and two alphabets (Latin and Cyrillic) are further evidence of the village's stagnant condition.

The pace of progress has not left these people completely untouched, however. Some homes are styled according to more modern standards, and many older houses contain western-style kitchens and bathrooms. Likewise, most people own cars, colored Tvs, VCRs, telephones, washers and dryers. Local discotheques are scattered everywhere, and many villagers outwardly reflect western culture by their taste in cigarettes, clothing and hairstyles.

During much of the 20th Century, the Croatian, Serbian and Muslim people in former Yugoslavia found themselves politically enslaved by Marshall Tito's brand of communism. While his particular flavor of oppression was a little less restrictive than neighboring Albania, former Yugoslavians have nonetheless lived fifty years of forced rule and pretentious class struggle. The western part of Bosnia, where Medjugorje sits, is primarily inhabited by Roman Catholic Croats. And often, over the centuries, it has taken violence to ensure their viability.

A bit of insight helps the layman better understand the tough yet sensitive heart-core of these people. During World War II, Yugoslavia was split apart by totalitarian extremists and invading forces. The Nazis occupied the country and nurtured right-wing elements, while Tito led a Marxist force that promoted and enforced the ideals of an atheistic left wing. Out of a population of almost 15 million, 1.7 million were killed. Century-old internal rifts were exacerbated during the wars, all of which have led to the modern-day tensions. Thus, while Yugoslavia was perhaps the most open Eastern block country before the fall of the Iron Curtain, according to Amnesty International, it held the most political prisoners.

Medjugorje is a Slavic word that literally means *"between the mountains."* The neighboring village, Bijakovici, sits at the base of two hills, Crnica and Podbrdo. Like Medjugorje, Bijakovici is a small village of white stone houses, tobacco fields and grape vineyards.

Just like Bosnia itself, these joined villages of Medjugorje and Bijakovici have a curious history of conflicts and vendettas that are rooted in history and blood.

In spite of the internal struggles, however, the Catholic residents of these villages all share Saint James' Church as their place of worship. Saint James' is an oversized church for the region and population. It actually serves the needs of five villages and about 530 families. The curiously large church was built from 1937 to 1969, and during its formation, many people wondered why it was being built so big. Although none could say for sure, one villager supposedly saw the church prefigured in a vision, and he claimed to have seen the Madonna floating above it.

While the roosters crow loud and strong each morning in Medjugorje, the dawn of June 24, 1981 was different.

Indeed, that particular morning was very different. A horrendously violent thunderstorm with lightning, rain and hail blew in with a force and intensity so strong that it frightened even the hearty villagers. Some said it reminded them of Judgment Day, while others paralleled the strange events to prophecies forecasted in The Book of Revelation. Just in case it was somehow of a diabolical origin, one woman fought back by splashing holy water in all directions.

June 24th was a Wednesday, the feast of Saint John the Baptist. At about 4:00 PM, two local teenage girls, Ivanka Ivankovic and Mirjana Dragicevic, were on their way home from a sheep pasture. It was a trip they had made many times before along the rocky path of the hill known as Podbrdo.

Suddenly, Ivanka saw a glowing silhouette. It was a distinct shape. In the center, a young lady in a gray robe, whose face glowed, seemed to materialize.

"Mirjana, look!" cried Ivanka. *"It's the Gospa (Our Lady)!"*

"Don't be idiotic," replied Mirjana.

At first, Mirjana didn't bother to look. But seconds later, she did. And there, before her eyes, she too saw the vision. Together, the girls quickly fled from the sight. When they later returned with others, they discovered it truly was the Blessed Virgin Mary.

The rest is history.

The word spread quickly, and the world came to see. The Communists didn't like it, to put it mildly, so the government persecuted both the children and the Franciscan priests at Saint James,' even going so far as to detain them. Although the local Bishop was at first sympathetic, he quickly evolved into the greatest foe of the apparitions.

Over the years, the supernatural consistently meshed with the natural world in Medjugorje, as over twenty million people from all religions, races and nations came to see for themselves. Many visitors claimed to witness the incredible. Angels, words and figures made of clouds appeared overhead, they said. As at Fatima, the sun danced and changed colors. Some claimed to see the huge thirty-foot cross on Krizevac elevate and spin, all the while glowing fluorescently. Mysterious fires on the hills that would vanish upon close inspection were also witnessed.

The faces of Jesus' and the Virgin were detected on the surface of stones, in the clouds, on the sides of buildings and on flower petals. Others said Mary spoke to them. For a few of the extremely fortunate, the Madonna herself would suddenly appear. Over and over, the Virgin Mary or something unusual would pop up in photographs after many returned home.

As the years passed, reports of the supernatural at Medjugorje continued. But numerous stories of miraculous physical and spiritual healings concurred something unique was transpiring in Medjugorje, something unique in the history of the world itself.

While apparitions of the Virgin Mary have been alleged and verified on numerous occasions throughout the centuries, never before have public apparitions lasted this length of time, as the visionaries (the six privileged young people to whom Our Lady has chosen to appear) attest that she has appeared every day for over a decade. Indeed, the experiences reported by the visionaries have stood firm, defying all attempts to illicit contradiction. Numerous scientific and diagnostic tests have been conducted to rule out the possibility of any deception, and many of them have left the professionals more confused than ever. Hundreds of books have been published about the events in Medjugorje with no end in sight. Reportedly, even the Pope is favorable.

Although skeptics have surfaced, they are relatively few in number. Most prominent theologians and Mariologists have been favorable to the events, methodically disarming and muting critics. Likewise, the Bishop's attempt to deflate the importance of the visions was erased by Rome's calling for a new commission to investigate, which eventually ruled for continued observation of the events which have had such a lasting impression on so many.

But one aspect of Medjugorje has left the deepest mark. Throughout the world millions have returned home permanently changed, their lives newly or more profoundly converted to God. The Virgin's call to prayer, penance, faith, fasting and peace has been deeply internalized and answered by many. New entities called *"Peace Centers"* have cropped up, devoted exclusively to spreading the message of Medjugorje and Marian apparitions. All this has happened in response to the Virgin's requests at Medjugorje to *"live and spread"* her messages.

Ironically, and almost unbelievably, the simple, babushka-clad grandmothers and their big smiles also had something to do with the positive changes effected in so many. Their daily treks to and from Saint James' and their happy faces somehow struck a chord: the pilgrims saw their example and set out to imitate it. One pilgrim, who watched a grandmother making hay, noticed her shining expression and told her, *"How lucky you are to have been born in Medjugorje, in this village chosen amongst all others!"*

"To be from Medjugorje," the Bubba replied with a tone of wisdom, *"is not to be born in the village, but to do everything the Gospa asks!"*[1]

Indeed, it was a revealing statement. For in it, the old woman foretold that all hearts could become a "little Medjugorje" if the Gospa was allowed to fill them.

Back in South Phoenix, Arizona, Reyes Ruiz Senior's life was far from the tremendous peace offered in Medjugorje. Rosary in hand throughout the day, he would continually petition on his family's behalf, all the while asking his best friend, the Blessed Mother, to work the miracle he so needed.

Finally, in 1987, Reyes stumbled across a little newspaper published by a Lutheran southerner named Wayne Weible. The paper was all about Medjugorje, and it instantly inflamed Reyes' heart. Indeed, he immediately knew where he was headed.

Reyes Ruiz had never studied apparitions. He only knew of Mary's visit to Juan Diego in 1531 at Guadalupe, as any other Mexican Catholic did. He didn't care much about Vatican commissions or what their findings might be. He didn't care about Communists, conflicts or skeptics. With his Spanish accent, Medjugorje didn't even sound like Medjugorje when he spoke about it.

All Reyes knew was that it was her, his best friend, and she was really appearing on earth. His beautiful lady, his *"Mujer Bonita,"* had come down from Heaven, and his only desire was to be near her.

For she was the one he had prayed tens of thousands of Rosaries to over the years. She was the one he fell in love with at age seven, the one he talked to every day like a member of his household. She was the one to whom his grandfathers and great-grandfathers had prayed all throughout the days, dropping to their knees in the fields as they worked. For him, Mary's apparitions in Medjugorje were his destiny.

"Medjugorje," Reyes proclaims *"was supposed to take place,"* and he says it as if it were all planned by God just for him.

While he says this without selfishness or conceit, Reyes Ruiz truly believes that Medjugorje was his destiny. He believes this not just because of what would later result in his life, but for what he had always desired in his heart: to be with his Lady, to be with his beautiful lady personally, alone and one-on-one.

Mary had come now. She had come for all of God's children, and Reyes Ruiz Senior knew that he was one of them. He was certain of it. He believed he had a right to see her, too - not with his eyes, but with his heart, with his heavy, burdened heart.

He wasn't after any visible miracles; he only wanted to get close to her. So while she was here, physically on earth at a special moment and place in time, they could talk. They could talk to each other's hearts, which is exactly the reason why Mary was appearing to the world in the first place.

Reyes discovered that the Virgin told the visionaries at Medjugorje that her own heart was also heavy and burdened. Heavy from the sins of her children. Heavy with the secrets of the future. Heavy from the sadness carried in the hearts of her children, like her son Reyes Ruiz.

In fact, from the beginning of her apparitions in Medjugorje, the Virgin often declared that the pain of the world and the frustration of the current times were as heavy on her heart as her Son's crucifixion. Evil covered the planet, she revealed. Satan was now enthroned.

Thus, like so many of her statues, she was indeed weeping for her children.

Reyes Ruiz Senior carried a lot in his soul that late September night of 1988 when he arrived in Medjugorje by bus. And in his mind were a hundred petitions he longed to ask Mary to help out with, petitions for his children and his wife, for cousins, nephews and grandchildren, for his friends and for himself...

But above all, he carried one urgent request in his heart. It was for his youngest son, Little Rey...

CHAPTER TWO

"LITTLE REY"

They called him "Little Rey," but with a physique which strongly resembled that of former NFL lineman William "The Fridge" Perry, his nickname was a gross misnomer. Indeed, a local journalist compared him to a *"camper,"* and pointed out, *"There's nothing 'little' about Little Reyes Ruiz."*[1]

Whether he compared best with a camper or a refrigerator, "Little Rey" was a mountain of a man. But his awesome size was no obstacle to a life of pain. Day in and day out, that was what he endured, and that was what he gave others. Pain. Lots of pain.

But for "Little Rey" it wasn't all that bad. A long time ago, he had become convinced that this was his life. This was what he had to endure to be happy. For his type of pain, the bitter, penetrating pain which accompanied him every moment, was the accepted price he had to pay for living his kind of life.

And what was his "kind of life?" Drugs. Lots of drugs.

Pills, pot, coke, crack - a lifestyle of day-to-day chemical euphoria, complicated only by the depletion of his stash or the unappreciated remarks of those who happened to share his life. Sure, they were family. They cared. But Little Rey was resolutely indifferent to their care. The road he was on was too narrow for him to worry about anyone else's needs, even if they did happen to be his family, even though his life was destroying theirs.

By 1985, Little Rey already qualified as a pro in the deceptive drug game that made his afflicted life so desolate of love. Just twenty-eight years-old, he had been chemically dependent for over sixteen years. Still, he pathetically and blatantly boasted that he did not plan to put an end to his life of drugs. To friends he would brag, *"I'll be seventy years-old and still doing drugs."* Indeed, drugs weren't just a part of his life - they *were* his life.

And for Little Rey, that life took shape around a weak opinion of himself and a family that he believed wasn't there when he needed them.

The only one of four brothers who didn't attend college, Little Rey's life was entrenched in the streets by age fifteen. Feeling much pain, no peace, and a deep need to prove himself, he struggled to find out who he was in his South Phoenix neighborhood where the desperate preyed, and the innocent prayed.

Problems! That's what this section of Phoenix is known for. Big problems. Ugly problems. Violent and deadly problems.

Far from "Mainstreet, USA," this particular area of Phoenix rivals other big city combat zones. In a part of town that doesn't blink as law enforcement helicopters probe late at night with powerful search lights, drugs and theft are part of the local scene, along with random shootings and street wars. Every household reveals a multi-layered legacy of pain and desperation, where finger-pointing is a family pastime.

The Hispanic community that dominates this impoverished part of the city has seen hundreds of "Little Reys" recklessly emerge, and then disastrously submerge into misery and despair.

Likewise, the town's subculture of drug dealers and gang rivalries is no secret. Falling victim to racial prejudice and language barriers, South Phoenix's Hispanic youth face an inevitable uphill climb in life.

According to some, that climb is complicated by the state's educational philosophy of "immersion," a system that forces Spanish-speaking kids to learn their "three R's" in English. Thus, from early on, many Hispanic children are taught little that they can actually comprehend, which leaves them educationally deprived and feeling as though they have mastered nothing... nothing except despair.

In futility, many South Phoenix kids quickly master crime. Like millions of other children who are betrayed by television and false heroes, they search for their identity by establishing themselves in their *"hood."*

For Little Rey, that identity centered around life in a gang.

His day-to-day schedule was far from status quo. Hanging out, picking fights and doing drugs was the program. But Little Rey didn't perceive this troublesome lifestyle as being on the edge; in fact, he enjoyed it. Instead of frightening him, drugs and the streets were his oasis of peace.

At the time, other members of the Ruiz family were also experiencing their share of growing pains. Little Rey's three brothers - twins Armando and Fernando, and oldest brother Isidore - were breaking away, and were just too old to relate to him anymore. Although Little Rey remembers looking up to them, they were heading off in their own directions and out of his life.

His father, Reyes Senior, was busy trying to make ends meet for the large family that included sisters Becky and Rosie, and youngest member Tony, whom they had adopted. Around the same time, his mother, Estela, was forced to direct much of her attention to her ailing mother. This turned out to be regrettable for more reasons than one, as Reyes Senior had to pick up more of the slack, and Little Rey was left to make sense of all the remaining pieces.

In retrospect, the circumstances that led to Little Rey's downfall

Estela and Reyes Ruiz with youngest son Tony Valverde.

seem blatantly clear. Back then, however, they were not. The Ruiz family had problems, but they were always close. While arguments and a lack of respect for each other did dominate at times, divorce between Reyes and Estela was never an issue. They were committed as a family. And most importantly, God was present in the home.

Indeed, long before Medjugorje, Reyes Senior was no stranger to religion. A daily Mass attendee for over thirty years, Papa Reyes awoke to his Rosary. Often it was tightly secured around the top of his head, like a sweatband worn at night. Images of Jesus and Mary canvassed their home, while Sunday church for the family was the rule.

Most importantly for Reyes Senior was the fact his best friend was watching over his family. His closest confidant since childhood just happened to be the Blessed Virgin Mary, and he trusted that she could certainly keep an eye on the kids even when he couldn't.

But none of that meant much to Little Rey. He wasn't into "religious" stuff. With his mother and father busy, the streets beckoned and the Virgin couldn't put a leash on him.

Fortunately, the gang he entered was "minor league"; that is, his early agenda centered mostly around being "*cool*," and experimenting with different things to get high, things like marijuana and alcohol. However, he soon found out that booze wasn't his bag. His father never drank, and liquor just didn't excite him.

However, for little Rey, smoking dope did.

His introduction to pot happened early when, at the local parochial school, a friend quickly showed him the ropes. Seventh graders who craved their after school "joint" would gather behind a chicken coop at the church's Convent, unbeknownst to the nuns who harbored little idea that the final bell signaled "party time."

Little Rey's very first marijuana cigarette was opium laced, and getting high soon became a ritual. After that first "joint," he says his mind was made up. *"I think I want to do this for the rest of my life,"* he vowed. It was not a hollow promise.

For Rey, marijuana was love at first sight, and his best friend was not about to let him forget it.

Sidekick, Bucky, was always operating in a higher gear. Together, their experiences quickly multiplied. And it wasn't a matter of desire or preference; their good times centered around availability. If a drug was available, Bucky and Little Rey did it.

Bucky didn't secure his "stuff" from invisible friends. This twelve year-old had connections that even the big boys would envy.

About a year or so after his first encounter with pot, Bucky introduced Rey to downers right in the middle of a junior-high classroom.

Flaunting a bag of "reds" just inches away from the presiding teacher, Bucky invited Little Rey to try yet another experiment, and of course, Rey couldn't refuse. As he eyed the bag, he still recalls his thoughts: *"Well, you know what? I'm going to have to try this stuff. I'm going to have to try everything that comes at me at least once so I can find out what I want to do."*

For Little Rey, it was a philosophy he would embrace for years, with every new pill that came his way. And there would be all kinds of pills: big ones and little ones, downers and uppers, reds and yellows. You name it, he swallowed it.

Little Rey's relationship with illegal substances didn't stop with his own personal habit. Soon, he went into business - the drug business. He had no choice. In his world, selling and using went hand-in-hand, like two sides of the coin that was needed to buy into the game. And this was a game that many kids needed to play just in order to survive.

Reys dad kicked him out at nineteen, after stumbling across some pot under the car seat. But ejection from home was a gift in his eyes, for his new freedom allowed him to indulge his cravings and deal drugs all day long. With his exile, Rey soon discovered himself in drug paradise.

Indeed, his hands were never empty.

Besides the downers, Little Rey was no stranger to hashish, quaaludes, amphetamines, peyote, mescaline, cocaine, mushrooms and other substances that bore no name or definition. Day after day, night after night, Rey sniffed, snorted, smoked, dropped, popped and injected.

By his teenage years, Rey smoked weed every day. It was his *"main thing,"* along with reds and tequila. Seven nights a week was the program. But as time went by, Little Rey felt he needed more *"peace,"* a deeper, better peace. He wanted, he insisted, a longer-lasting peace, a peace he could *"maintain forever..."*

It was a woman who turned Rey on to heroin. Her addiction was in its tenth year, and she couldn't break loose. Instead she broke in new partners, young drug aficionados willing to try anything at least once.

Rey listened to her stories about the big H and knew he couldn't violate his own commandment. *"Well, I got to try this...at least once, and see how it feels,"* he remembers telling to himself.

Little Rey harbored no fear of syringes. To him, *"needles were nothing,"* as he had trained to become a medical technician. In fact, he harbored no fear of anything at all.

He had to do it, he decided, for the peace - the peace only drugs could give him.

"Well, you want to try it now?" she coaxed.

With a life that consistently vacillated between intoxications of anguish and peace, Little Rey decided to strap on his boots and join the war that narcotic veterans insist is against a demon, a demon who seeks to turn fun-filled days of getting high into agonizing flirtations with death.

And so he went forward. After shooting his girlfriend up, Rey placed the heroin in a spoon and cooked some for himself. Absorbing it into a cotton ball, he then sucked as much of it as he could into the syringe and handed the needle to her. A moment later, Rey says, he felt *"automatically drunk."*

For some heroin users, the thought of overdosing or dying does cross the mind. But not for Little Rey. He was twenty-two years-old, and not a novice to risk. Accidents, overdoses, death - these concerns had all been previously processed and quickly removed. For Rey, talk of death induced humor, not caution.

By the time Rey mainlined heroin, he also had other new friends. These were friends more advanced, people who shared his creed and lived the deed. They were pros, the ultimate victims: battle-weary drug addicts who cradled their addictions to themselves, the kind of people whose days are filled with tears, pain and sorrow, but never sorrow to the point of regret.

To these poor souls, the high is heaven, the peace as if from God. But it is also a world of dire thoughts and deeds that drain every last drop of hope.

For these are people whose mornings, afternoons and evenings blur together, victims lost in time who know little love, few smiles, and no escape.

CHAPTER THREE

DANCING WITH THE DEVIL

While Little Rey's flirtation with heroin fortunately didn't stick (he shot up twice, concluding that puking from the high was not for him), his new friends did stick, and their numbers grew.

By that time, Rey had better connections, important connections. His inner circle consisted of about five comrades who were always available to service his needs. These were both pals and business partners.

Indeed, down on Sunland Street in South Phoenix, the action was fast and smooth. It was a dealer's derby, with everyone out in the open. The logic was simple: you can't make a sell if customers can't find you.

Little Rey understood the turf. Hidalgo — Fourteenth Avenue — Pecan Street. If you wanted to get high, this was where you went.

Likewise, when Little Rey shopped, he now purchased ounces and grams,not joints and lines. He needed quantity for convenience's sake. Some stuff, like hashish, was a great high, but too expensive. Rey liked to get high often, so he couldn't afford the good stuff. *"Rich man's taste,"* he would say," *but poor man's means."*

By now, Rey also had a new daily routine.

After washing his face in the morning, he would smoke a *"bong"* for breakfast (a pipe full of hash or marijuana). With that, he was out the door to get high or make a deal. His agenda wasn't complicated. He consumed, purchased or sold drugs every day, all day.

But although Rey seemed comfortable with his life, he knew he was on a fast track. Deep inside, he sensed he wasn't in control.

Somewhere in the crevices of his mind, he felt a cliff was waiting for him.

He just didn't know where.

He was right.

By the mid 1980's, his fear manifested itself. It's name? CO-CAINE. And with it came CRACK. Indeed, dangerous times were now at hand. And Little Rey began to walk the tightrope.

Slowly he began losing his grip. He found that his cocaine habit involved a deeper and deeper hunger, not like his marijuana life. Indeed, he now sensed a need to feed a beast that was inside him; for with cocaine, his guts begged for more and more. Money also became more of a problem, as the coke was far more expensive than the weed. And then there was the fact that Little Rey liked to fire up *"eightballs,"* mixtures of 3^1/$_2$ grams of cocaine and heroin that he would smoke until he dropped. At three hundred bucks a pop, one eightball amounted to only a single night's consumption for the big fellow.

And then one evening it happened. He refers to it as the *"experience,"* the moment that shocked him to his senses... at least temporarily.

Around midnight, after purifying some crack, Rey shoved the dope into a special pipe and drew a hit. Then another hit, and another and another.

For the next six hours Little Rey smoked crack unceasingly. If the pipe emptied, he refilled it. Over and over, hour after hour, he treated himself to an all-night crack-smoking smorgasbord. Around 6:00 AM, he was left in a state of terror.

As the sun rose above the horizon, Rey found himself uncontrollably shaking and sweating. His lips, tongue, and mouth were blistered and swollen. And he was in trouble, serious trouble.

Soaking wet from perspiration, his catatonic drug state left him unaware that, for hours, he was inhaling pure flames of fire, flames that charred his throat and even his lungs.

Scared out of his mind, he stormed out of his house and hurled his crack paraphernalia into the asphalt parking lot behind his backyard fence. His fear awakened him, for he sensed he was flirting with death.

"I can't do this anymore, I can't smoke crack anymore," he admonished himself nervously after destroying his glass pipes.

But it was a pathetic triumph. For in his moment of rage, he still clutched to the hand of the enemy as he added, *"From now on, I'm just going to snort this stuff..."*

It was now 1987. And although Little Rey no longer used heroin and crack, nonetheless he was hooked, hooked on getting high and on blasting his brain, hooked on a life of danger and despair, with no light at the end of the tunnel.

Indeed, by now, nothing mattered - not getting busted, not family, not friends, not women. Nothing. But something strange was about to occur.

While the year of 1987 saw both Pope John Paul II and Mother Teresa of Calcutta, India, come to Phoenix, Arizona, God permitted a visitation by someone else to Little Rey.

Early in the year, Little Rey broke his foot. While being treated, he suffered a setback that scared him; scared him about the life of drugs he was leading. After this experience, he decided he needed to get help for his addiction.

He entered Saint Luke's, a rehab hospital for detoxification. And one afternoon during the second week there, it happened. He had a dream like he had never experienced before. It was a dream, he says, from God. Later, he would insist he wasn't really asleep.

In the dream, Little Rey found himself entering a room. It was a room of sin. All types of sensual pleasures were taking place before his eyes. There were people doing drugs, some were drinking and others were indulging in a bloody ritual of murder. All kinds of sexual acts were also occurring in the open, with no limitations or inhibitions.

In his mind, Rey says he became ecstatic. Except for the bloody attack being made on the woman, the sights enthralled and enticed him. As he walked through it all, he hoped to become involved. And he did.

Out of nowhere, a beautiful woman appeared walking toward him. She was almost perfect in every way. Voluptuous and very sexy, he recalls.

The woman guided him to a private room. In the room, they stood together as she began to caress him. As Little Rey started to become sexually involved with her, he suddenly could see that her face was physically changing. In seconds, the beautiful Lady became transformed before his very eyes into an ugly beast.

Pulling back from her face, as he had been kissing her, he was given the most shocking of realities.

It was Satan himself that he was embracing in love. Truly, he was dancing with the devil.

The demon then spoke to him. *"You...are mine. You are mine..."* Laughingly, the demon persisted, *"You are mine!"*

"No...No!" cried Little Rey in horror. *"...I am not yours!" "I am not yours!!"*

"You are mine!" the devil repeated over and over, in a tone that sent shivers through Little Rey.

Struggling to escape the clutches of the devil, a profusely sweating Little Rey awoke from the vision. Immediately, he realized it was not just a dream. It had been, he says, truly some kind of an experience with Satan himself.

For days, Little Rey remained in terror, physically shaking and crying. He even disclosed the experience to his family, begging for their prayers.

But by then, the rest of Ruiz family were heading in many different directions, each one going about building his own little "kingdom," and dealing with their own dreams and nightmares. Oldest brother, Isidore, moved to California. While brothers Armando and Fernando were becoming big-time politicians. Even Mama Estela was climbing up the ladder; earning a Master's degree while pulling down a hefty salary as a school administrator. It was a family on the move.

People attempted to help Little Rey. People tried to talk to him. His mother would never quit asking, *"Mi hijo (my son), how come you're doing these things? How come?"*

But for the most part, family members distanced themselves from Little Rey. Indeed, everyone was just holding their breath, as if waiting for the inevitable to happen.

Little Reyes Ruiz continued on the move too. His drug business flourished, with crystal amphetamine his latest high. And despite his daily habit, Rey somehow even managed to hold down a job as an ambulance driver.

Like something out of a slapstick comedy, he says that his work *"was the best time to get high."* And if someone was dying in the back of the ambulance? It meant nothing! *"You don't worry about dying. Not your own death or anyone else's, because it doesn't matter - not your pain, not their pain, none of it matters. None of it!"*

Indeed, Rey even witnessed one of his friends die while smoking crack, only to be somehow miraculously revived through CPR. Moments later, they immediately began smoking crack again.

By 1988, Little Rey's father was a desperate man. An assortment of evils including power, politics, drugs and money had invaded his home. Those evils even included a gun battle fought and survived by Little Rey one night, which Reyes Senior knew nothing about.

While the family patriarch prayed his Rosary all day long, he sensed his world was caving in. The family he loved so much had fallen astray, into danger. And this danger he knew could become deadly for Little Rey.

Reyes Ruiz Senior knew he needed a miracle to bring them back. A big miracle. A miracle which, he believed, only his best friend could provide.

And so for him, it was not a difficult decision to journey to a Yugoslavian hamlet named Medjugorje... Even if it was almost 5,000 miles away. For in Medjugorje, Reyes Ruiz Sr believed, there had to be an answer to his prayers.

FOR THE SOUL OF THE FAMILY

CHAPTER FOUR

GOD, MARY AND FAMILY

Steeped in wisdom and led by God Himself in every step, Reyes Ruiz can be likened to a modern-day Abraham. An assortment of adjectives apply to him, all positive and worthy of his being: kind and loving, wise and discerning, confident and careful, strong, yet humbly insecure. He is not a contradiction in terms; he is all these things combined.

But above all, his friends will tell you, Reyes is a rock. When his strength begins to wane, he quickly turns to God to bolster him. When his mind becomes confused and overwhelmed, he petitions the Virgin to help him. In times of uncertainty, he clings to the recitation of his Rosary until sleep beckons to end his day. He struggles, at times, like a true warrior. But each day is a victory, a victory for Reyes himself, and a victory for God.

Thus, with his spiritual armor, Reyes Ruiz resembles many Old Testament heroes. He has complete faith in everything he says about God and the Blessed Virgin Mary. In the eyes of Reyes Ruiz, another parting of the Red Sea would be no great surprise. Undaunted in his faith, his attitude is one of admonition toward those who may doubt.

The son of Mexican immigrants, Reyes' heritage clearly becomes him. He is considerably dark-skinned, with shiny, jet-black hair that he combs straight back. Like the villagers of Medjugorje, his face reflects a life of joy and hardship with its deep, weathered lines.

While his hands and eyes are constantly in motion, it would be inaccurate to say Reyes is a nervous type. He is not nervous. His non-stop activity reflects an energy, an enthusiasm which makes one feel as if Reyes is about to explode with life. And that great life within him is usually derived from, and nurtured by, his constant conversation and communion with God.

In spite of his active exterior, Reyes is a genuinely peaceful man. He is a man who can easily pull up a chair, place his Rosary between his teeth, and make himself comfortable with almost anyone.

And before any more is said, one must understand about Reyes and his Rosary.

Like his arms and legs, Reyes' Rosary is almost an appendage of his body. It would be misleading to say Reyes "prays" his Rosary. Rather, he lives it. He lives it and he works it, almost like a classical pianist who can't break away from the feeling which his fingers create on the keys.

Indeed, Reyes is always doing something with his Rosary. He wrestles with it, massages it, pulls it and bites it. He stretches it and squeezes it. He kisses it. At night, he wears it. It is something that must be dealt with before he can shake someone's hand. At dinner, it's next to his plate and silverware. When he speaks, it becomes a focal point. Like a conductor whose baton is an extension of a certain pace, rhythm and feeling, it is almost as if Reyes uses his Rosary to direct and synchronize the words which flow from his mouth.

Reyes rises early in the morning to start to work the beads. But somehow, by late at night, he still hasn't finished. This phenomenon occurs daily. Indeed, Reyes only stops reciting Hail Mary's when he is eating or speaking, two activities he would have you believe deprive him of his daily prayer quotient.

Upon meeting Reyes for the first time, his fellow pilgrims journeying to Medjugorje that September were probably both awed and perplexed. A dual thought crossed their minds.

On one hand, it was apparent that Medjugorje and Reyes Ruiz were meant for each other, like bread and butter. On the other hand, they wondered what this soul could possibly find in Medjugorje that it did not already possess.

Without a doubt, Reyes probably attended more Masses and prayed more Rosaries than the entire group of pilgrims had done in their lifetimes. And certainly, Reyes Ruiz wasn't looking for faith. As a faithful servant, he had long ago pledged to serve his Master.

Indeed, Reyes Ruiz Senior was a soul seeking only to reflect his Creator's perfection, just as Scripture had invited him to.

But to Medjugorje, Reyes Ruiz journeyed. God had sent for him. Perhaps the outside world was puzzled by his zeal, but as far as Reyes was concerned, his was a journey like Saint Paul's trip to Damascus. There were things like Providence and destiny involved. In the book of Ecclesiastes, God reveals that there is an 'appointed time for everything and a time for every affair under the heavens.' Reyes' mission to Medjugorje fell under the banner of this truth.

His time had arrived.

Thus, the journey was important to both God and His servant. Like all mystical encounters, it had been preordained, and it had to be fulfilled. Reyes Ruiz, from all eternity, had been commissioned to Medjugorje, and he knew it. He knew it even before there was a Medjugorje. And, one suspects, God knew it before there was a Reyes Ruiz.

And so, with an open mind, much love for God and the Virgin, his Rosary in hand and many intentions on his heart, Reyes traveled to Medjugorje. His faith-filled journey was inevitable. God had sent for him. It was a trip that would change his life, and that of his family, forever.

As it is evident that Medjugorje and Reyes Ruiz were spiritually made for each other, the culture, history and geography of the country were also more than just compatible to him.

The rural hamlet of Medjugorje, in fact, was strikingly similar to Reyes' homeland, though Bosnia's Mediterranean terrain contained more foliage. Medjugorje's humble, agricultural lifestyle, coupled with a strong religious heritage, touched a familiar place in Reyes' heart.

Almost immediately, the village felt like home to him, with its little trails, the loving people, the mountains, the hills and the church. With a family history of Catholicism going all the way back to Our Lady of Guadalupe's 1531 appearance in Mexico, Reyes was instantly comfortable in Medjugorje due to its strong commitment to the faith, the Church and the Virgin.

Reyes soon learned the origin of that commitment.

Indeed, the faith in Medjugorje is strong, strong and tested. Like the Irish, Polish and Hispanic cultures, Croatian Catholics in Bosnia have weathered many storms, both natural and man-made. The village of Medjugorje has historically been committed to the Church and the Virgin. Not only is this found in recorded history, the Virgin confirmed it herself, right from the start of her appearances.

When asked by the visionaries why she chose Medjugorje, Mary responded it was because the faith *"was strong."* In fact, some say the Way of the Cross is part of the reason why the deep lines are permanently etched in the people's faces.

Likewise, since as far back as the Twelfth Century, religions and cultures have clashed in this area of the Balkans. Like Mexico's bloody history of Aztec human sacrifices and later Spanish atrocities, Bosnia has weathered religious crusades and Turkish invasions, all of which have tested and fortified the faith of its victims.

Over the centuries much blood has been shed, and much suffering has been endured. Through it all, however, the Franciscan priests and nuns stationed in the area have shared the people's sorrows and nurtured hope. As bishops, teachers and doctors, they have provided the necessary courage and morale, just as they had in Mexico. It was to the Franciscan church in Tlaltelolco that Juan Diego hurried that beautiful morning of December 9, 1531, when he first saw Mary. And it was near the Franciscan church of Saint James that the Medjugorje apparitions began in 1981.

Bloody trials. Suffering peoples. Inherently loyal churches. Apparitions of Mary. Franciscans around the world had seen these phenomena, and had taken part in the miracles and the struggles. It was as if the Franciscans were an advance party sent by the Virgin to prepare her way. And now, like so many others, Reyes Ruiz was the faithful servant being called by the Virgin to complete another of her many tasks.

While Reyes couldn't imagine what was to come, he was not oblivious to divine intervention as he shuffled along the dirt paths of the tiny rural village. He felt his calling, his calling to this little piece of heaven on earth.

Medjugorje! Like an exhilarating breath of fresh air that fully satisfies the body's hunger for oxygen, many claim that it's a spiritual sigh like nowhere else in the world. Indeed, those who have visited there say that every soul should experience the deep spiritual enrichment which Medjugorje offers. Like a mystical umbilical cord that connects earth with heaven, Medjugorje has nourished many with its heavenly peace.

And Medjugorje, with its peace, was now surrounding Reyes Ruiz. Indeed, it was the perfect place for a soul like his. Reyes couldn't get enough of it.

In church, Reyes cried. But that is nothing unique. Almost everyone who goes to Medjugorje cries in Saint James' Church. People cry and cry and cry. Tears are followed by more and more tears. The incredible surroundings, and the penetrating presence of God, lead many to cry, to think about their lives, and then to cry some more. In fact, many can't stop crying, not because of their pain, but because of how good it feels.

But "Medjugorje crying" is unique. It is different. It's the kind of crying that empties the mind and then the body, and finally the heart and soul. It flushes out the bad, and stirs up the good. It knocks on the door of each person's heart, helping to open up the places which have been locked up for so long.

Most of all, Medjugorje tears rouse up, and purge out, past sins, regrets and pain. The tears help to reconcile the memory of dead loved ones long missed and still longed for. Maybe thoughts of the words that were said, and regretted, come to mind, or perhaps words which one never had time to say. Some say the finger of God seems to touch each soul who steps into Saint James' Church. Inner memories are somehow "switched on," beginning a spiritual and emotional roller coaster ride which often leads to exhaustion, fatigue and emptiness.

But then it happens. Out of nowhere, it happens. A deep feeling of refreshment and happiness fills the soul. One senses exhaustion, but with it comes satisfaction and a triumphant awareness of God previously unacknowledged. And then, one realizes, an exhilarating feeling of peace has filled the heart, overwhelming and consuming it entirely.

It is His peace, God's Peace!

Gone now are all sorrows, regrets and pain. With each tear that falls from the heart to the eyes, down the face and into an abyss another memory is dismissed. The past is truly dead and only the future and eternity await. The tears are not isolated and personal, but rather, they consume generations and histories. A genetic healing that transcends the physical often appears to occur, which is why the Queen of Peace wears her crown and proclaims such a title at Medjugorje.

During his week-long pilgrimage, Reyes Ruiz never sat alone in Saint James. Oh, there were the others from the pilgrimage, like Rebecca and Dr. Neil. But there were also those who hadn't come on any plane, who only Reyes knew were present. They were friends whom he had secretly brought along, friends whom he couldn't possibly have left behind in Arizona. For all his life he never left them anywhere. Indeed, to travel to Medjugorje without them would have been unthinkable.

Back in the rear of Saint James, Reyes Ruiz sat quietly with his father, Isidoro, and with the departed souls of four generations of family members whom he personally knew from so many stories.

The son and grandson of Mexican farm workers, Reyes grew up in Virden, New Mexico, during the 1930's, the oldest of twelve brothers and sisters. When Reyes was just seven years old, his father, Isidoro, was run over by a car while he was on his way to work in the fields. He was 33 years of age. Reyes deeply felt his father's death, and it became the turning point in his young life.

Reyes became angry with God. It was a deliberate anger, a deep anger, an anger he believed God deserved. To fill the void left by his father, he fell in love with a beautiful lady, a lady from Heaven. It was to be a romance which would last forever. By age thirteen, Reyes insists that he was *"totally in love with her."*

In Mary, he found the release for his pent-up emotions. In Mary, Reyes found himself again. Mary understood, he believed, and she would talk to God for him. She could talk to God about his disappointments and his anger. She could talk to God about his father, the father he missed so badly.

While his father's death deepened his love for the Virgin Mary, it was his mother's side of the family which nurtured his spirituality. The Villalba family was steeped in generations of slaves for the Virgin. Born in the mid-1800's, Reyes' great grandfather, Teofilo Bejarano, had a special commitment to the Blessed Virgin. Like Reyes, his every moment revolved around service and devotion to Mary until he died in 1947 at age 86. Indeed, great grandpa prayed Rosaries, lots of Rosaries. All day long he prayed Rosaries.

Likewise, the prayer life of the entire family revolved around the Rosary. Since there were no Churches specifically for Mexican-Americans to attend back then, Reyes' first Holy Communion was made at home. In fact, it wasn't until age fourteen that he even stepped into a church.

Mother. Grandmother. Grandfather. Great-grandfather. Greatgrandmother. Like the respected family members of ancient Hebrew tribes, these were the religious elders of Reyes' times. Priests were far and few. Thus, his family members were the teachers of the faith. And with a dozen or more of them crammed into a small two-bedroom house, Reyes' home was his church, and vice versa.

Out in the fields, where migrant workers picked watermelons, cantaloupes, tomatoes, onions and corn, Reyes' relatives set up their shrines. Like an outdoor sanctuary, pictures of the Virgin hung at each end of the field, and indeed, throughout the entire farm. As busy as beavers one moment picking crops, grandmother Anastacia Villalba, and great-grandfather Teofilo, would drop to their knees as their work drew them near the devotional images. And not just prayer would flow, but holiness. Over and over, at the end of each row of crops, this reverence would be repeated. All day long, every day, year after year.

The prayers were beautiful, Reyes recalls, beautiful and fromthe-heart. They were prayers filled with love, like the angels are said to sing to the Virgin. And it wasn't just that way in New Mexico. These devotional practices had been part of the immigrant worker's day for many, many years in Texas, Arizona, and many parts of Mexico.

But it was the Rosary which the family prayed the most. Everyday, beginning at 4:30 a.m., the Our Father's, Hail Mary's and Glory Be's would commence. And from sunrise to sunset, they never ceased. In Reyes' family, an average day was 16 hours in the fields, 16 hours of picking crops, talking and praying to the Virgin of Guadalupe.

For Mexican-American families, no words can describe the Virgin of Guadalupe's importance. Proclaimed *"The Queen of the Americas"* by Pope Pius XII on October 12, 1945, she is the centerpiece of every Mexican's Catholic and ethnic pride.

After work, relaxation included chopping wood and sitting down to, once again, pray the Rosary. Late at night, with four or five bodies nestled together in one bed, Reyes would often awake to find his great-grandfather staring into space and, of course, praying the Rosary. Perhaps the particular day had been short on prayer, and a few hundred more Hail Mary's were in order.

Reyes remembers Our Lady of Guadalupe since early childhood, as a statue representing her stood at the entrance to the farm. He also remembers that his mother and grandmother were likewise devoted to Our Lady of Mount Carmel and Our Lady of Fatima. Nonetheless, the Virgin of Guadalupe was definitely Reyes' favorite. Her dark complexion, he admits, helped him with a complex he had from youth about the dark color of his own skin.

By age thirteen, Reyes had developed a deep spirituality. Mary crafted her work within him, and he loved her like a real mother. He could talk to her, and she would understand. He could sing to her, and she would listen. He could paint her, and she would smile. Mary became his brother and sister, his mother and father. It was a strong, trusting friendship.

As Reyes grew older, he learned to fast, especially during Lent, and Mary and God grew closer to him than ever before. Although he went through some growing pains, his commitment to her never ceased.

In 1955, Reyes married Estela. As the years passed, seven children came their way. Indeed, Reyes had his work cut out for him, but he was trained by the Virgin and the Lord for the challenge. After learning brick laying, Reyes traveled to Phoenix to find work. He built his own house, and tried to raise his kids the best way he knew: with love, prayers, daily Rosary, and the Mass. The family even found a real church to attend. Reyes consecrated all of his children to Mary.

In the 1960's, the Catholic Cursillo Movement, a trend growing in momentum at the time, strengthened the faith. His family grew. Reyes began to work as a contractor and both his life and family were beautiful and happy.

But then, something strange happened.

During the '60's and '70's, his children started school, and soon problems and trouble followed. They all set out in different directions, and even became outright rebellious at times.

For Reyes Ruiz, Sr., it was all a mystery. The kids received a warm family upbringing. They were raised with God. They went to college, and so, Reyes thought, they should have been happy. They should have been thankful and content he figured, but they weren't.

Indeed, Reyes Ruiz's family was in a struggle, and Little Rey wasn't the only one affected. All of them, each family member in his own way, was in the struggle of a lifetime.

Likewise, something strange was happening throughout America. Kid's weren't just growing their hair long. They weren't just opposing their parents and the Vietnam war. They seemed to be downright opposing God. It was a spiritual rebellion and the Ruiz family was just a microcosm of it all.

Back in the rear of Saint James, Reyes Ruiz sat quietly with his secret friends. Surrounded by so much peace, and so much faith, he couldn't help but ponder it all.

And he couldn't help but wonder. Was there any hope for his family against such great odds? Was there any hope for America? Was there any hope for the world?...

FOR THE SOUL OF THE FAMILY

CHAPTER FIVE

TWO SIDES TO THE SAME COIN

Reyes Ruiz had much more than his son, Little Rey, on his mind as he spoke to Our Lord and Our Lady in the back of Saint James' Church. While Little Rey undoubtedly needed lots of prayers, Reyes' heart was full of many other intentions which he whispered quietly and repetitively to his celestial listeners.

Reyes was praying to drive out the demons. Indeed, he was praying for an end to the problems and hang-ups which affected Little Rey, but unfortunately, some of those same demons were now bothering the rest of the family. While Little Rey had built himself a kingdom that fulfilled his needs at the expense of others, the rest of the family was beginning to show signs of the same traits.

Reyes' sons Armando and Fernando were more than twins. They were life-long friends, two guys who not only shared the same looks, but also the same path.

College-educated and charismatic, the Ruiz brothers nicely fulfilled the emerging demand for minority leaders in Arizona. The Ruiz brothers came into their own at the right time and in the right place,as the Hispanic population exploded during the '70's and '80's in communities along the border states.

Indeed, America's Hispanic population was beginning to flex its muscle. By 1990 the US census counted 22.4 million predominantly Catholic and Mexican Hispanics, and this was recognized as an undercount. At that time, Mexican-Americans also constituted approximately 40% of the USA's Catholic population, with most of them living in the southwest.

More significant than the numbers was the age profile. It was very young. In 1988, the median age of the total non-Hispanic population in the USA was 32.9 years. For Hispanics, it was 25.5 years. Almost twice as many Hispanics were below 15 years of age (39%) as non-Hispanics (21%). But all of this was, and still is, complicated by income. For in 1988, only 10.3% of all American families were below the Poverty 3 level, while almost 26% of Hispanic families fell into that category.

At the same time, census figures revealed that almost half of all Hispanic families were headed by a female, many of whom had children out-of-wedlock and were not part of the work force. These conditions constituted a grave social crisis of serious proportions, a crisis not only for the nation, experts say, but also for the Catholic Church.

In spite of the problems, the future of the USA and the Church is seen to be very Hispanic when childbearing factors are examined. Indeed, contributing editor Joseph P. Fitzpatrick in Sank's and Coleman's book *Reading the Signs of the Times*, notes this effect on the future of the Catholic Church in America: *"These Hispanics are, by baptisms and background, Catholic people. If present trends continue, they will be the dominant influence of the Catholic Church in the next century.*

"Just as the destiny of the Church of the Twentieth Century in the United States was determined by the Catholic immigrants who came during the Nineteenth Century, so the destiny of the Church in the Twenty-First Century will be determined by the immigrants of this century, primarily the Hispanics. From the viewpoint of people, and from the viewpoint of a preferential option for the poor, the context of ministries that predominates over all other factors is the presence and significance of the Hispanics."[1]

But, these masses of Hispanic people could not change the world and the Church by their numbers alone. They needed leadership, strong leadership, young leadership. They needed the type of leadership that big party machine leaders were looking for as candidates for state and national offices. Educated and Catholic leadership would be ideal, as both parties knew that developing and supporting the right leadership could help gain votes from the Hispanic community when needed.

In South Phoenix, Arizona, Armando Ruiz was the man!

Politics: the art of legal arrogance. A game of power, money, influence and, for some men, women. It's all there for the taking, and that's what Armando Ruiz did. This is not to imply that Armando was corrupt or insincere in his motivations. He wasn't. But he certainly was ambitious.

A graduate of Loyola Maramount University in California, Armando freely admits that his addiction was ambition. He had a voracious appetite for success, especially political success. And after his successful campaign for state senator, the world was his oyster. Or at least, Arizona was.

By the early 1990's, the bureaucratic party machine from the newly proposed Hispanic District Six knew they had their man.

Youthful, attractive, experienced, respected, and most of all liked, Armando Ruiz was headed for Washington. Already divorced twice, his cavalier attitude toward women and family were viewed by veteran politicians as pluses to insure his success.

Rival politicians admired his style. They said Armando knew how to play his cards close to his chest. They said he knew how to make all the right moves.

Indeed, by age thirty, Armando was a pro: cold and cavalier toward those who could hurt him or challenge him, but warm and open toward the little people on the streets. Young and admiring kids scurried after him as if he were a star athlete. Glued to his every word and action, they looked to him as their hero and mentor.

"Do this!... Support that!... Don't listen to him!" he cajoled his listeners, and his legions of followers trusted his every word. Highly likable and profoundly personable, Armando certainly had his share of followers, whom one newspaper reporter described as *"street urchins who follow him around like ducklings."*[2]

But that was O.K. to Armando. That's what he wanted. He wanted people to follow him. He wanted them to listen to him and to respect him. Most of all, he wanted them to vote for him.

And of course, that's what it was all about. Armando needed their vote.

And when he couldn't get their votes on his own, twin brother Fernando did. Like two sides of the same coin, the "Brothers Ruiz" comprised their own political machine, right in the family.

Armando and Fernando had always been very close, sharing everything and even lived within a mile of one another. When it came to politics, however, the two of them had very different lifestyles.

Fernando Ruiz's politics wasn't just family politics. He was a wheeler dealer, someone who looked 'em in the eye and slapped 'em on the back. He was a vote hustler, someone who got the job done. Most importantly, he could get his man elected. Fernando, political hacks said, was motivated to win.

And win he did.

After flirting with the priesthood as a young man, Fernando turned to politics with a passion. Where Armando failed or missed out, Fernando was always there to patch and proceed. Never the candidate, he instead became an organizer, and a good one. Fernando managed his brother's successful House and Senatorial campaigns and developed a name for himself. He helped his wife, Leticia, become elected to the school board, and he was South Phoenix's principal organizer in ex-mayor Terry Goddard's campaigns.

Upon graduating with a Bachelor's Degree from Loyola Maramount and a Master's from the University of Colorado, Fernando secured an executive job with an insurance company. Leticia, an assistant high school principal, was also quickly climbing up the success ladder. Together, the husband-wife duo began to rake in the cash, while dabbling in the world of politics for fun and power.

Sound familiar? Armando and Fernando are not alone. The same story is lived by countless others across America who conceptualize life as a game, a game of multiple consumptions and whimsical drives. It is a game that never ends. Neither winning nor losing brings satisfaction. For always there is something more, something bigger, something better.

It is an endless road with countless turns and millions of mazes. It is the wide road that Christ so clearly denounced in Scripture. By 1988, the Ruiz brothers were roaring down it with a vengeance. And at the same time, it seemed as if the whole country was merrily traveling down the same path.

Indeed, Reyes Ruiz had much in mind as he sat in his back pew in Medjugorje...

CHAPTER SIX

AMERICA: GOOD, BAD
AND VERY UGLY

Though very individual in their styles, Armando, Fernando and Little Rey were three peas in a pod, a pod containing stereotypical elements of a modern-day American family. It is a sad picture, one downright inimical to America as a whole.

Studying the lives, motivations and downfalls of the Ruiz brothers helps to paint a general picture of the current state of affairs in "America, the Beautiful," a picture which is anything but pretty. Indeed, America seems to be experiencing a tremendous trend toward ugliness, an internal ugliness coming from its people. Drugs, power, politics, divorce, violence, greed, lust — like the nation, the Ruiz family was traveling along the wide, easy path of moral decay.

But how does one begin to examine what went wrong with the Ruiz family, or for that matter, with countless other families struggling to survive in American society? A good starting point is to try to identify what has gone wrong with the nation at large.

What has happened to America?

Some sociologists blame the country's many social ills on the rapid advances in technology — the communications networks, television, computers, etc. They claim that American society emerged from the Industrial Revolution and entered into the Technological Revolution unable to adapt to the swift progress of science. This has led, experts continue, to a Pandora's box of ethical questions, many of which were basic and simple to answer years before. But because many individuals have somehow become confused as to what is ethical and what is not, a moral crisis in society has emerged.

These dilemmas, sociologists insist, are a natural by-product of societal evolution. The pace of science has always clashed with religion, they say, pointing to such examples as the Vatican's recent vindication of Galileo. Traditionally slow and resistant to change, religion just has not been able to keep up with the "modern" world.

The argument certainly holds truth. But it would be quite inaccurate to blame technology for the country's woes. There would still be much to explain, for most ethical problems are centered around people. Individuals choose what is right and wrong within themselves, regardless of the promptings and temptations of technological progress.

But what *is* right and wrong? Unfortunately, this has become the question. While technology has spiraled us into new dimensions and realities, the most basic of all questions has emerged as a growing mystery. In two-inch typeface, *Newsweek* magazine's cover story on June 8, 1992, boldly asked, *"Whose Values?"* The magazine's subheadlines added, *"Whose justice? Whose Morality? Whose Community? Whose Family?"*

Indeed, *Newsweek* columnist Joe Klein probed this issue in depth. He postulated more ethical questions: *"Who makes the choices? Who is to blame for our problems? Who will be accountable?"*[1] Wrote Klein:

"There was a time when America's culture was hegemonic, placid and family-centered. It was called the '50s. As it happens, the pristine image wasn't entirely a myth. The American Dream became a reality for a generation that had suffered through a terrible war and a Great Depression. Divorce rates decreased after a post-war spurt; disposable income increased. It was a unique moment. There was an economy of abundance and a psychology of scarcity, says Barbara Whitehead, a research associate in the Institute for American Values. The families of the '50s hunkered down, saved money, lived conservatively in anticipation of the next depression. Ironically, what we have now is the exact opposite, Whitehead adds. An economy of scarcity and a psychology of abundance."[2]

Klein's article asked the questions, covered the history, and explained the present moral state of America, religion and God. His conclusion directed the reader toward an *"ecumenical"* solution for peace in America through compromise, individual choice and tolerance for each other's views. This, he ventured, would solve America's problems.

But Klein's "solution," many critics say, is in fact the problem. For tolerance isn't merely the acceptance of different views and moral codes. It is often the acceptance of, and indifference toward, sin. And sin, along with a lack of moral justice, is destroying the nation.

In America, compromise has always been hailed as a virtue. But traditionally, this "virtue" has been subordinate to higher values, those based upon principles and truth. While many individuals seek compromise in the name of tolerance, critics explain that an ecumenical peace maintains that people can come together under the mantle of some sort of "universal truth," one that everyone can accept.

However, the same shortcoming surfaces here, as this "universal mantle of truth" refuses to recognize the existence of sin, thus pushing God and His laws of justice entirely out of the picture.

The proposed "truth," then, emphasizes individual liberty as the supreme virtue which, according to many, is the greatest error which currently dominates Western thinking. Indeed, it is precisely what Pope John Paul II has been trying to point out so courageously, though his wise comments are often labeled *"old-fashioned"* and *"unrealistic."*

Mr. Rocco Buttiglione, one of the most renowned, modern-day Catholic philosophers, and one of Pope John Paul II's most trusted advisors, sums up the Pope's position in a brief, yet concise statement: *"For Wojtyla, the fundamental, modern problem is a concept of liberty which does not include obedience to truth. His solution: devotion to Mary. Mary is the model of human freedom, a freedom which discovers itself in obedience to truth. The man who obeys only his own instincts is a slave..."* (*Inside the Vatican*, October 1993)[3]

Few would deny that, in the United States, individual liberties and sin reign supreme. A perplexing majority of people have chosen to blatantly reject leaders and institutions which teach obedience to truth.

Indeed, a year after the *Newsweek* article, *Time* magazine (April 5, 1993) concluded precisely this. Reflecting on the country's problems, *Time's* cover story read, *"The Generation That Forgot God."* The article noted that people crave spirituality, but reject churches that preach right and wrong. The article was, more or less, the continuation of *Newsweek's* "Whose values?" argument; however, the basic premise was applied to church ideology; that is, it questioned, *"Whose God? Whose Commandments?"*

As America struggled to formulate a new concept of faith without rules and laws, said *Time*, *"New ecumenical-type churches in every denomination were popping up."* These were churches that didn't label individual choices as *"binding upon the soul."* Rather, they emphasized the needs of their members. Today's churches, the article stated, should be *"seeker friendly."* Wrote *Time* correspondent Richard Ostling:

> *"There was a time in America when a spiritual journey meant a long, stormy crossing of the soul, an exploration mapped by Scripture and led by clergy. Through the family, Catholic you were born and Catholic you died, or Methodist, or Jew. Of the generation born after World War II, 95% received a religious upbringing, and had they behaved like before them, the churches and synagogues of their childhood would be thriving.*
>
> *Today, a quiet revolution is taking place that is changing not only the religious habits of millions of Americans, but the way churches go about recruiting members to keep their doors open. Increasing numbers of baby boomers who left the fold years ago are turning religious again, but many are traveling from church to church or faith to faith, sampling creeds, shopping for a custom-made God* (April 5, 1993)[4]

For America, this "religion shopping" does not signal a coming revolution; rather, it is a sign of a people emerging from one, from a revolution of errors that have now produced a country in chaos.

Worst of all, a new generation of leaders now fully embraces error as truth. To the world, America promotes a philosophy which demonstrates that disorder of the mind begets disorder of the heart, and consequently, disorder of the streets. Moral theologians explain that this current state of affairs is the apparent culmination of theories which began in the 16th and 17th Centuries, during the Age of Enlightenment. The present-day proponents of the philosophies of relativism, rationalism and humanism have come into power at almost every level of society.

Thus, the writings and beliefs of Nietzsche, Descartes, Kant, Leibniz, Voltaire, Diderot, Cherbury, Darwin, Engels, Marx, Freud, Crowley, Lenin, Mao and Sanger have been fused and mutated into the prevailing mentality of the times. It is a metamorphosis that has resulted in the widespread dominance of Voltaire's *"Anti-God — Pro-Man"* precepts, which are even more worrisome today than when first brought into the public eye.

This social wave began to emerge with a vengeance during the 1960's, as the decade marked the beginning of many changes in America. A brief look at the history of the current chaos can go a long way in explaining how the situation has reached such serious proportions.

Playboy magazine, Woodstock, hippies, peyote, marijuana, Hell's Angels and Black Panthers, escalating divorce and premarital sex — the sixties freely offered all of these, and more. Meanwhile, mainstream opinion of the decade debased school prayer, virginity, monogamous relationships, traditional families, decency and basic self-respect.

But it was more than the decade of *"free-love"* and *"anything goes."* From Greenwich Village to Haight Asbury, the country became covered with modernistic, cultural crud. Rock music and long hair concealed a much deeper peril, though no one could have recognized what was brewing at the nation's core. By the end of the decade, *Time* magazine declared that God was *"dead"*; meanwhile, man's first steps on the moon heralded another success for his expanding intellect.

By the seventies, things became even worse. "X-rated" movies were now considered "R-rated," and former "R-rated" films were thought of as family entertainment. Contraceptive tools such as "the Pill" became mainstream, and for those uncomfortable with taking a drug, intrauterine devices were conveniently available. Reproductive *"freedom"* for females was exploding, supposedly bringing with it a new *"female liberation."* And with the 1973 Roe vs. Wade decision, the country legalized the ugliest form of birth control of all in the form of abortion.

By the mid-1970's, the term "role model" referred to people who were socially cavalier and politically defiant. And it was senseless to marry before you *"shacked up."* The Vietnam War ended, resulting in a demeaning and belittling attitude toward national service.

Undoubtedly, the seventies were the *"Me"* decade, a time for the emergence of Eastern meditation, human potential, mental programming and ESP. National television became increasingly an Antichrist, belief systems crumbled, and people living *"alternate lifestyles"* actively sought recognition.

Michael Brown, in his book, *The Final Hour*, sums it up:

> *"The western hemisphere was being swept...by a surge of witchcraft and paganism. It wasn't precisely the type of paganism they had in ancient Greece, but is was paganism nonetheless. Televisions became our Coliseum. The youth were looking inward for the answers instead of upward. We talked to plants. We sent telepathic waves. We searched for the vibes of success. Women now competed with men, and the distinction between the sexes blurred. Our trends and lifestyles were shaped by a small cadre of nonbelievers who wrote the scripts for prime-time television.*
>
> *"The television set became the great idol of our century, and our addiction to it made us superficial and deviant. Materialism dominated as never before. An epidemic of pride and egoism infected all segments of society. We were now too busy for anything but our careers, we were certainly too busy and important, too sophisticated, to get on our knees and pray.*
>
> *"So consumed was American society with itself, and so unwilling to make personal sacrifice, that the divorce*

and abortion rates exploded. An unborn child was unceremoniously terminated if it stood in the way of a career or was otherwise the least bit inconvenient. "[5]

By the eighties, this undercurrent was swiftly becoming mainstream. America, while still singing, "God shed its grace on thee," was acting like God never had anything to do with the country in the first place.

"Man built America, not God," became the new credo. And man deserved the credit. In fact, if he looked inside deep enough, man would discover that he was God! The New Age movement said so! The time was emerging for the full evolution of paganism, pantheism, secret sects, Eastern philosophies, and downright demonic occult spiritualism. With growing materialism and sensualism thrown into the recipe, America was adversely "discovering" herself. Indeed, when the Pope and an American president were shot, the country showed more concern for beached whales and Wall Street.

By the late eighties, this whirlwind of confusion, lies and "tolerance" had taken its toll on the family. The problems in America's homes soon spilled over into the streets: violence and drugs, thousands upon thousands of illegitimate children, millions of teenage pregnancies and runaways. But none of it mattered, for everything was relative, everything was situational. Greed, sensuality and capitalism became the gods of the eighties, along with rap music and MTV. The *"Me"* generation of the seventies had become the *"My"* generation of the eighties.

By the early 1990's, the problems were evident. But the minds supposedly behind the solutions were even more troublesome than the problems themselves. In Washington, D.C. and throughout the fifty state capitols, elected officials now condoned, through legislative actions, a myriad of laws whose mere mention thirty years earlier would have caused a riot.

Individual rights reigned supreme. Family values were openly mocked, and everybody seemed somehow involved in it. The unions, the media, the teachers, the intelligentsia, and the courts had all become abominations. Judges moved to legalize homosexuality, and juries couldn't determine if murder was murder. And regrettably, the nineties' trend toward "political correctness" (P.C.) began to legally cement the whole mess. The country had become, as noted author and poet Robert Bly pointed out in his book, *The Sibling Society*, a nation of selfish, bickering adolescents, who care for only ourselves, no matter what our age. We are a culture, he concludes, that is *"shipwrecked."*

With our family problems erupting on the streets, the confusion and violence now flowed back into our homes. Late at night everything from psychic readings to numerology, astrology and sex could be found just a phone call away. The whole country was *"tolerant"* as long as each person could do what he wanted. Indeed, it was madness to the maximum, and dangerous to the point of no return.

Most frightening, America, the *"land of the free and home of the brave,"* began to openly denounce Christian teaching. Traditional Christians (both Protestant and Catholic) were depicted as the most dangerous people alive, individuals whose *"intolerance"* should be avoided at all cost. Their views were now "extreme."

America's problems became monstrous in proportion, and remain so to this day. Our *"one nation under God"* has become insensitive, indifferent, and callous to evil. Today, the soul of America lies near death. Evil has swallowed the land, as the whale swallowed Jonah.

Like a misty fog infesting every nook and cranny of the country, no corner of the nation has been spared. Indeed, the evil has touched the young and old alike. It has reached the government, the schools, the churches and the factories. It's in ghettos and elite country estates, in the office and the kitchen.

Indeed, this evil is alive, and in America, it is everywhere. Just as Pope Paul VI foretold on November 15, 1972:

> *"Evil is not only a privation but a living, spiritual, corrupt and corrupting being. A terrible reality, mysterious and frightening. The testimony of both the Bible and Church tells us that people refuse to acknowledge his existence; or they make of him a self-subsistent principle not*

originating in God, unlike all creatures; or he is explained away as a pseudo-reality, a fantastic personification of the unknown grounds of the evil within us."

And where evil reigns within people and nations, death is usually not far behind. For the ultimate result of evil is death, often bloody death. History proves that cultures which endorse evil usually feed their false gods a diet of blood. And by the mid-1990's, four thousand babies a day were being sacrificed in America. Still worse, some leaders were making plans to export this carnage to every country in the world.

Back in South Phoenix, the Ruiz family, too, reflected all of this. It had been touched by the same fog that had reached the rest of the country, it had been bitten by the same bug.

Even Reyes' wife, Estela, was showing the symptoms. And by 1980, she was tired of her life, and those closest to her, especially Reyes, could feel her restlessness...

FOR THE SOUL OF THE FAMILY

CHAPTER SEVEN

POWER AND PRESTIGE

*"S*lick." *"Calculated." "Indifferent." "Cold."* Were these the adjectives used to describe drug hustler Little Rey? Surprisingly not. Instead, they were used in reference to his mother, Estela. Much like her children, Estela had a clear and controlled plan for her life, a sort of goal or mission. But unlike her husband, that mission had very little to do with God, Providence or the Blessed Mother.

A pillowy-shaped woman whose full head of silver hair reveals she's somewhat past middle-age, Estela is noticeably restrained and calm. Raising seven children through some good, bad and very difficult times, she has been formed by the trials and challenges of the life she has lead. Intelligent and quick-witted, she uses her eyes to listen as much as her ears, and seems to assess everything internally before uttering a word.

The youngest of four children, Estela Ruiz was born in El Paso, Texas, on April 8, 1936. She grew up in Lordsburg, New Mexico. Curiously, her maiden name was also Ruiz. She was the only daughter and youngest child of Manuel and Delfina Ruiz, and had three brothers: Inocensio, Gilbert and Arturo. Her father was a heavy drinker, and Estela characterized her youth as chaotic and turbulent, typical of life in an alcoholic's home. It was *"a crazy house,"* she says, *"with lots of yelling and screaming."* Fortunately, Estela says, her father never physically abused her mother.

Her mother was an exceptionally strong woman, one accustomed to life's many challenges and hardships. Over the years, Estela developed a deep love and admiration for her, one that even caused her to suffer serious illness as she agonized over and internalized her mother's slow death process.

But unlike Reyes' family, Estela's parents and three older brothers were not very religious. In an ironic oddity, Estela's father, while intoxicated, was struck by a car, just like Reyes' father. Although Estela's father did not die, he did start to pray. Nothing extraordinarily religious ever happened in her home, Estela says, except perhaps for the ever-present image of Our Lady of Guadalupe. Typical of most Mexican-American's, Estela's family believed that the Virgin was all they needed to help deliver their prayers to God. Mary was especially called upon during urgent times, in particularly difficult situations.

At around age sixteen, Estela remembers that her mother did, indeed, call upon God for a miracle when one of her brothers became very ill. Estela and her mother climbed, in their bare feet, a steep mountain named *"Christ the King"* to fulfill a promise to God. It was a difficult ascent which often left the climber bleeding and in pain, but the promise had to be kept, and according to Hispanic tradition, the price had to be paid.

Curiously, Estela remembers that during this climb, a mysterious force somehow lifted her up the mountain, as at one point she had become fatigued and felt she could not go on. At that moment, she remembers that a voice in her heart assured her of approval. It was a voice, she says, that was God's.

By the 1980's, Estela Ruiz was again climbing mountains. This time, though, the climb was all for herself, not for any family or favors, and especially not for God. Estela had forgotten about her experiences climbing the rocky, jagged path of "Christ the King," and she never promised God anything for achieving her own success. Unlike her mother, she never thought it was necessary.

Meeting Estela in those days was almost like meeting a bulldozer at a dump site. She had work to do, a ladder to climb, and rare was the individual who dared to get in her way.

From a personality standpoint, Estela was still the same. She was a good person. Friends will tell you she had a heart of gold and was liked by all. Many often sought her advice and compassion, for she was known to never turn a deaf ear. Even Reyes insists that his wife was always as nice a person that one could ever hope to marry. But now, these attributes were being used in a different way, for the ladder of success was what she wanted to climb and nothing was going to hold her back.

What caused her great desire for success?

At age forty, she had enough cooking, cleaning and washing clothes. She had raised seven kids. Dozens of grandchildren, nieces, nephews, cousins and neighbors were now in the picture, or on the way, all requiring or demanding an extra drop of attention from her already barren energy supply. She had been mom to the world, and she was tired of it. And she had certainly had her fill of Reyes, her *"holy roly"* husband.

By age forty, Estela Ruiz came to view Reyes as the quintessential fool. He was an archetype remnant of a Hispanic culture who somehow still believed Our Lady of Guadalupe was the answer to everything.

While there were problems galore in the world and family, Reyes Ruiz was busy painting pictures of his beautiful *Mujer Bonita*, or wearing his Rosary around his head at night, as if it were some kind of audio receiver linked to God. He lived in a world of make-believe, Estela concluded, always escaping to God for the answer. To her, he was not just a fool, he was becoming an embarrassment.

While husband Reyes was always minutes away from another talk with God, Estela was shuffling out the door to the supermarket, or racing to the emergency room with a crisis, or making sure the many family errands and social details were taken care of. Day to day, morning to night, she fulfilled her duty as family matriarch, with no rest, no peace, and no noteworthy personal achievements to gratify her existence.

The television shows, the movies, the newspaper and ladies' magazines all told her that she was *"unfulfilled,"* not a *"total woman,"* and she was really beginning to agree. A sense of restlessness and frustration was a part of her soul, and she desperately needed relief.

Estela Ruiz wasn't looking for a legal divorce, but she did want a divorce from Reyes' ways, a separation from his madness. Their path together was splitting, taking each one down his own separate trail. And while they were both interested in holding together, they weren't exactly interested in being together.

By 1980, Reyes's relationship with the Virgin Mary was spinning out of control. More than ever, he seemed to believe a woman from 2,000 years ago was listening to him constantly. He believed she was listening, day in and day, out as he told her how much he loved her, as he confided to her his every thought and dream.

To outsiders, Reyes was like a love-struck teenage boy, hopeless but not dangerous. He was fascinating, yet pathetic and sad. But to Estela, he was clinically obsessed.

Not surprisingly, Reyes had become someone she felt she couldn't talk to anymore. It just seemed like a waste of time. For as far as Estela could tell, Reyes never heard a word. He was always too darn busy talking and listening to the *"other woman"* in his life.

Emotionally, Estela grew slightly frustrated. She was his wife, the mother of his children. She was his partner, his lifelong friend and chosen one. Yet, her husband was truly in love with another woman. He was in love with the Mother of God, the Blessed Virgin Mary, and he was in love with her like she was alive and living right in their own house.

Indeed, Estela's world became a cauldron of contradictory emotions. She wasn't jealous of the Virgin, but yet, in a way she was. She wasn't angry at Reyes, yet she was. She didn't want to leave him, but she didn't exactly want to stay. She just wanted to separate herself somehow from Reyes' consuming passion.

But Reyes was just part of the problem.

Like other American women of her generation, Estela felt a pressure building within her which centered on her role as a woman. She began to secretly share thoughts which were openly espoused by many feminists. Being female was, in a way, a bondage, she started to believe. She was a talented, intelligent woman. She could do more than just cook, clean and take care of grandchildren. She had brains and ambition, but like many women, she feared that it was all going to waste.

As Estela looked around at the world and at her family, she finally knew what she wanted. Her son Armando's political success had convinced her that the Ruiz family was powerful. And that power, she came to believe, was almost preordained.

Indeed, Estela encouraged her sons in the political arena. She admitted that she convinced them in a *"very, very big way"* that being in politics was the right thing for them to do. In fact, they *deserved* to be in politics, she would tell them, they deserved to make decisions for other people, to control other people's lives. And soon after convincing them of their political destiny, Estela began to feel the same way about herself.

In those days, Estela Ruiz had no problems with social issues like the "pro-choice" movement. Sure, abortion was wrong, she thought, but she could easily empathize with the abortion rights advocates. In fact, Estela easily embraced many positions promoted by the feminist movement. Needless to say, her husband Reyes was surprised by his wife's bold turn away from what they had always known to be true, from values they had always believed in. He couldn't understand why she couldn't read the writing on the wall, and she couldn't understand how he could be so closed-minded and *"intolerant."*

But Estela wasn't about to let herself get bogged down with thorny social issues or causes. She didn't just want a cause, she wanted freedom.

And most of all, she says, she wanted prestige. *"I wanted to have power!"* she boldly admits when questioned. *"I wanted to be one of the important ones who made the big decisions."* Prestige would sure feel good, thought Estela. It would give her recognition, the kind of recognition deserved by a minority woman who stages a tremendous mid-life comeback from the tyranny of an oppressive lifestyle.

Yes, Estela could see the headlines: *"Mother of Seven Earns Degrees, Rises To The Top of Her Field."* She couldn't wait for the reporter to do the interview. She longed for recognition, for fulfillment and triumph as a woman. And when that same reporter did a background check, the world would know that her triumph had occurred while living in a South Phoenix neighborhood filled with desperation and hopelessness. What a story!

Indeed, she thought, the "Estela Ruiz Success Story" could be big, very big. The world would discover that the family power and talent rested not only with her children, and they would look to her as the source and mentor. She would then earn the recognition and prestige she deserved, both as a talented working woman, and as mother of the famous "Ruiz Brothers."

All of this was no pipe dream. Estela acted aggressively on her desires.

She accepted a job as a teacher's assistant. Within a few years, she earned her Bachelor's degree from Ottawa University and then a Master's degree from Northern Arizona University at Flagstaff. Through this time, she worked her way up to a directorship position in the school district. By 1988, she had earned a powerful administrator's seat, along with $40,000 a year and a new car. At mid-life, the run-of-the-mill Hispanic mother of seven was changing everything. She had changed her role, changed her self-concept. She had even changed places with her husband as the breadwinner, with Reyes' salary totaling one-half of hers.

Inside, she had also changed.

Hard. Tough. Strong. Directed. To some, an egomaniac. People did not exactly compare Estela Ruiz to Mary Poppins. But it didn't matter to Estela. She simply forged ahead, her eyes on the goal,

Estela's Graduation (Masters Degree in Education)

even grabbing a few self-assertiveness courses along the way to help steamroll those who still had any ideas of crossing her.

But the climb up the mountain of success had, indeed, petrified her heart. According to her son Armando, Estela had evolved into *"someone who knew how to play the game."* And play the game she did.

Her desire for power had become a lust. She hungered for prestige. Over a period of years, her rise in the Murphy school district was sure and swift. She eventually became Bilingual Program Coordinator for the entire district's special language programs at a time when the issue of bilingual education in Arizona was smoldering due to the state's philosophy of "immersion."

Estela took it upon herself to spearhead a change. In her district, which was 75% Hispanic, she pushed for Spanish-speaking classes until students could read in English. After receiving a $100,000 grant, she wrote a manual that became the prototype for her district and others across the nation. Her actions on this issue transcended academics, as her Ruiz blood spurred her to search for a political resolution to the problem.

Unabashed, Estela picketed for bilingual education. And behind the scenes, she politically backed candidates for the school board. Sometimes working *"twenty-four hours a day to get the job done,"* according to husband Reyes, Estela soon became a bona fide state leader in bilingual education. Estela's boss, school superintendent Bob Donofrio, eventually uttered the words she longed to hear: *"Estela Ruiz,"* he noted, *"was a power in the state in mandated bilingual and ESL programs."*[1]

Indeed, she had arrived. Finally, the prestige Estela hungered for was hers. She had broken the shackles of a tyrannical lifestyle that had "oppressed" her for so many years.

But once she had obtained her goal, it was no longer enough. She wanted more.

Her kids were raised and out of the house, so she had nothing to hold her back, nothing to make her feel guilty. Likewise, she detected no problem with Reyes. So she figured, why not go for more? More power, more prestige, more liberation...

Ah, yes...liberation! Estela Ruiz had been liberated, and she proudly wore her new clothes and jewelry as confirmation. But even without her fancy wardrobe and new style, the family could see what was happening to her. Says Armando, *"Professionally, she was very sophisticated. I would describe her as a hatchet person; ...[someone who would] come at you and take your head off, and you don't see it coming. A lot of times you didn't know it was her. She was very manipulative, very successful. She loved her children and grandchildren, but there were conditions. There was an appropriate time."*[2]

By 1988, Reyes Ruiz cooked dinner most nights. In the mornings, Estela was often long gone before the family even woke up. Likewise, she usually arrived home very late. It was the price of liberation. And although Reyes kept pestering her about the Rosary, daily Mass and the Virgin, Estela never heard a word. She had come too far to listen to his song, too far to see her husband's loneliness and frustration. *"You over do everything,"* she would tell Reyes. *"I go to Mass every Sunday. That's all the Church asks us to do. You're just a holy roller. Santucho! You're a fanatic! Our Lord doesn't ask us to go to Mass every day. And you take away from Jesus when you talk so much about Mary!!!"*

Indeed, Estela believed she could do everything herself, or her family could do it. They were powerful. She was powerful. She was destined for something great. And her destiny, she believed, did not involve climbing rocky, treacherous mountains to fulfill promises to God or the Virgin of Guadalupe.

But her husband Reyes was not too "important" to climb mountains for God. By the end of his week-long pilgrimage, Reyes climbed the Medjugorje hills and mountains four times. He kept going back up Mt. Krizevac and down Krizevac, up Podbrdo and down Podbrdo. He kept feeling he had to climb some more. For he kept remembering more things that he needed to discuss with the Virgin.

Reyes had a lot to tell his lady. And Mary kept calling him back to talk. In his heart, he could almost hear the Virgin's voice:

"Mi hijo, mi hijo, te oigo. I hear your prayers. I hear your prayers. Don't you know?

"And don't worry, ya vengo. I'm coming. I'm coming for you... and for your family...

"...and for America."

CHAPTER EIGHT

"LET IT CONVERT ALL THE AMERICAS"

Rare is an early Medjugorje evening without a good deal of sun-gazing. As the orange ball that illuminates the sky sinks beneath the horizon, many pilgrims can be seen looking curiously and pointing overhead. While the Franciscans warn visitors not to stare into the sun looking for miracles, few can honestly say that they don't cast a hopeful glance. Most hunger for just a glimpse of the *"Miracle of the Sun."*

Witnessed by thousands at Fatima on October 13, 1917, news of this phenomenon repeating at Medjugorje escapes few pilgrims. Many search for it in earnest, hoping to have something to tell others when they get back home.

Depending on whom you speak with, the Miracle of the Sun usually encompasses four elements. First, the sun is mysteriously bearable to direct observation. For some reason, it doesn't hurt or damage the eyes to stare at it, even after twenty minutes or more of constant exposure. Next, some say, a black disc-like object materializes and shields the sun, somehow protecting the eyes. After this, many say the sun spins wildly and throws off a kaleidoscope of colors in all directions. Finally, for the very fortunate, Jesus or Mary may appear in the sun or on top of it, or sometimes a cross will appear. Cries of awe can be heard in the air, and arms can be seen extended overhead, all pointing toward the sun. These phenomenal sightings are said to be quite distinguishable, although not exactly three-dimensional.

Experiencing the miraculous at Medjugorje is not limited to solar phenomena. Strange and unique sightings and sensations abound everywhere. According to many authors who have written about Medjugorje over the last two decades, nothing has compared with it since Christ walked the earth. Medjugorje is like standing, some say, on the porch of Heaven. The Virgin's words to the visionaries there confirm this opinion. While hundreds of apparitions have occurred over the last two centuries, Mary emphasizes that the grace God is giving at Medjugorje is unprecedented. Never in the history of the world, the Virgin insists, has this occurred, and never will it again. And these are to be her last apparitions, she says — the last time God will send her to earth as His messenger.

At Medjugorje, Mary declares, she is setting the stage for a final showdown between her and Satan. This revelation is a confirmation of what visionary Sister Lucia of Fatima reported in the 1950's when Mary led the nun to understand that the *"last times"* had arrived. According to the Virgin herself, the confrontation between her and Satan will be decisive.

Mary likewise indicated that Medjugorje is the place God has chosen for the final step that will allow her to crush Satan's head. Michael Brown, in *The Final Hour,* poignantly describes this prophetic fulfillment, and Medjugorje's role in it all:

> *"I've never encountered anything quite like the sensations of Medjugorje. Not at the tarmac at Fatima nor the grotto at Lourdes nor the mountainside of La Salette. Not at Guadalupe or Pochaiv or Knock. Not at charismatic services in New York City or Mass at the Church of the Annunciation in Nazareth.*
>
> *Not since Christ appeared in glory to His apostles has there been a more direct interaction with the supernatural.*
>
> *The feeling is that of standing at a point halfway between Heaven and earth.*
>
> *The feeling is also one of standing in the middle of all the action. Since Fatima there had been at least 210 presumed apparitions, and within just the next few years there would be a minimum of another fifty notable reports. But none had the economy of language, the sweet grace, and the tranquil power of Medjugorje. It was the hub from which the spokes of other apparitions rotated, the very epicenter,*

along with Fatima, of twentieth-century interventions, at the vanguard of God's response to the devil, with roots all the way back to the Miraculous Medal (Rue du Bac).

And there was an ominous scent in the air. **I have come to call the world to conversion for the last time,** *Mary told the youngsters.* **After this period I will not appear any more on this earth.**

So began the final and most powerful stage of apparitions, the phase we find ourselves in now, the climactic period that has spawned dozens of similar apparitions on every habitable continent.

Yes, there were apparitions every decade; we've seen how they continued since Rue du Bac; so many, that we confuse them.

But Medjugorje is something else. Medjugorje is the touchstone for an entirely new flurry of reports. Medjugorje is the announcement that the era which began at Rue du Bac is about to end.

The Blessed Mother was calling mankind to prayer, penance, and fasting for a final time.

The hours of the apparitions follow a progression, Fatima specialist Luigi Bianchi points out. At Lourdes, they took place in the morning. At Fatima, at noon. At Medjugorje, in the evening.[1]

The details of this great supernatural mystery are numerous. Like major wars between nations, there is a wealth of information, both speculation and fact. Thousands of apparitions have occurred in Medjugorje, along with the transmission of thousands of celestial messages, such that understanding the full picture of God's work there is like trying to comprehend Michelangelo's *Final Judgment* at the Vatican's Sistine Chapel. The total picture presented by the mystics and visionaries in the world today is a massive mural, one that leaves many believers hungering for as much as they can absorb.

But the total picture can also be quite overwhelming. It's too big, too complicated, too uncertain and too frightening. For some, an extended glance is more than enough, as the whole story can be overwhelming and intimidating, especially the dark, serious side of it all.

Though many prefer not to acknowledge it, Mary reminds us that the evil flooding the world has a source. His name is Satan. He exists. He's real. And his infinite hate is in constant rebellion against God's infinite love.

Not to be confused with the cartoon-like character with a red suit, tail and pitchfork, the devil is a quantifiable being, a real entity, a source of tremendous power. As Scripture tells us, his downfall was pride and rebellion. Unlike ever before, he seeks to spread these same vices throughout the world.

Affecting families and nations, Satan is the source of a spiritual cancer that now covers the planet. He is the source, Mary insists, of destruction, divorce and death. He has set up his kingdom from one end of the world to the other, transforming the entire planet into a modern-day Babylon. Most significantly, Mary has revealed at Medjugorje that Satan's power is now at its peak.

But soon his kingdom will crumble, soon Satan will fall. The end of his reign is assured, with the final battle clearly disclosed in Scripture. Mary, too, reportedly distinctly foretold his downfall at La Salette.

Though hope is on the horizon, the war is not over yet. And in spite of the many confirmations for the devil's existence, those who acknowledge that he is real are ridiculed and dismissed. The world tells us that believing in a satanic being is superstitious, childlike and ignorant. Nonetheless, Pope Paul VI courageously and vividly described the reality of evil, followed in 1986 by Pope John Paul II, who did not hesitate to give evil a name. On August 13, the Holy Father spoke directly of the devil:

> *"The whole world lies under the power of the Evil One. The influence of the evil spirit can conceal itself in a more profound and effective way. It is in his interest to make himself unknown! Satan has the skill in the world to induce people to deny his existence in the name of rationalism and of every other system of thought which seeks all possible means to avoid recognizing his activity."*[2]

Indeed, in an apparent microcosm of the Holy Father's words, Satan attempted to deceive one of the visionaries by concealing his identify. In 1982, Lucifer appeared to Mirjana while she was living in Sarajevo. Mirjana was expecting the Virgin's arrival as she waited in her room one evening. Instead, God permitted a test. Satan appeared in place of the Virgin, and the event was one which Mirjana would remember with dread for all time. One of the Franciscan priests stationed in Medjugorje, Father Svetozar Kraljevic, O.F.M., explored this event with Mirjana:

Father Svet: You have never discussed what happened [with Satan] into my tape recorder. Please try to describe it now, so I can record it.

Mirjana: *It was approximately six months ago, though I don't know exactly and cannot say for sure. As usual, I had locked myself into my room, alone, and waited for the Madonna. I knelt down, and had not yet made the Sign of the Cross, when suddenly a bright light flashed, and a devil appeared. It was as if something told me it was a devil. I looked at him and was very surprised, for I was expecting the Madonna to appear. He was horrible - he was like black all over and had a... He was terrifying, dreadful, and I did not know what he wanted. I realized I was growing weak, and then I fainted. When I revived, he was still standing there, laughing. It seemed that he gave me a strange kind of strength, so that I could almost accept him. He told me that I would be very beautiful, and very happy, and so on. However, I would have not need of the Madonna, he said, and no need for faith. She has brought you nothing but suffering and difficulties, he said. But he would give me everything beautiful - whatever I want. Then something in me - I don't know what, if it was something conscious or something in my soul - told me, 'No! No! No!' Then I*

> *began to shake and feel just awful. Then
> he disappeared, and the Madonna ap-
> peared, and when she appeared, my
> strength returned - as if she restored it to
> me. I felt normal again. Then the Madonna
> told me, That was the trial, but it will not
> happen to you again.*[3]

Mirjana needed to understand the stark, blunt reality of Satan's existence. A visionary chosen by Heaven, and therefore a messenger to the world, Mirjana received the vision not just for herself, but for everyone.

College-educated and rather sophisticated, Mirjana's experiences lend credibility to the reality of Satan. Theologians judge Mirjana's testimony as being consistent and authentic. She is a strong person, the eldest of the six visionaries, and the first one to receive the ten "secrets," a term commonly used in Medjugorje to refer to the impending, worldwide events revealed by the Virgin that involve the end of Satan's reign and the future of the world.

Besides the secrets, Mary has entrusted much information to the six Medjugorje visionaries. During one apparition, Mirjana claims that the Virgin confirmed the truth of a vision experienced by Pope Leo XIII. Approximately one hundred years ago, Pope Leo XIII reported that he received a vision of God and Satan. In it, he claimed, Satan was permitted one century of power to test the Church and the world. According to the vision, the twentieth century is that century. Again, Father Svetozar's interview with Mirjana reveals the validity of this frightening truth:

Father Svet: Did the Madonna say anything else?

Mirjana: Nothing else. She told me it would not happen again and that she would talk to me about it later.

Father Svet: You said that the twentieth century has been given over to the devil?

Mirjana: Yes.

Father Svet: You mean the century until the year 2000, or generally speaking?

Mirjana: *Generally, part of which is in the twentieth century, until the first secret is unfolded. The devil will rule 'till then. She told me several secrets and explained them to me; and I have written them down in code letters, with dates, so I won't forget them. If, say, tomorrow a secret is to be revealed, I have a right, two or three days before, to pick whatever priest I want and tell him about it. For example: The day after tomorrow, such-and-such will happen. The priest, then, is free to do as he thinks best with that information. He can write it out before it happens, then read it to others after it happens. He can also tell it to the people: Tomorrow, such-and-such will happen. It's up to him to decide what to do with the information.*[4]

Secrets, secrets, secrets. The ten secrets being revealed by the Madonna in Medjugorje will affect the world. But prior to their announcement, Mary says, God's other plans must be in place. The stage must be set.

Throughout the world, a mystically-coordinated, massive campaign is underway to prepare for the coming events. The secrets involve future warnings, miracles and chastisements; they involve the end of Satan's reign, the healing of the world and an era of peace. It is no wonder, then, that so many millions of people who have been touched by the Lord's presence in Medjugorje and elsewhere are busily preparing!

Reyes Ruiz prayed for healing while he was in Medjugorje. He prayed for peace, too. He begged the Virgin for healing and peace for himself, his family and the world.

Little Rey was in the most serious trouble. Undoubtedly, the youngest of his flock was involved in the fight of his life. But the rest of the family was also far from God. Wife Estela and sons Armando and Fernando seemed headed out of orbit with grandiose plans for their lives, and Reyes' other children were also struggling.

Oldest daughter, Rebecca, was mired in a troubled marriage, while youngest daughter, Rosemary, was painfully experiencing life's ups and downs. Meanwhile, another source of anguish for Reyes was his oldest son, Isidore. While not in any extraordinary difficulty according to worldly standards, his departure from the Catholic Church wounded Reyes' heart deeply. Reyes was simply heartbroken over his family's condition, with all of his children far from the Virgin of Guadalupe's safe arms, far from Our Lady of Medjugorje's call to peace, prayer, penance and conversion.

Rebecca Ruiz and son Sergio

The miracles and phenomena at Medjugorje excited Reyes. But he was not hunting for a celestial magic show. He was searching only for peace, for healing and spiritual enlightenment for his loved ones.

At the same time, Reyes knew it wouldn't be easy. He was certainly familiar with Satan's existence, he was a "believer" in the snares and tricks often set by the Prince of Lies, even though his own family considered him eccentric and old-fashioned.

Indeed, at Reyes' level of spirituality, his battles with the devil were almost of Biblical proportion. In fact, in early 1988, just prior to his trip to Medjugorje that September, he endured quite a serious encounter with the Evil One. It was an encounter which Reyes, like Mirjana, wasn't sure that he would survive.

Like Saint Catherine of Siena who was tormented for years by degrading temptations from Satan, Reyes found himself in the fight of his life. Out of nowhere, temptations of the flesh began to attack his mind. Over and over they came, like tidal waves battering a shore on a stormy night.

Prayers, spiritual communions, Mass twice a day — nothing seemed to help. At night Reyes awoke and beseeched God for hours on end to help him, to *please* help him! He couldn't understand, he told the Lord. Why was he being put through this?

In spite of his prayers, the attacks continued. The devil was mauling him. The temptations became so great that Reyes began to pray constantly. On the inside, he shook and shook. On the outside, he cried and cried.

By early spring Reyes would get up twice a night to pray. By late spring, the number had risen to three times a night. While in prayer, he would sense footsteps. Evil would radiate upon him, as if Satan's shadow was over him.

Reyes called upon his friend, his best and most trusted friend, but the Virgin didn't seem to hear. He prayed to Our Lady of Guadalupe. He prayed to Our Lady of Mt. Carmel. He prayed to Our Lady of Grace, of Fatima, and of Medjugorje. Still nothing happened, and the darkness got deeper.

As days and weeks passed, the mental assaults continued to come, as did the footsteps. Reyes ordered the enemy to depart, but it didn't work. A vacation in Las Vegas made it worse. After a few days, he cut it short and came home. Depression sank in. He had waged a spiritual battle for twenty-eight years. But now, his life seemed to be caving in on him.

As months went by, even Estela realized something was wrong. The devil was now in Reyes' dreams, taunting him, distorting his every thought and emotion.

By the end of May 1988, Reyes began to believe he couldn't bear much more. By now, he was mad at God. His wife confronted him, *"There's a fight going on inside of you,"* to which he replied, *"And it's a big fight. Satan won't leave me alone!"*

Indeed, there was only one thing left to do. Reyes began to fast, to fast and pray like never before. And he begged God to take him home. Life for him was over.

One morning, he awoke crying and headed for church. Estela followed. As he sat in a rear pew, everyone present could see their strong friend was in serious trouble.

Suddenly, out of nowhere, a woman walked up and handed Reyes a baby.

"Reyes," she said, *"babies can be sometimes the most beautiful thing for you."*

As he took the baby, the woman added, *"Her name is Maria."*

It was all he needed to hear. A river of tears flowed from his eyes, and he exploded inside. And amazingly, something else happened. The attack suddenly lifted.

Reyes had one final conversation with the Virgin, begging her for her love and her kiss. And as quickly as it all began, it was over.

Peace filled his heart, his mind and his soul. God's presence overcame him, and he felt as if the Virgin herself had embraced him.

Filled with both agony and ecstasy, 1988 was a strange year for Reyes Ruiz. He felt he was being prepared by God for something. At Medjugorje, the Virgin had come to teach, and once he arrived there, Reyes could definitely feel her knitting an important work in his heart. He felt forgiveness toward his family and toward himself. But above all, he felt forgiveness toward Estela, his wife, so distant from him in every way, who had taunted and mocked him before he left for Medjugorje.

"You think you're so holy! You think you're so right!" Estela had lashed out at him before he departed. *"I live my life the way I want to!"*

Reyes forgave Estela for those piercing words. He forgave her for saying *"no"* to daily Rosary and Mass with him. He forgave the kids. He forgave everyone.

Indeed, forgiveness was a full-time job for Reyes in Medjugorje. He busily crisscrossed the village all week long, thinking, praying, and forgiving. If something popped into his mind — a prayer, a petition — he would ask for it immediately. If it was important, he headed back up the mountain or over to Saint James' Church. After all, if there was any time to ask, it was now. He was in Medjugorje. His heart was next to Mary, his beautiful *"Mujer Bonita."* And somehow, he felt that she could hear his every word even more clearly than before.

"I want Little Reyes to be healed," he demanded of Mary. *"I want my family to be converted,"* he told her all week long. But every day, he would amend his petition slightly.

"I want them committed totally to God," he asked one day.

"I want Estela to be my prayer partner, a prayer warrior. I want her to go to Mass every day," he later insisted of the Virgin, as he headed back up the hill.

But toward the end of the week, he felt as if he were shortchanging himself. So he asked for more. He realized that he had nothing to lose.

"I want them to be saints... I want all of them to be saints! I want everyone in my family to be a saint!!!"

Finally, he had said it. His family's holiness was truly the heart of all of his prayers, and he saw no reason to hold back. Medjugorje had filled him with a spiritual boldness, with a rejuvenated, intense faith, which gave him confidence that his prayer would be answered. It was a petition that undoubtedly shook the heavens.

In Saint James, at the approximate time of the Virgin's daily apparition, Reyes would sit next to his friend, Rebecca, and silently pray. But at the moment of Mary's apparition, Reyes would suddenly break into tears and cry out loud. He couldn't help it. He could feel Mary kissing his heart and taking his hand. He could feel her giving him Heaven's blessing.

At that same moment, he would often intervene for the visionaries too, imploring the Virgin:

You take care of them... They don't know how hard it is! They don't understand how hard it is to live a...a life of God... You have to protect them... You continuously have to be with

them, because it's going to be very, very hard for them...
They have to be protected... You've got to protect them!

Like most people who visit Medjugorje, Reyes didn't want to leave. No one can say exactly why, but leaving seems like an agony. Many wish to stay forever, consumed by a heavenly peace that they can't imagine living without.

For some, the magic lies in Saint James Church. Others are drawn to the hills and mountains where Mary has appeared. Still others find a warm feeling of attachment to the visionaries, the Franciscans, the Croatian people and their simple rural lifestyle of agriculture, ancient customs and traditions.

But in the end, the real draw is the peace.

Medjugorje offers peace to souls — total peace. It's no wonder that Mary declares that she is appearing at Medjugorje as the *"Queen of Peace."* For truly, if the feeling many derive from Medjugorje could spread throughout the world, it would be a tranquil, better place.

Reyes' final night in Medjugorje was painful. With his friend, Dr. Neil, he crisscrossed the village in the Medjugorje twilight one final time.

The two advanced up the path toward Podbrdo, where the apparitions first began. One final Rosary was in order. Even though it was two in the morning, and the bus was already waiting almost a mile away for departure in thirty minutes, Reyes felt the urge to go to the hill. Just one last time, he wanted to go back to where he hoped Mary would be waiting for him, back to the oasis of peace.

Sitting near the cross, Reyes stopped halfway through his beads. He glanced at Dr. Neil and asked, *"Will you finish the rest?"*

Neil had no objections. When they finished praying, Reyes begged his taller friend, *"Would you please place this Rosary on top of the cross?"* Again, Neil complied. He placed the beads on the large, homemade cross that had marked Mary's point of arrival and departure for numerous apparitions since 1981.

Turning to leave, a thought flashed through Reyes' mind. A final petition overcame him and pierced his very soul like a bolt of lightning.

Several days before, at that very spot, the visionaries had disclosed how a brilliant light from Heaven always accompanies the Virgin. This light, they said, reflects off the top of the cross and throughout the valley.

Reyes imagined this reflection traveling from Heaven to the village of Medjugorje, and then to the surrounding countries of the world, and for some reason, he was suddenly led to ponder this. Then logic set in. He knew inside himself that he needed to say one more prayer.

"Now I am leaving this Rosary here," Reyes addressed the Virgin and Jesus. *"I am leaving it here, and I am consecrating my family...all of my family, all of our friends, the city of Phoenix...then the state of Arizona, and then each one of the states, to You. I am consecrating the entire United States to You!*

"And when that light from Heaven comes tomorrow," Reyes' prayer continued, *"let it reflect on that cross."*

"And as it reflects on the cross, then let it spread throughout our land, throughout the world.

"Let it convert all the Americas, and then let it convert all of God's people...!"

With this prayer, Reyes again could feel Mary's touch and her blessing. And feeling a bit more at peace with the thought of leaving, he hurried back to the village to mount the bus for his trip home.

FOR THE SOUL OF THE FAMILY

CHAPTER NINE

"GOOD MORNING, DAUGHTER"

While the atmosphere Reyes would encounter upon returning home was sure to differ from Medjugorje's penetrating peace, the humility and simplicity of his small stucco home on downtown Phoenix's East Cody Drive was not much more elegant than the homes of the Croatian villagers.

Only a block away from Central Avenue, the Ruiz family's house is modest in size and sits just a few feet away from the sidewalk. It is enclosed by a wire fence that surrounds the building, with a good-sized yard on one side and in the back. The property outside has been tastefully decorated with Reyes' personal version of "home improvement," that is, statues of Jesus and Mary, and an image of Our Lady of Guadalupe.

The statues sit in marked contrast to an open field of rocks and cinder right across the street, the by-product of a fire which now serves ideally for parking or sports...or for carrying a life-size crucifix around in circles at all hours of the day and night, as Reyes' brother Fernando did a few years back.

All things considered, though, it's home. Except for the businesses that line Central Avenue, this house and street could easily be mistaken for dozens of others that fill South Phoenix.

Occupying a flat, sprawling area of land that ends at a group of classic rocky mountains, this arid desert community is home for tens of thousands of Hispanic families. Usually, the sky is clear and intensely blue, and the sun's strong presence is acutely noted, both by the heat felt, and by the fact many cars have windows tinted almost black.

Flying into Phoenix, one's first impression is that of cactus, prairie bushes, and canals. With so much sand, such arid temperatures and such little water, it's obvious that people didn't always live here. Like Las Vegas, Phoenix was the product of entrepreneurs who couldn't bear to see all the beauty and pleasure of the surreal environment go to waste. Today, it is one of the fastest growing metropolitan areas in America.

Known as *"the Valley of the Sun,"* Phoenix proper is huge. The entire metropolitan area is spread out over 450 square miles of Sonora Desert. Maricopa County, where Phoenix and surrounding communities are located, is 9000 square miles or about the size of Vermont. Miles of boxy, stucco buildings, and strip malls and "walled" communities line very wide, straight streets that appear to stretch into the horizon. Some say it is a never-ending suburb without a city. *"Phoenix is like a little kid who grew up too fast,"* says Arizona Republic columnist E.J. Montini, *"It has size and strength, but no maturity."*[1]

By late 1988, Phoenix was spreading out and flexing its muscle. And keeping the pace with the city's growing prestige, Estela Ruiz forged ahead too, more and more sure of her goal. Her tone of authority and commitment to her job were unmistakable. She was on the move. One could see the resolute firmness in her face. Her eyes were like steel, while her tightly squeezed mouth pulled her lips in and caused her jaw to protrude like an army general. She had become a fighter, a true career warrior, and she even dressed in typical, stylish yet no-nonsense, career "battle garb." Like icing on the cake, her large-framed glasses accentuated her image as the consummate professional woman.

Indeed, Estela was prepared and ready for battle, and she seemed to be sinking deeper and deeper into the trenches. Although Reyes had known her for decades, his Estela was now a different person. She became hard as anthracite and cold as ice. Reyes' attempts to get her to pray the Rosary or to go to Mass in the evening were not just declined, they were explosively received. And by September of 1988, this was something Reyes Ruiz was having a hard time dealing with.

By now, most members of the family were becoming weary of each other. As Reyes would say, *"They were all being called by the world."* And they were all, like Mama Estela, coming to view their patriarch as one who had a few screws loose.

Often, the kids tried to reason with their father. *"Dad,"* they would ask, *"do you think that...that all this stuff you're doing — going to daily Mass and going to daily prayer, daily Communion — do you think it's worth it? Is it all worth it?"*

Reyes, Sr. always held his ground. Like a good counselor, he responded to their questions with a question: *"What do you think?"* Reyes would reply. *"What do you think, is it worth it or not?"*

Heads would drop. Silence would fall. No one could muster up the courage or find the certainty to challenge dad. Whether it was because they didn't want to hurt him, or because they just didn't want to answer to God later, no reply ever came forth.

"Then you have already answered it!" Reyes would quickly proclaim without hesitation.

Seizing the victory like a soldier proudly raising his flag after a battle, Reyes wouldn't let these encounters be perceived as a draw. They were triumphs, triumphs for God and for his friend, the Virgin, and he would readily claim them as such. Time and time again, he would witness his family wilt and then raggedly retreat from his question, like beaten dogs that have lost their bark and bite.

While Estela could explode in Reyes' face if he approached her with his "religious stuff," most of the time she was prepared. By now, Estela looked at him differently. He was simply an embarrassment. He was odd. In fact, after objectively contemplating his psychological makeup, Estela even concluded that her husband was truly *"gone."*

Her conclusion was a logical result, she felt, of Reyes' own behavior. But it also sprung from her own lack of belief in the supernatural.

Apparitions, visions, weeping statues — it was all too much for her. Like her husband, back in the 1960's Estela became involved in the Cursillo Movement for a while, but the fire soon died. Once-a-week Mass on Sunday became the bulk of her relationship with God. As far as supernatural events were concerned, skepticism was safe ground.

On the other hand, a real-life supernatural occurrence was all Reyes needed to earn his trip to the padded cell. And that's exactly what happened to his personality when he found out about Medjugorje. The animated religious zealot became almost unbearable to live with after he heard that the Virgin was appearing there.

The proverbial saying about gasoline on a fire would have been an understatement. More accurately, Reyes was like Babe Ruth getting his first chance to be in the majors, or Clark Gable auditioning for his first film. Like the dark night sky that never fails to embrace the rising sun, Medjugorje and Reyes Ruiz were perfect for each other.

Reyes' first victim after hearing of the Madonna's arrival in Medjugorje was, of course, Estela. Potential mine field or not, Reyes approached.

"Read this!" he ordered her, convinced that she would have to apologize for being wrong about him for the last thirty years. For in Reyes' mind, he now had proof. The Blessed Virgin Mary was appearing daily to six children in Medjugorje, Yugoslavia, and there was even a newspaper written by professional journalist Wayne Weible that said so. Case closed! He was right all along! She was the one who needed the help!

But Estela didn't have time to read his little newspaper. She was far too busy. By now, she was marching to the beat of a different drummer, and to her, Reyes was still the same, only now he was more nuts than ever!

Day after day, Reyes would ask, *"Have you read the articles?"*

"No," Estela would answer, either by word or look.

Days turned into weeks, and weeks into months. Estela still showed no interest in the newspaper her husband wanted her to read so badly.

"No."

"No."

"No!"

Same question, same answer. But Reyes still didn't stop asking. Though attempting to evangelize his wife was a lot like playing Russian Roulette, he never backed down. He would just reload and fire again.

And why not? It was simply a matter of time, especially now that he had proof. He had been right all along, and the newspaper backed him up. Estela would realize that the Virgin was in Medjugorje if she would only look at the facts.

Somewhere around August of 1988, Reyes stopped listening for his wife's reply. Instead, he began to hear another voice. It was his friend, the Virgin. She was calling him to herself, calling him to Medjugorje.

Now it was time to ask Estela one last time. Would she go to Medjugorje with him?

"NO!"

For Estela, Reyes now showed symptoms of needing a straight jacket and medication. The man she loved, the dark-faced Mexican son of sharecroppers with a sixth-grade education, was now beyond hope. He had lost his mind, Estela believed. People from South Phoenix don't travel five thousand miles to communist countries to see visions, not if they're sane.

The last thing in the world Estela wanted was to make a trip to Medjugorje. She didn't believe, and she didn't care. She didn't want to be with Reyes, and she was busy. Even if it were true, why couldn't Mary have picked somewhere a little closer or more convenient?

"I don't want to go! You go ahead and go," she told him.

That was it. Case closed. He would go and she would stay. End of discussion.

Within a short period of time, though, Estela's mind began to explore the possibilities of Reyes' departure in another light.

This would be, she realized, ten days of being alone. She would have ten days without having to hear about the little newspaper, ten days of peace, quiet and freedom.

On his part, Reyes didn't press the issue. The world was coming down on his family, especially Little Rey, and he had to make his move. He had to go. With Estela or without her, this was his calling. His kids needed the prayers. His wife needed the prayers. He needed the prayers. And from what Reyes read in the little newspaper, Medjugorje was the ideal place for all kinds of prayer.

Before leaving, Reyes asked Estela one last thing. *"Do you have a petition you want me to present to Our Lady over there?"*

Estela didn't say anything. The bottom line was that she really didn't believe in petitions, either.

But out of nowhere, it dawned on her. Estela had a fear of dying, a horrible, deep-seated fear of death. On a little piece of paper, she scratched a request to the Virgin: *"Please, Blessed Mother, help me get rid of the fear of dying."* And for good measure, she threw in, *"And I would like to go straight to Heaven when I die."*

Out the door, to the airport and across the Atlantic, Reyes traveled all by himself. It was quite a daring trip for a man of his background to embark upon, but with his eyes focused on his goal, Reyes forged ahead fearlessly. The date was September 8, 1988, the Church celebrated birthday of the Virgin Mary.

Packed with some clothes, a handful of petitions and a heart full of prayers, Reyes felt like a little boy about to enter a toy shop, like a teenager about to go on his first date with the girl of his dreams.

And in some ways, that is exactly what he was doing. For he had always been in love with this girl. Finally, Reyes was going to get a chance to be with her in person.

Estela felt like a bird that had been locked up in a cage and was now set free. Reyes was gone for ten days! No one would be asking her questions about God, or giving her pointers on how to improve her prayer life. Her youngest son, Tony, was the only one still living at home. Once the boy was off to school in the morning, that was it. The rest of the day was hers. The liberated woman was now emancipated to the fullest, at least for ten days. But they were going to be ten of the best days of her life!

Or so she thought...

On the third day her husband was gone, Estela Ruiz awoke, climbed out of bed and headed through the living room to the kitchen to make a pot of coffee. Tony was still asleep, and she wasn't yet dressed for work. As she passed the portrait of Our Lady of Guadalupe painted by her husband, she distinctly heard a soft voice, the voice of a woman, which spoke to her out loud.

"Good morning, daughter," the voice beckoned, as if calling to her and expecting a response.

For a second, Estela paused.

What in the world was that?

Her immediate thought was, *"Oh, come on now, I think I'm hearing things."* But in her mind, a thought of what it could have been surfaced. She instantly rejected the idea.

"That's silly, I don't believe in that stuff..."

Estela brushed it off. After waking up Tony for school, she headed out the door for work. It was over. It didn't cross her mind for the rest of the day.

Two days later, as Estela retraced her steps from the previous morning, the same thing happened. She heard a voice. This time, it was clear as day. And this time, she knew where it came from.

The painting of Our Lady of Guadalupe, the same painting she was thinking of taking down since Reyes had turned the house into a shrine, was talking to her. Yes, this time she was sure that a voice in the direction of the picture had spoken to her. Again, it was the voice of a woman.

"Good morning, Daughter," the voice melodiously intoned.

This time, without blinking an eye, Estela answered back.

"Good morning, Blessed Mother," she replied to the wall with the picture hanging on it.

"Yikes!" she thought to herself upon hearing her own reply.

Panic gripped her. Her spoken reply had been an involuntary response, a reflex action. But it had happened, and she had to accept it.

She had heard the voice emanating from the direction of the painting. It spoke out loud. She had heard herself answer. She answered out loud.

"My God," she thought, *"what in the world is going on?"*

Stunned and confused, Estela tried to rally a little. But she couldn't. *"I'm really going crazy now,"* she thought. And then another thought struck her, worse than the first. *"Reyes is crazy, and now I'm going crazy! I'm going as crazy as my husband!"*

Estela knew that if she hadn't answered back, she could have gotten out of it. She could have let herself off the hook. Her mind could have rationalized the voice. But once she heard her own voice reply to the Virgin, *"Good morning,"* she knew she was stuck.

Indeed, Estela was now in a jam. Her husband, long ago diagnosed in her mind as a major loon, was off in Medjugorje seeking the Virgin's graces. And here she was in Phoenix, taking up where he left off. The Ruiz home was par for the course, she thought. Now amidst the gallery of pictures of Jesus and Mary, there was still someone to talk and listen to them.

Quickly, Estela made a pact with herself. *"I will never tell any-one what happened — they'll think I'm crazy!"*

She was serious. There was a lot at stake here. Estela Ruiz was an educated administrator with two degrees. She made good money. It wouldn't be smart if this got out. Her career might take a nose-dive. Worse than that, her son — the noted, respected State Representative on his way to being Senator — could quickly become a state-wide spectacle. A big-time politician whose mother talks to paintings and whose dad visits communist nations would most definitely not go over well at the polls. It would be too much to explain. Wise, old, politician-minded Estela knew that the opposition was always digging for something. Forget drug and sex scandals — this really had the potential to be a permanent knock-out punch to her son's career. She could see the headlines: "The Honorable Armando Ruiz has loony parents that speak to paintings and are possibly spies."

Several days later, on September 17, Reyes Ruiz triumphantly returned home from Medjugorje. At the airport, Estela noticed his face. It was different. Her husband didn't look the same.

Like Moses coming down from Mt. Sinai, Reyes' face radiated, it had a certain glow that was not there before. The radiance was not so much visible as mystical. Estela couldn't put her finger on it.

"Gosh, he looks different," she thought. *"Something happened to him over there. Something beautiful happened to him..."*

From that moment on, Estela says, she began to see Reyes in a completely different light. It was almost as if she had never known him. After thirty years, her partner who had almost become like the furniture to her, had a light radiating from him. Reyes was a different man.

Maybe he really saw the Virgin Mary, Estela began to wonder. Maybe the Virgin really did speak to him out loud.

Maybe he wasn't so crazy after all, she thought...

Something must have happened to him...

CHAPTER TEN

FROM BLOOD TO ROSES

Though Reyes definitely did seem more bearable, and even some how likable, Estela still wasn't talking. Her recent experiences with Our Lady of Guadalupe were still buried deep within her heart, and she wasn't sure how, or if, she was going to let them out.

Unfortunately, Our Lady of Guadalupe had never been an important part of Estela's life. Unlike most modern-day Hispanic households, and certainly the traditional ones, in which Our Lady of Guadalupe is almost an honorary family member, Estela had never developed a truly close relationship with her.

The majority of Hispanic Catholics, however, honor Our Lady of Guadalupe with special devotions, statues or paintings of her scattered throughout the home, and elaborate celebrations and Holy Mass on December 12, her feast day. In Phoenix, she is even the Patron Saint of the diocese.

To understand the significant role which the Virgin of Guadalupe plays in the lives of many Hispanic families, it helps to know the story of her first appearance in Mexico to the now beatified Juan Diego.

It began with a dream.

It was a dream which occurred hundreds of years before the Virgin of Guadalupe spoke to Estela Ruiz through the painting fashioned by her husband.

Her name was Princess Papantzin. She was the sister of the Aztec Emperor Montezuma II, and in the year 1509, she had a mystical experience.

As she lie in a coma, a glowing angel with a black cross on his forehead appeared to her. The angel led the princess to the ocean shore, where he showed her ships sailing to the pagan Aztec nation. These ships were unlike any she had ever seen, as their white sails were emblazoned with black crosses similar to the one on the angel's forehead.

The angel told Papantzin that the Aztec's tyrannical rule over pre-Columbian Mexico would be overthrown. Her nation would be conquered and brought to the knowledge of the true God. The oppressed Indian people would be liberated, set free by white-skinned invaders, the angel declared.

Upon hearing of it, Montezuma brooded over his sister's prophetic dream.

And with anxiety and uncertainty, he awaited its fulfillment.

At that time, Montezuma's reign was a bloody one. He and his Aztec predecessors were dedicated to offering their gods as much blood as they could. There was one barbaric condition, however: the blood had to be human.

Through their sacrificial religious practices, millions of people were fed to a myriad of Aztec false gods. The Aztec's complicated mythology called for them to worship celestial bodies and natural forces. In order to avoid natural disasters and to insure health and military victories, the Aztecs offered an estimated 50,000 victims a year to their gods of the sun, moon and rain. Approximately one in every five children was sacrificed.

Their hungriest god of all was named Quetzalcoatl, who came into their lives after certain Aztec ancestors viewed a cataclysmic event in the heavens. A great comet, they reported, appeared in the sky in the shape of a fiery serpent. After it disappeared, the Indians believed that it became the planet Venus, the "Morning Star"! They named it Quetzalcoatl, meaning "*feathered serpent,*" and they fashioned numerous stone idols in its image. Soon after, they began to offer these idols human sacrifices.

In 1487, just five years before Columbus arrived, an estimated 80,000 people were sacrificed during a four-day, bloody orgy near Mexico City. This offering was made to the false god Avitzilopochtli.

The Aztec society at the time was quite advanced, even sophisticated. They had made great progress in mathematics, architecture, astronomy, and engineering. Mexico City was the capital of the Aztec Empire and said to be one of the most beautiful cities in the entire world.

Yet, bloody rituals were at the center of its culture. Long lines of people, stretching for miles, could be found constantly marching toward pyramids where, on all four sides, they would ascend to be slaughtered.

These prisoners would climb more than a hundred steps to meet with *witch doctors*, dressed in black robes with long hair, who would slice open the victim's chest with a knife. Then, as they lay slain upon an altar, the witch doctors would remove their hearts while they were still beating. Every fifteen seconds an Indian would be killed and then fed to the wild animals in the zoo. Some of their body parts would be ritualistically indulged upon by the Aztecs. If a new temple were dedicated, the traditional ceremony called for at least 20,000 sacrifices.

The Aztecs regarded themselves as *"people of the sun."* And in order to preserve their divinity, they fed their god of the sun a regular nourishment of human blood, for fear that the sun would leave them. The worst stories known involve people being eaten alive, a bloody horror of unimaginable description.

Other Aztec gods were likewise fed regularly. Xochipilli was the stone god of abundant food, pleasure and love. Coatilicue was a monstrous idol in the shape of a woman, with jaguar's paws for hands and eagle's claws for feet. Tona Tiuh represented the sun, and his image in stone shows his protruding tongue, representing his thirst for blood. Finally there was Tonantzin, the great mother god, whose temple once stood on the summit of a small hill named Tepeyac, near Mexico City.

After Papantzin's prophecy, Montezuma became downright gloomy. Known primarily for his sinister nature, he was nonetheless respectful of prophecies. Even before his sister's vision, soothsayers were predicting his downfall. White men from the ocean, mystics warned, were on their way.

In the late 1400's, Columbus arrived from Spain with his fleet in search of the "New World." America was that "New World," and he immediately claimed the land for Spain.

The white men had arrived.

Conflicts between the Spaniards and the Aztecs were on the horizon. Once begun, they were numerous and bloody. But Montezuma was no match for the Spaniard's thundering cannons and blazing muskets. Almost as soon as the battles had begun, Montezuma became convinced that the Spaniards were invincible. The Spanish invasion of 1519 sent the emperor into retreat and quickly brought an end to his tyranny. Defeated by Cortez, and a growing allegiance of Mexican tribes who detested Montezuma, by late that year it was all over.

Almost immediately, the practice of offering human sacrifice to the gods was abolished. The pagan temples were destroyed, and the Catholic faith was instituted throughout the country.

From what the Spanish soldiers witnessed of the blood-soaked pyramids and temples, one conclusion was drawn. The Aztecs had been victims of Satan, prisoners sacrificed because of Lucifer's thirst for blood and hate for God. The bloody assassination of the innocents had been no accident, the Catholic explorers concluded; on the contrary, it had been totally conceived of and instituted by the Prince of Darkness.

The whole scenario was nonetheless puzzling to the Spanish soldiers. When they looked at Mexico City, it was apparent that the Aztec civilization was at its peak. But like Rome and countless civilizations before them, there appeared to be a relationship between the fall of the civilization and its degenerate moral condition. Often, that degenerate condition was filled with false gods and the bloody persecution of the innocent.

With Montezuma's regime in ruins, Spain moved quickly to bring the Aztec people into the Christian faith. After eradicating the temples and spreading images of Jesus throughout the land, missionaries spread out in all directions. Churches, schools and hospitals opened, all bearing the cross of Jesus and all preaching love and forgiveness. And to help bring greater order, Spain dispatched a distinguished scholar, Prior Juan Zumarraga, who was appointed the first bishop of the New World.

Both pious and versatile, the Bishop brought printing presses, textiles and new foods to the Mexicans. He also tried heroically to encourage baptism and faith in the true God. But the Indians didn't want to hear it. Few converted, and the Bishop was ridiculed. Fed by their pagan past, the people claimed they had *"no souls,"* and soon an insurrection mounted.

Sensing his own powerlessness, Bishop Zumarraga turned to a higher force. Addressing the Virgin, he begged, *"Intervene, dear Lady."* The Bishop then proceeded to ask for a sign that she had heard his desperate prayer — some Castilian roses. So what if there were no such roses known to grow in Mexico. In order for him to be sure she had heard him, the sign had to be pretty difficult to accomplish!

At the same time, back in the "Old World," another type of insurrection was taking place throughout Europe. Martin Luther, formerly a devout Catholic, was leading a revolt in the Church. The "One Church" instituted by Christ was beginning to separate.

The Church had other problems, too. Bishops were becoming wealthy men. Time in Purgatory could be eliminated by hefty donations. Priests were taking up with women. And all the while, Popes were busy solving political problems or promoting the Renaissance. On the eve of the Protestant Reformation, the Fifth Lateran Council met in Rome (1512). Under Pope Leo X, it argued for five years and finally brought reform.

But it was too late. Luther had ignited a revolt.

While at first Luther did not intend to separate from the Catholic Church, this quickly changed. Lutheranism began and was quickly followed by more radical forms of Protestantism. Jean Calvin, Huldereich, Zwingli, Thomas MÅnzer and a host of other religious zealots emerged, each with his own version of the truth, his own interpretation of the Bible which the Catholic Church had preserved. Murder, unrestrained sexual mores, and a variety of ills resulted as Rome moved to further reform itself.

Still, Catholic evangelization continued. In the Far East, Francis Xavier traveled to India and Japan, while a host of new religious orders spread throughout the globe.

Back in Mexico, the missionaries weren't turning up too many miracles. The Indians were just too resistant, too set in their pagan ways.

However, one unseen sign, one great flicker of hope did occur at the time.

Princess Papantzin, Montezuma's sister who had received the vision of the *"luminous being"* and had foretold her brother's downfall, was again stricken by the providence of God.

In 1525, Princess Papantzin was baptized Catholic, becoming one of the first Mexicans to enter into the faith. She was joined by a poor Indian couple from the village of Cuautitlan, some fifteen miles northeast of Mexico City, who adopted the new baptismal names of Juan Diego and Maria Lucia. And six miles away, in the village of Tolpetlac, Juan Diego's uncle was brought into the Church: Juan Bernardino.

Juan Diego and his wife didn't just join the faith, they began to live it. Frequently Juan and his wife would walk fifteen miles to Tlaltelolco to attend Mass and receive the sacraments.

Rising before dawn so as to arrive on time, Juan Diego's daily round-trip walk of thirty miles had become routine. The Franciscans had taught him about the importance of early arrival, and he had obviously taken it to heart.

Juan also continued to educate himself in his new faith. At the Franciscan convent in Tlaltelolco, Juan learned about the love of God and Santa Maria (Holy Mary) with hundreds of other Mexicans.

After his wife died in 1529, Juan moved in with his Uncle Bernardino. While caring for him and doing farm work, Juan Diego was now only nine miles from the church, and only days from his destiny...

CHAPTER ELEVEN

THE WOMAN CLOTHED
WITH THE SUN

In 1531, Juan Diego was an experienced 57 years old. The work, the long walks and the loneliness he felt after his wife's death were all beginning to take their toll on him.

It was a cold, starlit morning on Saturday, December 9, 1531, when Juan rose early to begin his long walk to Church. He was scheduled to assist at Mass that day. This Mass was in honor of his newly-adopted Mother and Queen, the Virgin Mary, as December 9th was then celebrated as the Feast of the Immaculate Conception.

As he approached Tepeyac Hill, a place surrounded by memories of the former pagan temple and diabolical sacrifices, Juan started to hear music.

He stopped. But the music continued. As he approached, he heard it more clearly. The melody coming from what seemed like a celestial choir was sweet and captivating to his senses. As Juan searched for the source of the beautiful, yet bewildering sounds, he noticed a glowing white cloud emitting a kaleidoscope of colors that formed a brilliant rainbow. The little Indian peasant was stunned.

Then, the music stopped, and a gentle voice called to him. The voice was female, soft yet persuasive.

"Juanito... Juan Dieguito," the Lady called.

The diminutive peasant felt no fear. Racing up a 130 foot summit, Juan suddenly found himself face-to-face with a glowing lady, whose beauty and brilliance were overpowering. He was mesmerized.

While the hill was boulder-strewn and covered with mesquite bushes and prickly plants, Juan Diego was oblivious to the potential for harm. All he could see was the glowing Lady. Her dress shown like the sun, and she appeared to be young, perhaps about fourteen years-old.

The amazing apparition magnetized him, and he drew nearer. After several steps, Juan dropped to his knees, overwhelmed by a feeling of love and peace.

"Juanito, my son, where are you going?

"Noble Lady," he replied, *"I am on my way to the church in Tlaltelolco to hear Mass."*

The Lady smiled and said to him:

"Know for certain, dearest of my sons, that I am the perfect and perpetual Virgin Mary, Mother of the True God, through whom everything lives, the Lord of all things, who is Master of Heaven and Earth. I ardently desire a teocalli [temple] be built here for me where I will show and offer all my love, my compassion, my help and my protection to the people. I am your merciful Mother, the Mother of all who live united in this land, and of all mankind, of all those who love me, of those who cry to me, of those who have confidence in me. Here I will hear their weeping and their sorrows, and will remedy and alleviate their sufferings, necessities and misfortunes. Therefore, in order to realize my intentions, go to the house of the Bishop of Mexico City and tell him that you have seen and heard. Be assured that I shall be very grateful and will reward you for doing diligently what I have asked of you. Now that you have heard my words, my son, go and do everything as best as you can."

Juan bowed and replied reverently, *"My Holy One, my Lady, I will do all you ask of me."*

Hurrying down Tepeyac, Juan Diego raced toward Mexico City. As he arrived at Bishop Zumarraga's house, his worst fear unfolded. Physical abuse he could stand, but what if the Bishop didn't believe him?

And of course, that is what occurred. Although Zumarraga eventually saw the Indian after he had waited for hours, the Bishop merely listened and then dismissed him. It was simply too much.

Why would the Mother of God appear in Mexico on a hill where there was once a pagan temple? The story was interesting but highly unlikely, concluded the educated bishop. Nonetheless, he promised Juan Diego that he would reflect on it all.

Once again passing by Tepeyac on the way home, Juan's second-worst fear was about to be realized. Mary was waiting for him, just as he suspected.

On his knees before the glowing Virgin, the bewildered peasant recounted his miserable day. *"Noble Lady,"* he sighed,

> *"I obeyed your orders. I entered into the Bishop's audience chamber, though I had difficulty in doing so. I saw His Excellency as you asked me to. He received me kindly and listened with attention, but when he answered me, it seemed as if he did not believe me. The bishop told me, You must come again some time, my son, when I can hear you more at my leisure. I will reflect on what you have told me, and I will take careful consideration of the good will and the earnest desire that caused you to come to me. I knew by the manner of his response that he thought I was inventing the story of your desire to have a temple built here... So I beg you, noble Lady, entrust this message to someone of importance, someone well-known and respected, so that your wish will be accomplished. For I am only a lowly peasant, and you, my Lady, have sent me to a place where I have no standing. Forgive me if I have disappointed you for having failed in my mission."*

The Virgin smiled and said,

> **"Listen to me, my dearest son, and understand that I have many servants and messengers whom I could charge with the delivery of my message. But it is altogether necessary that you should be the one to undertake this mission, and that it be through your mediation and assistance that my wish should be accomplished. I urge you to go to the Bishop again tomorrow. Tell him in my name and make him fully understand my disposition, that he**

should undertake the erection of the teocalli for which I ask. Repeat to him that it is I in person, the ever Virgin Mary, the Mother of God, who sent you."

Juan replied,

> *"Holy Lady, I will not disappoint you. I will gladly go again at your command, even though once more I may not be believed. Tomorrow toward sunset, I shall return here and give an account of the Bishop's response."*

The next day was a Sunday. Once again, Juan awoke early and headed back to the Bishop's residence, somewhat dreading that his worst fear would again materialize. Rejection and dismissal were sure to be dealt him again, he thought, and he would have to endure another embarrassing confrontation with the Virgin over his failure. After muttering a prayer to Mary, he entered the Bishop's house.

Again, he encountered resistance and another long wait. Finally, the Bishop saw him.

Bishop Zumarraga was stunned. The little Indian had returned with the same story. The Virgin was appearing in Mexico and wanted a church built. Though the Bishop's inclination was to dismiss the peasant immediately, Juan Diego's tears caused him to inquire more.

"Where did you see her?" the Bishop asked. *What was she like? How long did she stay?"*

Juan Diego consistently recounted his story. Cross-examination failed to unravel it. No error surfaced. No contradictions were elicited.

The Bishop began to believe... but only a little. He needed a sign, any kind of sign, and he would leave it up to the Virgin, he concluded with Juan.

Back to Tepeyac, Juan Diego raced, followed by spies sent by the Bishop. But as Juan reached the crest of Tepeyac, he somehow vanished from their sight, which caused the Bishop's men to return in frustration, without a clue.

Again atop Tepeyac, the radiant Virgin appeared. She listened to Juan's appeal for a sign and promised to deliver one the next day. She also assured him that the Bishop's change of heart was imminent.

That evening Juan went to visit his uncle and found him deathly ill. The following day, Juan urgently needed to care for his uncle, and he therefore could not make the trip to the Bishop's office. After finding a doctor for his uncle, he waited. Though he was distressed over his uncle's health, Juan became even more worried about the Virgin. He had failed to keep his appointment, and Mary would be displeased, he thought.

His uncle's condition grew worse. On Tuesday, December 12, Juan hurried to Tlaltelolco to search for a priest who could give his uncle Last Rights.

But there was a problem. Juan would have to pass by Tepeyac, and he suspected that the Virgin would be there, ready to question him. It was a dilemma. He wanted to retrieve the promised sign for the Bishop, yet his uncle could die if he lost too much time. Also, he still had to explain to Mary why he didn't show up the day before.

To solve his problem, Juan Diego decided to take an alternate route and bypass the heavenly visitor. It was good thinking, he concluded.

But as Juan scurried across the rough trail, his plan soon failed. A flash of light appeared on Tepeyac and zoomed in on him at an angle that intersected his path. Embarrassed, confused and ashamed, Juan Diego was again face-to-face with the Queen of Heaven.

"What is the matter, my little son?" the Virgin compassionately inquired. *"Where are you going?"*

With his head bowed low, Juan Diego mustered up enough courage to explain.

"Noble Lady, it will grieve you to hear what I have to say. My uncle, your poor servant, is very sick. He is suffering from the plague and is dying. I am hurrying to the church in Mexico City to call a priest to hear his Confession and give him the Last Rites. When I have done this, I will return here immediately to convey your message.

Please forgive me and be patient with me. I am not deceiving you. I promise faithfully to come here tomorrow with all haste."

Instead of reproach, the Virgin comforted her son: *"Listen and let it penetrate your heart, my dear little son,* she said consolingly...

"Do not be troubled or weighed down by grief. Do not fear any illness or vexation, anxiety or pain. Am I not here, who am your Mother? Are you not under my shadow and protection? Am I not your fountain of life? Are you not in the folds of my mantle? In the crossing of my arms? Is there anything else you need?"

Mary paused and then added, *"Do not let the illness of your uncle worry you because he is not going to die of his sickness. At this very moment, he is cured."*

Reassured, and trusting in her words, Juan Diego raced to the summit of Tepeyac, where the Virgin promised him he would find the sign — flowers — especially the Bishop's Castilian roses.

"Gather them carefully," the Virgin insisted. *"Assemble them together, and then bring them back and show me what you have.*

On the hill, Juan Diego did indeed find the flowers and even the roses. Though the December soil was frozen and hard, the flowers were somehow growing anyway, and the roses were in full bloom. Covered with morning dew, the flowers filled the air with a magnificent fragrance.

Removing his cape, or tilma, Juan Diego filled it with flowers and hurried back to the Virgin.

When he returned, Mary hastily arranged them with her own hands and gave him his departing orders:

"My little son, these varied flowers are the sign which you are to take to the Bishop. Tell him in my name that in them, he will recognize my will and that he must fulfill it. You will be my ambassador, fully worthy of my confidence. I enjoin you not to unfold your tilma, nor to reveal its contents, until you are in his presence. Then tell him ev-

erything: explain how I sent you to the top of the hill where you found these flowers growing in profusion, all ready to be gathered. Tell him once again all that you have seen and heard here to induce him to comply with my wishes so that the teocalli I asked for may be built there."

Once again, Juan Diego was off. The fateful moment had arrived. Again, he would have to argue his way into the Bishop's quarters, but it would be worth it. He had his sign.

Upon arrival, the servants detained him again. But the sight of the flowers changed their ways. The Bishop emerged and Juan addressed him.

"Your Excellency," Juan began,

"I obeyed your instructions. Very early this morning, the celestial Lady told me to come and see you again. I asked for the sign which your requested and which she had promised to give me. She told me to climb to the top of the hill where I had previously seen her, to pick the flowers growing there. I knew quite well that the summit of the hill was no place for flowers to grow, especially at this time of the year, but I did not doubt her word. When I reached to top, I was astonished to find myself surrounded by beautiful flowers, all brilliant with dewdrops. I plucked as many as I could carry and brought them back to her. She arranged them with her own hands and replaced them in my robe in order that I might bring them to you. Here they are. Behold, receive them."

With that, Juan Diego opened his tilma, and the flowers, mingled with Castilian roses, fell to the floor.

The Bishop and his associates were speechless.

Then, as they all stood before Juan Diego stunned and amazed, they noticed something even more spectacular. Juan Diego's tilma, woven from cactus fibers, now had a stunning, color portrait of the Blessed Virgin Mary upon it. The image glowed as if Mary were somehow present within the fibers, and the eyes of all those assembled were almost frozen in wonder.

"It is the Immaculate One!" exclaimed the Bishop.

One by one, all fell to their knees. Apologetically, Zumarraga turned to Juan Diego, who was more perplexed than all of them. There, on his own tilma, was an exact replica of the celestial Lady he had encountered on Tepeyac! Her image, now imprinted for all eternity, was before him in the Bishop's very office!

A chapel was quickly erected in Tepeyac, and the story spread like wildfire throughout the land. Later, it was discovered that Mary had also appeared to Juan Diego's uncle, Juan Bernardino, bringing to him healing at the exact time in which she had assured Juan Diego of her assistance.

Through what historians refer to as a series of errors and "misunderstandings," the Virgin's apparition at Tepeyac became known as the "Miracle of Guadalupe." Time has shown, however, that it may be the historians who are in error.

Juan Bernardino had told Bishop Zumarraga that the Virgin referred to herself as *"The Ever Virgin, Holy Mary of Guadalupe."* This astounded the Bishop, for it was the name of a famous Marian Shrine in Estremadura, Spain.

In the year 1326, the Virgin was believed to have appeared there in order to reveal where a hidden statue of herself holding the Christ Child had been hidden in a cave some six hundred years earlier. The cave was situated on the banks of the River Guadalupe, a word that means literally "Wolf River." Upon finding the statue, King Alfonso XI of Castile ordered that the Royal Monastery of Guadalupe be built to house the statue. The King then placed it in charge of the Franciscans.

The shrine soon became the most celebrated in Spain, where it is said that Columbus prayed before his momentous voyage. And it was Columbus who named an island in the Atlantic *Guadalupe*, after being shipwrecked there on his return trip to Spain.

However, theological scholars of 1666 believed that the Virgin, in her conversation with Juan Bernardino, had probably used the word TEQUANTLAXOPEUH (pronounced Tequetalope), which means *"Who saves us from the devourer."*

At that time, the devourer referred both to Satan and a terrible pagan god. But by the 19th and 20th century, most experts believed Mary actually used the word COATLAXOPEUH, which means *"she who breaks, stamps or crushes the serpent."* This was an Aztec word, and the Aztec serpent god Quetzalcoatl had seemingly been put out of business. There remained only a dreaded memory of years of human sacrifice which the people had endured. Indeed, this deduction made sense, especially considering the image on the tilma and the promise in Genesis (Gn 3:14, 15) of the woman *crushing the head* of the serpent (I.e., Satan). For years, Marian scholars have agreed that the Virgin of Guadalupe represents not only the woman in Genesis, but also the woman described in Revelation (Rv 12:1).

The image on the tilma seems to precisely fulfill Saint John's prophecy. Mary appears as the apocalyptic Mother of God, *"clothed with the sun,"* with the moon at her feet. On her head is a faint crown, and she is surrounded by golden rays, while at her feet lies the symbol of the crushed serpent, fulfilling her prophetic role in Genesis as well as symbolizing the end to the Aztec serpent god of blood sacrifices, Quetzalcoatl. Mary's clothing in the tilma image, extremely colorful and symbolic of royalty, reflects the Aztec culture of the time.

In Mexico, the serpent was now truly crushed, as the greatest mass-conversion in history commenced after the apparitions. Within a few years, over nine million Aztecs converted to Catholicism. Juan Diego himself would lay great emphasis on the fact that the visions had occurred on Tepeyac, the former site of the temple to the pagan mother-goddess Tonantzin, which had been destroyed by Cortez. Juan Diego believed it was a sign that Christianity was to replace the Aztec religion.

Juan Diego, Bishop Zumarraga and Cortez all died within a year of each other, after the miraculous work of God and the Virgin of Guadalupe had been courageously begun through them.

After the first nine million converts, tens of millions more would follow over the centuries. The Virgin had come to the Americas to free her children from Satan, and to present them to God.

She had come, as Pope Leo XIII would declare on October 12, 1895, as *"Queen of the Americas."* Fifty years later, on October 12, 1945, Pope Pius XII ordered the tilma image to be crowned again, and proclaimed Our Lady of Guadalupe as *"Empress of All the Americas."* The Pope also declared, *"We are certain that, as long as you are recognized as Queen and Mother, Mexico and the Americas will be safe."*

Indeed, twelve years later, Pope John XXIII again named Mary the *"Mother of the Americas,"* and the *"Mother of all those who lived united in this land."*

As recently as 1979, Pope John Paul II made it even clearer. The Virgin of Guadalupe, Our Lady of the Americas, was destined to be the *"Star of Evangelization."*

It was as if the Holy Father had said that Princess Papantzin's dream had not yet been fulfilled. More work remained — more evangelization, more conversions, more intercession through the Queen of the Americas. Quite simply, Mary was calling her children to sainthood!

Our Lady of Guadalupe had come in 1531 to put an end to human sacrifice, to stop the violence and bloodshed. It was therefore logical, as much as any other reason, that this was why she had come again, to a humble yet devoted household in South Phoenix. A household that reflected a land that once again was in serious trouble.

Indeed, Francis Johnston, the acclaimed English author whose two books *Fatima - The Great Sign* and *The Wonder of Guadalupe* are highly noted, wrote shortly before his death:

> *"Our Lady of the Americas may have been intended as a tangible pledge of hope in order to sustain us during the worldwide rationalist revolt against God which has arisen over the past few centuries and is now reaching its terrible climax.*
> *"The darkest hour will inevitably melt away in the radiant dawn of Our Lady's Triumph over the serpent."*[1]

CHAPTER TWELVE

A DECISIVE BATTLE

Mary's decisive victory over Satan did not start at Guadalupe. Down through the centuries, numerous prophecies have echoed repeatedly. Old and New Scripture foretell its coming. Good and evil, the prophecies concur, will do battle one decisive time.

It will be the ultimate confrontation, a showdown. The event will be more important than any other in the history of mankind since Christ's crucifixion. Not surprisingly, this clash between the forces of God and Satan has been anticipated by every generation. The wise seek to prepare since, when it climaxes, the world will apparently be consumed by chaos:

> *"When in the world there shall appear quakings of places, tumult of peoples, schemings of nations, confusion of leaders, disquietude of princes, then shalt thou understand that it is of these things the Most High has spoken since the days that were aforetime from the beginning."* (Ez 9:3-4)

> *"Little children, it is the last hour, and as you have heard that Antichrist cometh, even now there are many antichrists: whereby we know that it is the last hour."* (1 Jn 2:18)

In addition to Scriptural references, many older prophecies forecast Mary's victory over Satan:

> *"The power of Mary over all devils will be particularly outstanding in the last period of time. She will extend the Kingdom of Christ over the idolaters and Moslems,*

and there will come a glorious era in which Mary will be the ruler and Queen of human hearts. (Saint Louis De Montfort, 1673-1716)"

"In the last times, the Lord will especially spread the renown of His mother: Mary began salvation, and by her intercession it will be concluded. Before the Second Coming of Christ, Mary must, more than ever, shine in mercy, might and grace in order to bring unbelievers into the Catholic Faith. The powers of Mary in the last times over the demons will be very conspicuous. Mary will extend the reign of Christ over the heathens and Mohammedans, and it will be a time of great joy when Mary, as Mistress and Queen of Hearts, is enthroned. (Venerable Mary of Agreda, d. 1665)"

"We expect that the Immaculate Virgin and Mother of God, Mary, through her most powerful intercession, will bring it about that our Holy Mother the Catholic Church, after removal of all obstacles and overcoming of all errors, will gain in influence from day to day among all nations and in all places, prosper and rule from ocean to ocean, from the great stream to the ends of the earth; that she will enjoy peace and liberty... that all erring souls will return to the path of truth and justice after the darkness of their minds has been dispelled, and that there will be then one fold and one shepherd. (Pope Pius IX, d. 1878)"

"Hearken, thou, until I relate things that shall come to pass in the latter ages of the world. Great carnage shall be made, justice shall be outraged, multitudinous evils, great suffering shall prevail, and many unjust laws will be administered. (Saint Columkille)"

"All the nations of the earth shall fall away from the faith; the Holy Roman Empire shall collapse; Antichrist shall come; Enoch and Elias shall return to preach; the Jews shall return to the Holy Land; the powers of heaven

*shall be shaken; the stars shall fall from heaven; wide-
spread earthquakes, tidal waves, lightning, wars, fam-
ines, and epidemics shall occur.* (Saint Alphonsus Liguori,
1696-1787)"

Likewise, saints and Popes have echoed the prophecies:

*"We believe that the present hour is a dread phase of
the events foretold by Christ. It seems that darkness is about
to fall on the world. Humanity is in the grip of a supreme
crisis.* (Pope Pius XII, 1939-1958)"

*"I sometimes read the Gospel passage of the end times
and I attest that, at this time, some signs of this end are
emerging...* (Pope Paul VI, 1977)."

In numerous apparitions, Mary insists that the times of these
prophecies are now unfolding, and many theologians agree, particularly after studying her words.

In 1830, Mary told Saint Catherine Labouré, ***"The times are
evil... the entire world will be distressed with afflictions,"*** and 150
years later at Medjugorje, Mary boldly revealed, ***"The hour has come
when the demon is authorized to act with all its force."*** The Virgin's
words consistently confirm that the times are at hand, and many are
beginning to wisely prepare by listening to her indications.

Since Our Lady first defined the world's desperate situation in
1917 at Fatima, the picture has become increasingly clearer. Simply put, these final days, this time of confrontation between good
and evil, are in Mary's hands. God has willed it to be her moment,
and she will indeed triumph over Satan and evil. This victory was
promised to her in Genesis. Mary is the ***"Woman Clothed with the
Sun,"*** experts say, who defeats the Red Dragon in Revelation 12:1.
Likewise, Mary has confirmed to numerous visionaries, ***"These
are my times... the times of the Triumph of My Immaculate Heart."***

Theologians studying Guadalupe in the 17th, 18th and 19th
Centuries were aware of some of these prophecies. After examin-
ing the events in Mexico, it became obvious to them that the miracle

there involved something very significant. The image on the tilma, they said, connected Genesis with Revelation. It was truly astounding, and it was more than a coincidence.

The tilma, they concluded, signaled that the decisive, final confrontation was near. And by the Nineteenth Century, many more experts agreed that the battle was close at hand.

Besides, perhaps, the Shroud of Turin, never in the history of Christianity has such an incredible miracle been granted. The miraculous image on the tilma was unprecedented. As time went on, the event grew even more amazing and miraculous.

Today, one of the greatest miracles associated with the tilma is its very existence. A cloak-like garment made of a coarse fabric woven from natural cactus fiber called a*yate*, the tilma cloth should have disintegrated ten years or so after the apparition, according to scientists. But instead of disintegrating or losing its color, the cloth has remained miraculously intact for more than 460 years.

Besides surviving the natural aging process, the tilma has amazingly resisted extreme forces of nature and the hands of pilgrims, who at times even plucked away at its threads. It has been touched by millions of people and even by swords, it has been consumed by smoke and humidity, and attacked by acid and bombs.

But to date, nothing has harmed Juan Diego's humble cloak. It has not been compromised in any manner, nor has deterioration of its fibers or intensity of its colors been detected. Indeed, it seems to be as good as it ever was, full of a vibrancy and newness which makes it appear almost alive.

The Virgin's image upon the cloth is likewise miraculous. Mary appears on the tilma as a *Mestiza,* a mixed-breed of Indian and Spanish. Experts say this unique imagery helped to unite two opposing races which then began to intermarry, forming *La Raza*, a new race of Mexicans.

Furthermore, the Virgin Mary is depicted with her head bowed and her hands folded in prayer. The bowing signifies humility to God, and her folded hands indicate that she intercedes to the one true God for her children. This is important. The early Indian converts were taught of Christ's death on the cross, His supreme sacrifice which was sufficient to save all mankind from Hell. Thus, human sacrifice was evil and unnecessary. Mary's humble posture perfectly represents this theme, and was, therefore, the perfect image to help the Aztec peasants embrace the Christian religion. Scientific and modern-day miracles have also surfaced from inspection of the tilma. In 1956, five opthamologists examined Mary's eyes on the tilma, and reported that they were amazingly life-like and human. Observation of the retina revealed the reflection of a man, with his hands extended in front of him and his palms upward, who was carrying something red. It is suspected that this is the reflection of Juan Diego with roses in his hands.[1]

Astronomers also recently reproduced a map of the stars as they would have appeared on December 12, 1531, the date of the appearance of the miraculous image. This astrological map was inverted and laid over the Virgin's image in the form of a transparency. It was discovered that the stars on the Virgin's mantle coincided exactly with the stars on the astronomers map, when considered from the point of view of someone looking down from Heaven.[2]

In addition, a transparency of the Virgin's image was superimposed on a topographical map of Central Mexico. Again, the conclusion observed was phenomenal. The colors of the major mountain ranges on the map coincided perfectly with the golden filigree flowers on the Virgin's gown. The result was nothing less than mind-boggling.[3]

In spite of the inexplicable phenomena associated with the tilma, the greatest miracle of all has been how Heaven has accomplished its work through it. After the initial conversion of nine million Indians and the complete halt of all bloody sacrifices, many more miracles followed.

In December of 1531, an Indian slain by an arrow through the neck was instantly resurrected after the tilma was brought before him. In 1545, a plague in Mexico City that killed 12,000 people came to an immediate end after a pilgrimage to Tepeyac was made to pray for deliverance before the tilma. In 1565, an image of the tilma halted a war in the Philippines and brought peace there between the Spanish and the Filipino Indians. In 1571, at the Battle of Lepanto, the Guadalupe tilma was credited with a miraculous change in the winds, which halted a Moslem advance and preserved Western Christian civilization. The list of victories and miraculous interventions secured by the Empress of the Americas continues up until this day.

But why was the miraculous image of the Virgin, clouded in such mystery and significance, given to the Americas? How was it related to the decisive showdown between Mary and Satan? Why would God grant the greatest sign of Mary's power to the New World? No one knows for sure.

But since 1531, history suggests that the Virgin of Guadalupe has consistently stopped bloodshed and instigated conversion in the Americas. She has brought about the healing of individuals, communities, races and nations — perhaps the most important kinds of healing which America again needs today.

Estela Ruiz knew little of these great spiritual implications when the image of Our Lady of Guadalupe spoke to her in September of 1988. As most Mexican-Americans, she was familiar with Mary's visit to Juan Diego and the conversion of the people. She knew that her own family and Reyes' family had been devoted to the Virgin of Guadalupe. But beyond that, her knowledge was scarce.

Caught up in her own life, she understood little of how modern times are in many ways as bad as, or worse than, Juan Diego's time. People, families and nations were in desperate need of all kinds of help, but Estela, Armando and Fernando just couldn't see it clearly.

Even Little Rey, so engulfed in his own problems, wasn't aware that his family members, too, needed help. In 1988, while their lives were going down the wrong road, they were blind to any spiritual danger or error.

Indeed, the Ruizes were just another American family in trouble and in pain. They lived with it all as if it were normal... and that was just the problem.

The sorrow and sufferings which Mary had healed in the days of Juan Diego were defiantly manifesting themselves anew, and the vic tims involved were again accepting their godless situation as normal. The sad picture was the same in families throughout America.

The blood in the streets and the sacrificing of the innocents in the form of abortion had become gravely serious, and were producing unimaginable consequences. America had, indeed, returned to the worshipping of false gods. Just as during the Aztec reign, death was bloody and was becoming accepted. And the shedding of so much innocent blood in particular confirmed the existence of the worst sacrilegious profanity scorned by all elements of Heaven.

During the sixties, seventies, eighties and nineties, a series of scandalous events from Woodstock to Watergate to Whitewater clearly demonstrated America's decline. But far from the headlines, it was mainly the little things that were destroying America, things like ruthless unaccountability for one's deeds, power struggles and lack of love. They were things that occur every day in almost every home, but neither Estela nor her family could see them in their own household. Indeed, they were blind to it all.

Strong prayer and faith were almost completely absent in their home, as were love and respect. Instead, they had been unrecognizably replaced by false idols like television, drugs, alcohol, money, success, and personal freedom.

And all across America, the story was the same. In every city and every home, people craved the good life and disdained suffering and sacrifice. Most American families of the '80s and '90s developed a common goal: to live as well as they could, and as comfortably as they could, no matter what it took. Lifestyle became everything. By the mid 1990s, the country was compromising life itself for life's "style."

Like the Aztec gods of blood, the old and the young alike were being grotesquely sacrificed to maintain the American way. America believed wrong was right and right was wrong. From abortion to euthanasia, America was now ready and willing to pay the ultimate price to maintain its standard of living, almost exactly as the Aztecs had been. Again, the Ruiz family was not immune to any of it. During the 1980's, abortion reared its ugly head. As if power, drugs, divorce and greed were not enough, the haunting shadow of this great sin ripped through the Ruiz family, leaving Satan poised for a knockout punch.

Time has made the comparisons even more frightening. Like Sixteenth Century Mexico, America is today a country at the peak of its power, yet possibly on the verge of total collapse. The handwriting is on the wall, as boldly forecasted by Pope Pius XII almost fifty years ago: *"Evil, under its myriad of forms, launches against good; the struggle of hate versus love, of evil habits against purity, of egoism against social justice, of violence against its peaceful life, of tyranny against liberty!"*

All of this, Pope Pius XII said, was materializing due to the decay of morals on all sides, and was *fostered by evil shows, evil books, evil newspapers,"* and *"the breakdown of the very foundation of society."*

No words said it better. So then, who could be better equipped to tackle this acutely American problem than the Virgin of Guadalupe, the Queen of the Americas? For it was in America that this hellish movement against life was strongest. It was in America, in particular, that Satan seemed to be preparing for the final battle.

Furthermore, the Virgin's apparition in Medjugorje, distinctly viewed as the most remarkable grace ever allowed by God, has caused a flood of millions of Americans to the site. Could this possibly be an indication that God plans to include them in that decisive showdown?

Like Reyes Ruiz, millions of people have returned home from Medjugorje since 1981 with a new vision of life, a new perspective on right and wrong. Once firmly on the path of conversion, Our Lady's children could see that a nation which ostensibly guaranteed freedom was blatantly promoting death and misery for itself and the world. The link between Guadalupe and Medjugorje was evident.

At Medjugorje, just as at Guadalupe, the Virgin seemed to bring to fulfillment Scripture's words of the woman who fled to the wilderness and then to the desert to a special place prepared by God (Rv 12:6). They were places that Satan would hate and then would attack with all his might, and then, Scripture says, he would depart to make war against the rest of her seed.

Indeed, since 1981, as God's people journeyed to, and then returned home from Medjugorje after hearing the Virgin's call, it seemed that many of these seeds were going back to America to fight the dragon, *"As he stood upon the sand of the sea"* (Rv 12:17)... or perhaps in reality, *"upon the land of the free,"* that is, ... *America.*

CHAPTER THIRTEEN

OUR LADY OF THE AMERICAS

Back in South Phoenix, everything seemed quiet, quiet and hidden. September quietly passed into October. Reyes quietly returned home from Medjugorje to South Phoenix where he detected no change. Estela quietly went about her usual duties, as did the rest of the family. And the Virgin quietly watched them all as she began her work in and among them.

Of course, Mary was busy elsewhere, too. By October 1988, Mary's work at Medjugorje had been in progress for over seven years. Indeed, those years had been busy ones! Thousands of apparitions and messages were given. Two visionaries possessed all ten secrets, while the other four continued to see Mary every day. In August 1988, the Pope proclaimed a Marian year, calling on Catholics to turn to the Mother of God for their needs. She was the answer, John Paul II insisted, as her motherly assistance could help God's children through the problems of our times.

In Eastern Europe, cracks in the foundation of the communistic systems were starting to reveal themselves. A decade-long upheaval in Poland came to a climax, putting an end to communism there. Likewise, from Bulgaria to Romania, Czechoslovakia to Yugoslavia, the Iron Curtain had rusted and was crumbling. Hard core enclaves of communist tyranny throughout Europe were about to fall. And an uprising in Beijing, China, revealed a surprisingly soft underbelly of an otherwise unbreakable communistic state.

Across the Atlantic, the situation was the same. Soviet satellites in Nicaragua, El Salvador and Honduras collapsed. In Africa, Angola and its neighbors were throwing out Cuban and Soviet advisors.

On the spiritual level, Mary was revealing to visionaries around the world that many of the changes occurring were a direct result of her intervention, as willed and ordained by God. Her little ones who were responding to her requests at Fatima, Medjugorje, and elsewhere, were uniting in the name of the true God. Through prayers and fasting, through consecrations and acts of reparation, the Red Dragon was dying. And as Saint John foretold, the **Woman clothed with the sun** was defeating him, along with her loyal remnant.

But though many positive changes were taking place, the war wasn't over. Nations long crushed by the tyranny of communism were in need of healing. And from the ashes of communism's collapse, a new and more insidious danger loomed, one that could prove even more harmful. Newly liberated, the people of the Eastern Bloc were being shackled by a new and much more deadly form of slavery, a spiritual tyranny of the body and soul.

The West, especially America, was already firmly in its grip. Greed, lust, practical atheism and deceit were main course items on the menu. Violence and death were the immediate results, while economic instability appeared on the horizon.

The West was also moving to export its diet of misery and sorrow to the rest of the world, especially to the naive inhabitants of former-communist countries. America's gods of materialism, lust, and power were forerunners to self-inflicted oppression and depravation. This wasn't just a hypothesis; the Virgin herself clearly outlined the scenario.

At Fatima, Mary foretold that Russia's conversion would secure an Era of Peace. However, this Era of Peace was not to be taken for granted. It would come, but at a price. This price depended upon people's prayers and sacrifices. It depended upon the world's response to God's call, particularly His call through the Virgin's apparitions. For at Fatima God made it clear that His victory was to be through Mary, it was to be the *"Triumph of the Immaculate Heart"* in the world.

Slowly, gradually, as Mary's plan around the world unfolded, things were happening. And it seemed obvious that America was destined to play a key role in God's plan to bring in the new times. For while America had a myriad of its own problems, it still possessed the ability and promise to evangelize widely throughout the world.

Even while admonishing America for its shortcomings, the Pope insisted that the nation use its gifts for the work God, Jesus Christ and His mother, Mary. Indeed, John Paul II proclaimed that America possessed the key to lead the Church into the new millennium.

Nonetheless, everything remained locked at the Ruiz household. Reyes Ruiz didn't return home from Medjugorje to greet a marching band and an award ceremony. Initially, little changed, with Estela remaining silent about what had happened to her, just as she had vowed.

The painting of Our Lady of Guadalupe, too, remained silent, and the rest of the family went about its merry way. Little Rey was still canvassing the town, buying, selling and using drugs. It was life as usual in South Phoenix, and in the Ruiz home.

Yet the stage was set. Something big was approaching.

There was activity stirring between Estela and Reyes. Somehow, they started praying the Rosary together. And what's more, some of their kids began to join them.

Reyes' enthusiasm from his trip to Medjugorje seemed to spark a slight spiritual renewal in his family, although no one knew how long it would last. Surprisingly, even Estela wanted to hear more.

Before Reyes' trip and her mystical experience, Estela felt that devotion to Mary detracted from Jesus. Now she knew it was just the opposite. The more she understood about Mary and her life of quiet devotion and sacrifice, the more she loved the Lord.

Then it happened.

Sometime in the middle of October 1988, the Virgin surprised Estela. This time with a dream. And just as with the dream of Princess Papantzin, an important message was to be delivered.

In an incredibly vivid dream, Estela witnessed the Virgin Mary having an intimate conversation with her husband, Reyes. Estela saw herself with Reyes in their own bedroom, and suddenly the room lit up like the sun had come out. In her dream she found herself awakening Reyes to prepare for Mary's impending arrival.

To Estela's amazement, Reyes showed little excitement at the prospect of their celestial guest. It wasn't that he lacked enthusiasm, but rather, it seemed to Estela that for Reyes, the Virgin's arrival was nothing unusual. It was like they were old friends who knew each other intimately. It was as if they had been visiting with each other for years, so one more arrival was nothing out of the ordinary. In her dream, says Estela, Mary appeared in a white dress with a blue mantle and white veil. Her back was to Estela as she stood and talked to Reyes. Throughout the dream, Estela couldn't hear anything, but Mary and Reyes kept acting like good friends.

Meanwhile, Estela found herself yelling, *"It's the Blessed Mother! Oh how beautiful! Beautiful! Beautiful! You're so beautiful!"*

All of a sudden, the Virgin turned around and stared into Estela's eyes. It was a glance, she says, that pierced her soul. Looking into Mary's eyes, she felt that the Virgin knew everything about her. And she felt a tremendous love as the Virgin reached out to embrace her, and she returned the embrace.

Suddenly, Estela awoke. The dream was over, and Mary was gone.

Estela opened her eyes in bed, and took a minute to orient herself. Yes, it was a dream. But it was so real! And Estela started to wonder: *"Perhaps the Virgin has been talking to my husband for years. Perhaps Reyes does really know Mary. Perhaps Our Lady of Guadalupe really did speak to me. Perhaps my crazy husband is right about a lot of stuff..."*

But Estela had a lot of adjusting to do. Everything was happening much too fast. Her intelligence and personal make-up were not condusive for radical swings of opinion. She needed more evidence. There had to be more investigation, perhaps another dream. Or maybe another painting would address her...

Fate was not to be tempted. After several generations of preparation, God would now make a monumental move.

Packed into a small bedroom in the back of the Ruiz home on Saturday, December 3, 1988, at around 11 PM, the family began to pray the Rosary. Estela was seated on the back of the bed, up against the wall in front of a small family painting of the Immaculate Heart of Mary. Her daughter-in-law, Letitia, who was pregnant, sat on the other side of the bed. Her husband Reyes and son Fernando both sat on the end of the bed, all staring at the same image.

It was the ninth and final day of a special novena the family was making. And it wasn't just any novena. Like everything else unfolding, it was divinely appropriate — the Novena to the Immaculate Conception.

The Novena to the Immaculate Conception is specially promoted by the bishops of the United States through the Shrine of the Immaculate Conception in Washington, D.C. The ninth day of the novena recalls how the bishops of the United States of America dedicated the nation to Mary of the Immaculate Conception in 1846. *"Into her hands,"* the bishops stated, *"would be all of America's cares and future. Mary was for America,"* they wrote, and *"America was for Mary."*

The novena continued, *"Mary would be a perfect model for America's women and a never-failing inspiration for their men."* In short, Mary would be the protectress of the nation and its families.

Suddenly, a brilliant white light flooded the room. Estela was taken off guard. Stunned, she was sure everyone else was seeing it. *"I became paralyzed, I couldn't see anything,"* she later explained. The light totally overwhelmed her.

Next, like the special effects in a movie, a mist-like cloud materialized around a painting of the Virgin. By now, Estela was having an anxiety attack, with her heart pounding like a drum as she was frozen in place.

The rest of the family, like toy mannequins in a department store window at Christmas, continued repeating the prayers. As with most apparitions, they were oblivious to what was unfolding. Recalls Estela,

> *"The picture of the Blessed Mother was on the wall and we prayed the Rosary. What happened was that I started looking at the picture and I could tell that she was trying to say something to me. I thought, oh gosh, I'm having one of those crazy feelings again like when she spoke to me a month earlier. It was peaceful and calm though.*
>
> *"What happened is that I shut my eyes tight, but every once in a while, my eyes would look at the picture... I got to the point where I was fighting a sense of opening my eyes. I began to see this cloud form around the bottom of the picture, but before the cloud, a bright light appeared.*

*I tried to let go of the Rosary to rub my eyes, but I couldn't;
it's like they were stuck. I felt like I was paralyzed, but not
in a bad way.*

    *"My heart was going bum bum, bum bum... I knew that
we were praying the Rosary, I knew what was going on."*

Estela gazed slightly above the painting. There, suspended in the
air and surrounded by white light and a fog-like brilliance, stood the
Queen of Heaven. She was looking directly into her eyes and soul.
Estela sat straight up. By now the mist cleared.

    "Oh my God!" she said aloud. *"She's here! She's here!!!"*

She then began to exclaim, *"You are a beautiful woman! You
are a beautiful woman!"*

By that point, the rest of the family knew something was happening. But only Reyes knew exactly what it was. As usual, he was
operating on another frequency. The stoic patriarch sensed immediately what was unfolding. Someone from Heaven was in the room,
and he suspected it was his best friend.

In seconds, the Virgin totally materialized into a three-dimensional form, smiling and floating as she stood on a cloud. Although full-sized, the vapors of the cloud covered Mary from the
knees down. She had deep blue eyes, and light radiated from her.
Her face glowed. And her hands, ever so slowly, motioned toward Estela.

    "Don't you know I'm going to take care of your children?"
said Mary to Estela in a soft and reassuring voice. It was a direct
response to Estela's prayer of just moments before.

While Estela heard the words, all she could say was one thing:
"You're beautiful — you're beautiful!"

    "I'm going to leave you now," Mary told her.

    "Don't go! Don't go!" Estela cried.

But the Virgin faded and vanished. As she departed, Estela
begged her, *"Take care of them! Take care of them!"* Letitia also
petitioned Mary to care for her children, for by then she was aware
what Estela was asking the Virgin to do.

In minutes, it was over. But the memory has remained crystal
clear. Recalls Estela, *"Her most dominant feature is her eyes. They*

steal your heart. They're full of grace, love, tenderness and mercy. There are so many beautiful things about her."

Three days later, the Ruiz family again gathered to pray the Rosary. This time they were in their living room, and more of the family was present. Little Rey and daughter Rebecca had not yet been told about what had happened. Again Mary appeared, this time wasting neither time nor words.

"I have come to ask you to be my messenger, and I want to know if you will do it," the Mother of God asked Estela.

Mesmerized by the Virgin's beauty and held prisoner by her words, Estela quickly replied, *"Yes."*

Later, she would explain how Mary's beauty, her radiance, and her abundant love were humanly irresistible. *"No one,"* Estela insists, *"could say no to this person. No one could do anything but comply."*

Again, as quickly as it began, the Virgin departed.

Seven days later, on December 10th, the diocesan Feast of Our Lady of Guadalupe, the Virgin suddenly appeared again to Estela above the altar inside the Immaculate Heart Church in Phoenix. Mary appeared directly above the bishop who was celebrating the Mass.

This time Estela had some questions. Husband Reyes needed confirmation of who the apparition was, and who had sent her.

"I am the Immaculate Heart of Mary," she assured Estela. *"This is my reign — this is the time of my reign. I am here to bring my children back to my Son. The one who sent me is God, our Father."*

And then Mary explained to her:

"I am the same one that has appeared all over the world. Look around this church and see all the different forms in which I have appeared. I am the Mother of God, and I have appeared in different places.

"There is only one and that is me, and I am all of these. But I come today, at this time, as the Immaculate Heart of Mary, as this is the reign of my Immaculate Heart."

Again, without a moment's notice, the apparition ended. But before Mary left, her parting words further revealed her mission to Estela.

The light from atop Cross Mountain in Medjugorje had, indeed, reflected back to his home, just as Reyes had prayed.

"I wish to be known," the Virgin told Estela, *"as Our Lady of the Americas..."*

CHAPTER FOURTEEN

A WOMAN MOLDED TO PERFECTION

What exactly is an apparition? To best answer that question, an explanation is in order. Technically, apparitions cannot be completely defined, as they have no objective scientific model.

To complicate matters, apparitions are virtually inconceivable to most of the world today. In the minds of many, they are fiction — they simply don't exist. So, many feel, why even try to understand their existence?

But for those who have experienced apparitions and for those who are convinced of their reality, the technical definitions or lack of facts are irrelevant. The need for a standard model vanishes in the smoke, much like the apparition itself.

Indeed, apparitions are matters of faith, and consequently, they go beyond technical standards and definitions. They enter into a dimension where such standards are meaningless, and while most apparitions cannot be experienced at will nor controlled, they are nonetheless very real. If they were not, how could so many lives be affected and changed — particularly the lives of those closest to them?

Those who experience visions, then, are always breaking new ground, redefining and re-exploring uncharted territory. Although reports of apparitions are found in early recordings of human events, no two visionaries undergo the same apparition experience, nor do they describe it in precisely the same fashion.

In reality, however, the whole concept is quite simple. Mystical events are just that — mystical. And what could be more mystical than attempting to define something invisible yet wonderful, startling yet tranquilizing?

And what is the general opinion toward those who claim to experience visions?

Without a doubt, most people believe it to be quite strange when someone claims to have had an apparition or mystical vision. A strange cookie, indeed, many secretly think.

And Estela Ruiz knew this right away, as she herself had been guilty many times of passing such a judgment. While her husband Reyes never claimed to experience visions, strange lights, voices, or to receive messages, Estela had believed for many years that her lifelong partner was very strange. And he never claimed to see the Virgin Mary!

But suddingly, out of nowhere. Estela Ruiz was claiming all of this and more. Worse than that, the Virgin told her from the beginning she wanted her to *"be her messenger."*

"Now," Estela thought, *"if I am to be her messenger, that means I have to tell the world about this — the whole world! And that means the whole world will think I'm nuts!"*

While Estela nervously pondered her plight, around that same time the gaze of much of the country was fixed on something else in Phoenix, something which many believed to be also quite odd.

Just one month after Estela's apparitions began, a yucca branch on a bush at Eleventh Street and Van Buren in Phoenix gained national attention. Many insisted the branch looked like Our Lady of Guadalupe, and it was even ripped down and placed in nearby Immaculate Heart Church.

According to son Armando, the Virgin confirmed to Estela that the branch was, indeed, a sign from God, so that people would *"begin to soften their hearts so they can accept [that] God has sent His mother to send messages specifically for America."*

Unfortunately, with that revelation, Estela began to realize, much to her own dismay, who this messenger *"for America"* was to be and what it all meant.

In reality, Estela Ruiz had had some time to contemplate this from the beginning. She knew that her encounter with the voice and the painting in her living room (September 1988) left her immediately susceptible to involvement in such a scenario. Indeed, her fear of possible ridicule produced her premeditated silence. *"No one can know,"* she concluded. *"That way, no one will tell anyone."*

But now, the safe, silent course was impossible. Her mystical experiences were repeating themselves. And Estela was convinced of their authenticity. While the devil would later try to create doubt, as he does with all visionaries, Estela knew in her heart that she had to do what Mary asked of her. Thus, she had to reveal her experiences to the world.

For Estela Ruiz, this would not be easy. Always a careful, deliberate person, her education and professional experiences cultivated these traits even more. At the time the apparitions began, she had developed into a calculating and methodical individualist, one who avoided rash pronouncements. Consequently, she took great pride in her reputation as a rational and sound professional. But that reputation, and the pride which went along with it, were now skating on thin ice, and she knew it.

In a way, though, the whole thing was kind of funny.

God couldn't have chosen a better or swifter way to humble Estela's heart. Nuts, crazy, kooky, weird, odd... Faced with the reality that these words now applied to her, Estela's mind fought for a way to try and save face.

But it wasn't to be.

Estela was, indeed, experiencing apparitions, experiences which left her edified and tranquil. Regularly, her whole being was consumed by visions which she couldn't deny. Reyes, her formerly kooky husband, knew it right away. So consequently, she probably would now be known as a "visionary." As one who claims to see apparitions is conveniently ordained with the title, visionary.

As far as Estela was concerned, this was the icing on the cake. An influential force in statewide politics, the holder of a Masters Degree and the Director of the Special Language Program for Murphy School District, Estela could now add the title visionary to her list of credentials. Wouldn't that make a wonderful impression on her prestigious colleagues!

But like it or not, she had indeed earned the title. According to Webster's Dictionary, Estela Ruiz was now *"someone apt to behold visions of the imagination, apt to receive or act on mere fantasies or whims as if they are realities, given to indulging in fanciful theories, someone given to impractical schemes."*[1] Fanciful theories? Improvement schemes? And she was supposed to be moving up in the world!

Indeed, the Virgin's plans for Estela *were* to move her up, but not by earthly standards. As heaven looked on, Estela's worldly influence and credibility would wane, while her heavenly reward would multiply by leaps and bounds.

While Webster's definition of Estela's mystical encounters was far from flattering, it's important to explain exactly what she claims to experience.

Far from a *"vision of the imagination,"* Estela Ruiz perceives with her senses some real object, in this case, the Virgin Mary's body. This perception is invisible to others. According to theological experts who have analyzed different categories of extraordinary mystical phenomena, Estela Ruiz's experiences are technically classified as sensible or corporeal visions, otherwise known as "apparitions."

While Estela also experiences locutions (voices), imaginative dreams and intellectual visions (infused knowledge), her supernatural experiences primarily revolve around her ocular or corporeal visions. Thus, Estela sees Mary with her bodily eyes as she would see anything else around her.

But despite her own certainty that these visions were not *"false imaginings,"* Estela was in a quandary. For if anything, she had always viewed herself as practical and realistic. But now God was pulling the rug out from underneath her.

After coming to terms with her situation, though, Estela offered little resistance. If she was to be Mary's messenger, so be it! Her practical, intelligent side knew that the apparitions were real. Moreover, her experiences seemed to be strikingly similar to those of many others before her who were plucked from their everyday lives and hurled into the world of the supernatural.

Indeed, Juan Diego reported no different a tale. Nor had Saint Bernadette Soubirous at Lourdes in 1858, or the three shepherd children at Fatima in 1917. All were unsuspecting participants in a divine plan that changed their lives overnight.

And just like Estela, each of them had to face public ridicule and a loss of "self-image."

Visionaries report visions that the rest of the world can't see. Some say these visions are creations of the mind. Thus, a rocky path unfolds for those who discover themselves in this situation.

At Guadalupe, Juan Diego struggled with this predicament so much that he decided not to keep his appointment with the Virgin on the third day. Saint Bernadette, already at odds with her parents over her experiences, was left even more bewildered after her second apparition. For at school, the nuns whom she trusted advised her, *"Put it all out of your head, my dear; it's an illusion."*[2]

Likewise, Lucia Santos, the eldest visionary at Fatima, became greatly confused after experiencing her mother's wrath. This was compounded by the local priest who concluded that her apparition *"doesn't seem to me to be a revelation from Heaven."*[3]

Wrote Lucia in her second memoir:

> *"I began then to have doubts as to whether these manifestations might be from the Devil seeking to make me lose my soul. As I heard people say that the Devil always brings conflict and disorder, I began to think that, truly, ever since I had started seeing these things our home was no longer the same because joy and peace had fled. What anguish I felt! I made known my doubts to my cousins."*[4]

Indeed, Estela Ruiz was now a member of a very exclusive club. Though the call was divine, the jury was human. But it was something she quickly accepted.

Soon, through television appearances on shows such as *Geraldo* (Rivera), *Sally* (Jessy Raphael), and *The Joan Rivers Show*, the whole world was to discover who she was and what she claimed was happening to her.

Yet, while Estela struggled, she often confronted her fears with humor.

"You know, they put people away for hearing little voices," she would laugh with others.

As the saying goes, behind every joke is the truth, and indeed, many of Estela's jestful comments were full of fact. But while she didn't expect to be put away for claiming to experience apparitions, what happened to her — and indeed, what happens to many visionaries — was perhaps even worse.

The public's reaction toward people who claim apparitions is a mixed bag. Alleged visionaries are defended and persecuted, attacked and loved. They are hounded, chased, followed, touched and grabbed. They are endlessly pursued. Like celebrities, they attract everyone, whether friend or foe, good or bad. The attention is unconditional and unavoidable.

After her experience at Immaculate Conception Church, Estela began to receive apparitions regularly. Gradually, as the public came to hear her announce the Virgin's messages, she accepted that her life would never be the same.

As the crowds increased, so did the Virgin's visits. To Estela this made it all worthwhile.

And for her, the apparitions were breathtaking, as the Queen of Heaven revealed her full majesty in a curiously hypnotic fashion. One Estela claimed that she could never tire of experiencing it.

Bathed in streams of brilliant white light, Estela says that Mary lights up the room as if *"the sun had just come out."* The Virgin usually comes to Estela dressed in a blue mantle and white veil, except at Christmas, Easter or a special Holy Day. On those days, Mary wears gold.

The mystical meeting usually commences with Mary appearing suddenly, materializing from a light, vaporous image into a three-dimensional, hologram-like shape. According to Estela, Mary's radiance is all pure, shining and brilliantly attractive. It's an attractiveness that is irresistible and magnetic, for Estela senses pure love totally emanating from her, as intensely as the light which radiates from her.

Consistent with dozens of visionaries who claim to have seen the Virgin Mary, Estela enthusiastically describes the Virgin as, *"Beautiful!! She is just beautiful!"*

Indeed, if it weren't for the primary purpose of the Virgin's appearance, her messages, Mary's physical appearance could easily leave Estela trapped in a mesmerized state of awe and wonder. For it's impossible, Estela says, to stop staring at Mary's radiance and mystical beauty. Ironically, she says, a painting of Mary painted by her husband comes closest to how the Virgin appears to her.

For Estela, it is the Virgin's eyes that leave the greatest impact. Her eyes, she insists, *"steal your heart and capture your soul. They are eyes,"* says Estela, *"so full of mercy, love, tenderness and grace, one almost fails to study their beautiful blue color and sparkling intensity."*

And she adds, *"Mary's eyes leave you feeling that she knows everything about you, that she loves you and everything is wonderful."*

Of course, the rest of the Queen of Heaven's beauty cannot be overlooked. Estela says the Virgin's hair is dark brown, long and hidden under her veil. Her face is slightly round, very beautiful and radiates affection and concern, while her voice is soft and uplifting, with a gentle maternal tone.

Estela does not fail to note that while Mary appears small and delicate, she actually comes across as a strong and powerful woman, a woman who knows her purpose and is far from meek. Despite her strength, though, the Virgin radiates a femininity that is total. She is kind and humble, yet strong and confident. She is in a mystical way, a total woman, but this totality emanates from humility and obedience, not arrogance and control. She is a woman who undertakes many roles, all quite confidently with action and determination, and always with great love. According to Estela, Mary is the *"quintessential mother"* and the *"ultimate lady"* molded to an incomprehensible perfection.

In short, says Estela, Mary is everything that many women, including herself, long to be. Mary's virtues of strength through humility, and respect through charity, reflect the way God really meant for both men and women to be. Unfortunately, the world now guides men and women down an erroneous path, one which seeks to gain power and respect through authority and aggression. Now, with her apparitions, Mary is showing us the proper way to be molded to God's perfection.

It is a way that can only come through prayer, sacrifice and faith. Prayer must come from the heart and be filled with childlike faith. This will bring change. And according to Mary, change must come. For God the Father wants to help His children, so many of whom are lost and confused in today's world.

As Mary told Estela one night:

"This evening I want to ask all of the world, and especially you, my children in the Americas, to help me in the work that I am doing by learning to pray with me to Our Dear and Beloved Lord so that all hearts who want to turn to Him shall find the strength and courage to do so. Those who are already praying to full capacity, continue to do so. But remember, there is always room for one extra prayer. To those who are beginning to learn, I ask that you move forward as fast as possible to learn to pray from the heart. And for those who have not started, begin without any more hesitation, as there is no more time for you to flounder around in doubts and exercises. You must begin to pray with the heart and the faith of a child.

"As a child looks to its parents for care, love and nurturing, so must you look to Our Father in Heaven for that same care. So must you look to my Son, Our Lord Jesus, for His great mercy and love that He wants to give you. And so must you look to the Holy Spirit to defend you against the ways of the world and to empower you with His courage and strength. As you see a little child reach out to his protectors, so must your heart reach out to your protector, Our God, who awaits to love you and nourish your soul. You must be of the faith of the infant, who clings to his caretakers to survive. You must also develop this same kind of faith, ever believing that Our God will never fail you.

"Remember that I as your mother in Heaven am always there with each one of you, guiding you and leading you to His love." [June 16, 1990]

CHAPTER FIFTEEN

"I WANT YOU TO LEARN TO LOVE EACH OTHER"

"*My child,*" said the Virgin Mary, "*the good God wishes to charge you with a mission.*"[1]

And so it began. Far from South Phoenix, over a century ago, the Blessed Virgin Mary came to Paris and spoke these words to Saint Catherine Labouré. Many years later, Catherine would write of her incredible experiences. As with many visionaries including Estela Ruiz, Saint Catherine's experiences began with a visit from Heaven's Queen.

Our Lady first appeared on July 18, 1830, the eve of the Feast of Saint Vincent de Paul. Saint Catherine relished it all. The first unexpected moments brought mysterious lights and then the Virgin herself. Mary's beauty, her heavenly mannerisms and her melodic voice were overwhelming. But like with Estela, the moments of ecstatic awe were not ends in themselves. There was work to be done. It was why Mary had come. And the work would be difficult, filled with joy but also with crosses.

"*You will be tormented,*" Mary told Catherine on her first apparition. "*You will be contradicted, but do not fear, you will have grace. Tell with confidence all that passes within you; tell it with simplicity. Have confidence. Do not be afraid.*"[2] The Virgin further instructed her, "*Give an account of what I tell you and of what you will understand in your prayers.*"[3]

With those words to Catherine, events of unprecedented magnitude were initiated. Many significant occurrences would result from her apparitions, and the Miraculous Medal would emerge as a gift for the faithful from Heaven.

Marian theologians today insist that the apparitions to Saint Catherine Labouré were the beginning of modern Marian times. Times, experts believe, that are about to culminate and conclude with a series of great events which have been preordained from all eternity, and which are so prophetic they can be referenced in Holy Scripture.

"The whole world will be upset by miseries of every kind," the Virgin told Saint Catherine before departing.[4] Indeed, this ominous prophecy now stands fulfilled before our very eyes. For today's world is submerged in misery and sorrow, disaster and sin.

Over 150 years later, in the Ruiz's humble Arizona household, the Virgin repeated many of her words. *"Yes, I have come to ask you to be my messenger,"* the Virgin addressed Estela on her second apparition. Like her words to Catherine, they were exciting, yet serious. For a great responsibility was now in Estela's hands, a crucial task of fulfilling the Virgin's work through her..

As Mary's work with Saint Catherine immediately involved attention to the Vincentian Fathers and Sisters of Charity in her religious community, likewise in South Phoenix the Virgin began her work by tackling the problems in Estela's fragmented family.

"I'm going to help you and your children make many changes," she told Estela. *"I will guide them — I will guide you. And I will be here with you. There will be a period of time when I will prepare the family."*

And Mary set out to do just that. The Virgin came so often that the Ruiz's could have with good reason set another place at the evening dinner table. Throughout the first months of 1989, Mary appeared almost daily and worked intensely with Estela.

For Estela, it was a time of great joy and expectation. She changed her work schedule so she could come home at lunch to talk to Mary. And their conversations were more than just personal. The Virgin would speak to her about herself, her life and her family. It was a mother-to-daughter chat, with many conversations focusing on what mothers love to talk about most — their children.

After their clandestine meetings, Estela would hurry back to the office, almost like a child involved in a secret activity. She would then try to assume her responsibilities, all the while contemplating the uncanniness of the whole thing. There she was, a professional surrounded by professionals, who daily had lunch with an invisible friend.

But while Estela never doubted what was happening, she did explore thoughts of a more humbling nature.

"Boy," she would say to herself, *"Our Lord really must be desperate if he has to use me."*

The Mexican-American homemaker wasn't being laconic about herself. Like Saint Catherine and others, she struggled to grasp the Lord's immensity and her nothingness.

Indeed, Estela's private lessons from the Queen of Heaven were intense. Things began to change in the Ruiz home. For the first two months, it was nothing but the Ruiz family and their Queen, living the ways of God.

"I want you to take up a study of the Bible," Mary told Estela, which the family immediately did. Like young recruits jumping at orders from their staff sergeant, the Ruiz family burned the midnight oil till 2 AM almost every night. Of course, they were exhausted the next day. Eventually, they discovered that a weekly program was more in line.

Each time Mary came, she brought more and more advice. By the spring of 1989, Estela knew she was to share these lessons with everyone.

But the problem was how to remember it all.

At first, Estela tried repeating the message to herself. Each time, she would journey out from her bedroom after an apparition and report the message to the family, all the while replaying it over and over in her mind. The family, in turn, would record the message and commence study and prayers, trying earnestly to digest and fulfill Mary's instructions. It was a noble effort from a family desperate to please Mary. But it was difficult, for Estela couldn't recall every last word for certain, and the family wasn't sure what they were studying.

Sensing the Ruiz's frustration, the Virgin comforted their anxieties by suggesting that Estela write down what was being told to her. While humorous to outsiders, the Ruiz family was so eager to fulfill Mary's desires that the idea of a verbatim transcript of her directives was most appreciated.

But now the family was on its way. Following those simple instructions, Estela had truly become the Virgin's messenger, just as Mary said she would.

Twice a week — every Tuesday and Saturday morning — the Queen of Heaven would come and leave a message. The messages were for the family, the community and for America. Word by word, phrase by phrase, Mary would dictate the message to Estela. Upon completion, Estela would enter it into a computer. From English it would then be translated into Spanish. As time went by, the messages in both languages would be faxed across the country and to Mexico.

By March of 1989, crowds began to descend upon the Ruiz home. As more people heard about the apparitions, more came. Likewise, Mary's messages began to get longer. On Tuesday and Saturday nights, Estela would address the crowd and read to them the Virgin's communication of that morning. And they always hungered for more.

"Tell us what her face looks like!"
"What does she say about fasting?"
"Did any angels come with her?"

For Estela, the Virgin's words to Saint Catherine concerning the weight of her cross were beginning to be felt. For with the crowds came controversy.

Nonetheless, bolstered by her family and especially by her devoted husband, Estela persevered. She followed the Virgin's personal advice. She began to attend Mass daily and to regularly receive the Sacraments. She began to pray the Rosary daily. And most importantly, she began to love everyone. Everyone.

Indeed, Estela soon discovered that this *love* was the core of the Virgin's messages. For with this love would come the necessary changes in herself, her family, and in the world. As Estela explained to a crowd one night:

*"The messages talk about treating each other, who-
ever it is in your life, with LOVE. The basic message is
this: she wants us all to be saved, and the road to salvation
is through **Jesus Christ** and by following the Command-*

*ments of **God**, the two greatest of which are loving **God** above all else and loving your brothers and sisters in the world. And that is essentially her message. Learn to love each other. She says, `**Even the ones that you think you cannot** — **those that you look down on, like the homeless, the mentally ill or those that have hurt you. Those are my children too. I want you to learn to love each other.'***

Personally, the Virgin requested little else of Estela. Mary gently suggested that she leave her prestigious position and dedicate herself to her family and ministry. Most of all, Mary urged Estela to balance her time between her husband, family, community and Church.

But the most visible change which occurred, though, was probably the Ruiz home. For where Reyes once formerly displayed his collection of religious paintings and statues only sporadically, now the home was entirely his domain to convert into his dream, inside and out.

Indeed, it was Reyes' moment of victory, the reward for a life of tremendous patience and faith. No longer would the house be merely speckled with religious paraphanalia; it would now become Reyes private sanctuary.

And it was the Virgin herself who initiated this process. Mary asked for a shrine in the backyard. Before the words finished coming out of Estela's mouth, Reyes was off and running. It was construction time.

Up went the wood and adobe structure which stands approximately ten feet high with an image of Mary in the center. It was built out of stone upon a base of red-colored cement. This was followed by a waterfall, statues, landscaping, paintings of Mary, and finally a life-sized crucifix.

A large statue of Our Lady of Guadalupe was placed in the far upper right-hand corner of the yard near a prickly pear cactus, guarded by tall candles and more cactus. To the left of this statue was placed a porcelain image of Our Lady of Fatima, followed by a small figurine of the Rosa Mystica which sits on a ledge in the far right-hand corner. Small angels, flowers and tiny pictures of those remembered in prayer by loved ones were then added. Here and there, colorful plastic rosaries can be found hanging on nails. As usual, for those who have forgotten their beads, Reyes is always prepared.

Backyard Shrine at Ruiz home.

The centerpiece of the backyard shrine is a handmade statue of the Sacred Heart of Jesus, complete with a red heart that lights up at night. Ironically, this stature sometimes serves literally as a light of mercy for desperate victims of South Phoenix who seek a sanctuary. But the culmination of the work was the sculpting of Christ's body for the fifteen-foot life-sized crucifix, formed from plaster casts of Reyes' own body. To perfect the project, Reyes even grew a beard and shaved it off when it got the right length. He then glued it to the grimacing face of Christ, a fitting tribute from a man who always sought to follow and imitate his Lord and Savior.

While Reyes felt fulfilled in his duties, the same could not be said for Estela. She was undergoing conversion. And while she had peace, a new cross was emerging.

Estela Ruiz was beginning to experience what many visionaries call a *"dark night of the soul."* This dark night is a restless inner torment that can only be fulfilled by the mystical experiences the visionaries begin to wait for. Indeed, their primary longing becomes awaiting their next heavenly visitation. In a way, this is logical, for it is said that once a person has felt a touch of Heaven, it is all they live for. It is all they desire.

For Saint Catherine Labouré it was no different. Father Joseph Dirvin, in his book *Saint Catherine Labouré*, noted this extraordinary cross endured this great saint, whose incorrupt body attests to the success of her mission:

> *"As for Catherine, these terrible days were a sort of triumph, for they went a long way toward vindicating her. She was not the victim of illusions, for the prophecies of her visions had come true. It was a horrible proof, and she could not bring herself to dwell upon it. Rather, her thoughts were fixed upon the future. The Blessed Virgin had spoken of a mission. What could it be? When would she see Our Lady again? The question set up a longing in her, a longing that seized upon her soul and gave it no rest by day or night."[5]*

At East Cody Drive, the same restlessness came upon Estela Ruiz. For although her cross was difficult, her soul couldn't help but long for more.

FOR THE SOUL OF THE FAMILY

CHAPTER SIXTEEN

THE DIAGNOSIS

L ike a physician, Mary entered into the Ruiz family's lives and began to help heal their wounds. And as she had done with Estela, the Queen of Heaven told them in so many words, what they needed to do:

> *"What is going to make peace in your family and in the world is if you focus on love. You must develop love within yourself and for others.*
> *"And only Jesus Christ can help you make this change."*

But as, Mary explained at Medjugorje, certain issues were critical for her to have success with the family. Primarily, the Ruizes needed to recognize that they were under spiritual attack. They needed to recognize that their problems were caused by sin and by a lack of love and respect for each other. And most of all, they had to acknowledge that they needed help.

Just like an alcoholic interested in recovering, the family first had to accept that there was a problem, Mary said. There also had to be faith that, by surrendering to His Will, God could bring them healing and peace of mind, body and soul.

If they agreed to all the above, they needed to remember one last thing: the Ruiz family had to understand that Satan was real and was not going to give up. The devil, Mary informed them, still wanted their souls. And as always, he was free to go after them.

And so, understanding that their best chance at victory was a good weapon, the family began to pray.

Gradually, they began to meet together at Estela and Reyes' home to pray the Rosary. They also participated in Scripture meetings and read the Bible on their own. One by one, each began to respond to Mary's call. Change was difficult, but things were at least on their way.

...except for Little Rey. He didn't buy it.

When Estela told him that Mary was appearing, it was borderline humorous to him. *"O.K....so what?"* he said, laughing it off.

It wasn't that Little Rey didn't believe. More serious than that, he just didn't care. Like Mary's instructions on how to pray, Little Rey's response came from the heart. He really didn't care if the Queen of Heaven was appearing to his mother or anyone else.

"Great, so Mary is appearing to mom. What do you want me to do about it?" he asked.

Before even waiting for a reply, the Ruizes' prodigal son was out the door. *"That's cool,"* he muttered to himself upon departure, *"I got to go get high!"*

The scenario was heartbreaking. While the family prepared for the arrival of the Virgin, Little Rey prepared for parties — drug parties. He even remembers getting dressed up one night as if heading to a black-tie affair, while everyone else awaited Mary's apparition.

Like a loving mother, Mary most certainly felt his absence. And since she had promised Estela she was going to care of the children, a message from the Queen of Heaven directly for Little Rey was in order. A few days after receiving it, Estela presented Little Rey with the news.

"Our Blessed Mother wants to know if you'll help her in her work," Estela said, trying to put it just right.

"O.K.," he surprisingly shot back, then added, *"but you tell Blessed Mother this — if she can't take me the way I am, then I wish to have nothing to do with her ... or her Son, Jesus Christ."*

And Rey concluded, *"Here I am. But she has to accept me the way I am or no deal."*

With that, the conversation was over. Little Rey had cut his deal with the Virgin, and then he headed out, just like usual.

It was not unusual that Ray reacted this way to his mother's news. Indeed, Little Rey always made deals, deals that involved compromise. For as far as he was concerned, if you were going to give something up, you had to get something back in return — even with God.

But Little Rey's not the only one. Again, it is the story of America itself.

According to polls, 90% of Americans believe in God. Yet, this belief comes as long as there is a compromise on who God is and what He wants. *Time* magazine polls reported that Americans wanted God, but like Little Rey, they didn't want to give up their lifestyle. More specifically, America wants God, but not His Commandments.

A 1993 TIME-CNN poll showed that 80% of America's Catholics were "free thinkers," people who believed it permissible to make up their own minds on moral issues rather than follow the Church's teachings.[1] Only 14% said that they should always obey Church teachings. Yet ironically, another survey of religious beliefs showed that 86% of Americans believed in Heaven and 71% believed in Hell.

Relatively speaking, these numbers were high in comparison with other populations. For example, only 27% of the people in Hungary believed in Heaven and 16% in Hell. And in East Germany only 19% believed in Heaven and 7% in Hell.[2]

Yet in America, while belief in Heaven and Hell is high, there appears to be little belief in a connection between one's behavior and one's arrival at either of these eternal destinations. Indeed, Americans are anxious to say they believe in God and want to go to Heaven, but they are apparently reluctant to conform to any lifestyles or rules which might be required to help them get there.

Again, it comes down to deals. Like Little Rey, Americans want to make a deal with God. For with a deal, they believe they can do whatever they want and still get to Heaven.

For Catholics, though, this is extremely difficult, as it is hard to belong to the Catholic Church without accepting its teachings. Consequently, many people are leaving or simply ignoring these teachings. *Time* magazine (April 5, 1993) labeled this phenomenon, *"The Church Search."* According to *Time* reporter Richard Ostling:

> *"Today a quiet revolution is taking place that is changing not only the religious habits of millions of Americans but the way churches go about securing members to keep their doors open.*

"Increasing numbers of Baby Boomers who left the fold years ago are becoming religious again, but many are traveling from church to church, or faith to faith, sampling creeds, shopping for a custom-made God...

"They believe in God though one-third also believe in reincarnation, ghosts and astrology.

"The God of their understanding is not necessarily the personal, all-powerful and all-knowing deity of orthodoxy. Nor is Jesus affirmed by boomers necessarily as the Son of God and unique savior of humanity."[3]

The fact that Jesus is not accepted as the Son of God and the Savior of humanity is not hard to understand. For once again, how could He be? Jesus denounced sin. He also came to redeem mankind of its sin and when you get down to it, it is apparent that Americans simply don't want give up their sins, their habits which are contrary to God's Commandments.

Indeed, much of the country is just too comfortable. Like Little Rey, Americans want to enjoy life. Thus, they have little choice but to make a deal with God, or to redefine God, Church and Christianity to conform to their own lifestyles.

The Virgin's words to Estela during the first twenty-four months crushed those false beliefs. The Blessed Mother exposed America for what it was, a nation of little humility and great pride, a nation on the edge of despair. Mary warned Estela that this needed to be reversed before it was too late:

"If you behave more and more without pride and malice toward others, always striving to become the servant rather than the one to be served, we will win many souls for my Son.

"The world is waiting for you, my children, and I am asking you to prepare your lives as you know you must!!

"LEARN THE HUMILITY OF TRYING TO BE LAST INSTEAD OF FIRST, LEAST IMPORTANT INSTEAD OF MOST IMPORTANT!

"Yes, my children, I know that it is difficult, especially when, in the Americas, the way of life is to be first, not last!

"But, if you have decided to say, yes, to me, that is what I am asking." [May 27, 1989]

Indeed, Mary's words laid the groundwork for a series of messages that totally stripped America to the bone. She brought to light the existence of the parasitic, spiritual disease devouring the country's soul. Likewise, the Virgin exposed the hypocrisy behind America's claim of believing in God, yet not living those beliefs. To Estela Ruiz, she presented the facts:

"This evening, I want to speak about faith.
"Faith is a word that is used commonly in the world. However, in the context in which it is used, it is totally MIS-USED! In the Americas, it is used when speaking about having faith in your country, your friends, yourself, your government, schools, and even your doctor!!! However, the word, as it should be used, is now rarely used, and that is when speaking about your faith in God!
"You may say you have faith, but your actions don't show it. You worry about everything in your life: your home, your cars, your children, clothes, time, space, money, friends, enemies, business, jobs, and oh, so many things!! This allows you little time to give your Lord attention. Your ears and hearts cannot, do not, open to hear my Son talk to you, reach out to you, console you, love you!
"The faith you must have to believe that He is constantly there, reaching out to give you what is necessary in your life to be happy, is lost in your worries; the faith you must have to believe that the things you constantly worry about cannot, will not, give you or bring you happiness; the faith to believe that only Our Lord, Jesus Christ, can bring you the happiness that you desire, the happiness that you were meant to have, which you inherited as part of the Body of my Son." [July 15, 1989]

According to Mary, America's lack of true faith has also instituted a false conception of charity. Again, the Virgin wasted no time pointing this out to Estela:

"Many of my children believe that charity is something which shows the world how great they are!
"They also believe that giving a small amount of their excess possessions will endear them to the world and to

an imagined God. In their minds, the God they imagine is a being whom they can throw leftovers, as if to AP-PEASE the imagined God. This makes them feel that, since they are capable of giving, this allows them to do other things that are highly offensive to my Son!! They give a few possessions, and then turn around and par-take of the evils of the world!

"Believe me, my children, this understanding of char-ity is wrong and very offensive to my Son. These people use their own meaning of charity to abuse others. This type of understanding will only cause those who do this to lose their souls to Satan.

"The virtue of charity is a virtue, which, if under-stood, can be cause for your sanctification. It is under-stood correctly when you care for your brothers and sis-ters in the world, regardless of who they are...whether they are those who are your superiors according to world cat-egories, or those who are not important to your way of life. Charity is understood when you can finally under-stand the words of My Son: Love others, as I have loved you...treat others, as you would like to be treated. Give to others with your heart, body and soul. Strive to be last, not first, so that you can be first in Heaven. Treat your brothers and sisters with love, dignity and respect. When you see your brothers down, offer your hand to assist them.

"My children, reach out to those who are hurting in the world! The more you give of yourself to alleviate the hurts of the children of God, the greater a place you have reserved in Heaven!

"Who are your brothers and sisters? Every human being with whom you come in contact throughout your life. And if in those, there are some who do not seem to need material possessions, then give them love! EVERY-ONE NEEDS TO BE LOVED!!" [July 18, 1989]

America's lack of faith and charity, according to Mary, has brought about a national crisis, a crisis of hope. She told Estela:

"IN YOUR HEARTS THERE IS NO HOPE!
"You don't look to Our Savior to give you healing of
body and spirit. The world no longer recognizes that He
is the hope you are looking for.
　　"You, my children, suffer, but refuse to give and of-
fer your pain to Him Who can turn it into love. You no
longer accept death as the reunion of your soul to our
God and you are afraid to die!!! You are torn apart when
someone close to you dies because you no longer under-
stand that DEATH IS LIFE!! Instead, your hope is no
longer in reuniting your soul to Our Lord, but in trying
to live forever!! If you could begin to understand that if
you die to the world by changing your lives and giving
them to my Beloved Son, you would be born to Him!!!
And then you would understand the faith, hope and love
that my Beloved Son tried to teach you! And through this
knowledge, you would also understand that it is through
dying that you will reunite with my Son and with me."
[August 5, 1989]

Mary explained that the end result of the loss of faith, hope
and charity in America is pain and suffering, a type of suffering
which Little Rey was quite familiar with. Mary told Estela that this
suffering is everywhere across our once-so-great land:

　　"I find that this evening my heart weighs heavy with
the pain of seeing my suffering children in the Americas
and the world. As I see all of you suffer with the pain of
living without faith and hope, and in a desperate way, my
heart feels sad. As your heavenly Mother, I don't like to see
you, my children, in pain. But it saddens me more to recog-
nize that a lot of your pain is much greater than it should
be because you have not yet learned to give it up to my Son.
　　"The world is in so much pain at the present time, and
I, as your Mother, recognize that you have lost the knowl-
edge of how to alleviate and ease the pain. If, long ago,
the world had not lost its focus and set its vision on other
things than Our Savior, my Son Jesus, there would not be

as much pain and despair as there is now. Men have assumed control themselves and, because of that, we see broken homes, adults and children using drugs to escape reality, the worship of material things, looking to achieve power regardless of the consequences, and many other things which are not from God.

"All those things that I have mentioned are not from God, and are not caused by Him, as many of my children seem to think. Our Lord has never wanted His children to suffer. There are things in life that are hard, but are tolerable, if you could just hand them to Our God's love and mercy. It is possible to overcome the things in life that are difficult. NOTHING IS GIVEN TO YOU THAT IS IMPOSSIBLE FOR YOU TO BEAR!" [September 19, 1989]

But Americans do not want to suffer. Voluntary acts of sacrifice and reparation are virtually out-dated. This has contributed to the evil tide sweeping the country, for the Virgin says that Americans turn to pleasure to avoid and soothe their pain:

"The reign of evil is so great and so strong that I come to let you know that the GREATEST AND MOST POWERFUL WAY LEFT TO BREAK SATAN'S GRIP ON THE WORLD IS THROUGH TRUE COMMITMENT TO PRAYER, PRAYER FROM THE HEART!!

"My young ones find themselves lost in the grip of evil, and they don't know how to release that hold.

"Parents and adults have made material things their gods, and don't know how to help their children because they, themselves, have lost the knowledge of the power and love of Our Lord. They cannot give the young ones something they do not possess. The world must, again, learn to look to God for guidance and strength to change their lives, and to help others change their lives.

"There are many who are unhappy with their present lives because, even with all the material comforts, their lives are empty and useless. This is because they do not know God!!!" [September 30, 1989]

Consequently, says Mary, people blame God for their suffering, for their own pathetic state:

> *"These are times when my children on earth seem to be suffering so much. Sadly, many times, Our Lord in Heaven is blamed for the problems that grip my children.*
> *"If you will but think for a moment, this is not possible!! The Lord Our God did not introduce what is now hurting you, my children...things like abuse of drugs, divorce, unfaithfulness in marriages, love of material things.*
> *"If we could but take inventory of the problems and concerns of man in the world, it would be easy to see that everyone of them has been caused by man himself!!"*
> [September 28, 1989]

Obviously, the Virgin's words present a painfully accurate assessment of our culture. Mary clearly outlines what the polls and magazine writers show: America, so advanced and full of comforts, is spiritually starving. On the outside, the country may seem to be thriving, but its soul is barren and desperate, on the brink of despair.

While painting a frightening picture, the Virgin also presents the solution for this dilemma: America must turn to God. Nothing else will bring it peace. And God, she says, is ready to respond to the people's pleas:

> *"The problems of the Americas are not so much physical hunger, as spiritual hunger. The Spirit of God is weak in you, and many of my children on your continent suffer from lack of faith; and because of this, charity, which is love for each other, is almost nonexistent. Many suffer from spiritual weakness but refuse to turn to God in hope.*
> *"Yet, I, as your Mother and your Lady of the Americas, tell you that never has my Son, Jesus, showered more Mercy and graces on your continent than during the present time. Never has the Holy Spirit been more powerful than now. God, Our Father, loves you so much that*

He is showering you with abundant blessings, so that you may find faith. Only those with bitterness and hard hearts may resist, but the love of God can break even the hardest of hearts.

"With the prayers and love of those who have heard my call, who are praying with me for the salvation of all my children, we will succeed in turning others to God's love. I ask that you not give up on your commitment to prayer. Sometimes it seems hard and can be tiring. Sometimes you may think your prayers are useless, but they are not. We are making headway. We will be victorious over evil. The angels and saints and the whole court of Heaven are with you, assisting you, the mighty warriors of God's love. Call on them often. I am forever with you, at each one's side..." [June 13, 1992]

While some in the Ruiz family struggled, Estela easily accepted the Virgin's words concerning herself. Her conversion progressed. Almost overnight, she saw herself in a new light. She recognized the hardness, the cold personality. She realized what ambition had done to her. She had, in her own words, *"gone overboard,"* as worldly success totally consumed her.

When Estela saw her true self in the light of God, she wept. She wept with shame and with joy. Most of all, she wept with appreciation for God's great mercy on her soul. For Estela realized that she had been traveling on a *"self-destructive path."*

As she recognized the long path of conversion which lie ahead of her, Estela had to laugh. Just imagine, she had actually petitioned the Virgin to ask God to send her straight to Heaven when she died. She had even written it down and given it to Reyes before his trip to Medjugorje! What a joke, she now thought. In fact, how embarrassing!

But Estela Ruiz was no different than the other 86% of Americans who believed in Heaven and smugly felt entitled to its key. A key many may never see. For the real key to Heaven must come through Jesus Christ.

And from what Mary was explaining to Estela, this key must be used to open one's own heart before it can open all eternity.

CHAPTER SEVENTEEN

OUR LADY OF CONVERSION

SAINTS AND SINNERS. People often speak as though the two are diametrically opposed, like parallel lines in opposite directions which never intersect.

But those with the scarlet letters and those with the halos know better. They'll tell you how it is. The truth is, many of the saints were once great sinners, and many of the great sinners had been well taught the rules.

Staying on one path or another is a conscious decision, but by far the better path is that which offers an eternal reward. Nonetheless, achieving that reward requires tremendous grace and mercy from God.

Sainthood! No person is ineligible for membership in this lofty club. Even in modern times, many people acknowledge the special power of saints. A 1980's national Catholic magazine reported that 67% of those surveyed prayed to saints, and 68% said they attempted to imitate them. But once again, there is a catch. Before the halo must come the conversion, along with a lifetime of exemplary holiness.

What wily old Estela Ruiz didn't realize when she self-righteously requested immediate admission into Heaven, was that this presumed she was of sainthood status, a woman of outstanding commitment to prayer and virtue. No wonder she laughed in retrospect. She couldn't help but laugh.

Like Saint Paul on the road to Damascus, the sight of her soul after her conversion was distressing. But not for long. With God's forgiveness, Estela decided to put her past behind her in complete trust that God had done the same.

Quickly, like a spark growing into a flame, she marched in the right direction. She took her heavenly Mother's advice by setting her feet firmly on the path of conversion. But, Mary warned, Estela deserved little of the credit, for it was entirely God who had deigned to correct her path.

Soon, many other conversions began to occur around the apparitions. Near the end of 1988, the forcefulness behind these conversions indicated something big was indeed happening in South Phoenix, something very big.

Just as the Virgin's work at Guadalupe was characterized by mass conversion like the world had never before experienced, the conversions surrounding Estela Ruiz's apparitions were profound and numerous. What's more, Our Lady of Guadalupe was often referred to as the "Queen or Empress of the Americas." The fact Mary was now appearing to a Hispanic woman as Our Lady of the Americas seemed to signal that she had come to continue the work she began at Guadalupe. Indeed, not only were the Americas again deep in sin, but theologians have insisted for centuries that the tilma's miraculously preserved state implies more than what the eye physically beholds. The incredible failure of the cactus fibers to disintegrate is, according to some, a sign that something significant is about to unfold in America.

Other signs seem to confirm this hypothesis. Two missionary images (i.e., exact replicas) of Our Lady of Guadalupe are now circulating the globe. Veneration of these images brings promises from Mary of conversion and heavenly graces. Many miracles are being reported.

Most significantly, just as in Sixteenth Century Mexico, millions are experiencing phenomenal conversions as a direct result of the Virgin's apparitions at Medjugorje. In fact, not since Guadalupe have such conversions occurred. People of all countries, races and religions who traveled to the Bosnian mountain hamlet are returning home radically changed. It is as if the Woman clothed in the Sun on the tilma of Guadalupe has sprung to life in Medjugorje. And dozens of healings accompany the stories, as God confirms His presence with these signs.

Again, these phenomena have not escaped the eyes of experts. The curious connection between Guadalupe and Medjugorje is being recognized. Father Robert Faricy S. J., author of numerous books and Professor of Theology at the Gregorian in Rome, says he has personally experienced the connection. *They re both alive,* insists Fr. Faricy...

> *"They're both still happening because the miracle is there! The miracle at Medjugorje, because the apparitions are happening there every day. And the miracle at Guadalupe, because that painting is a miracle. You can't explain that! Mary is active there. Something is keeping that painting from deteriorating. It's preserved. It's supposed to deteriorate. It doesn't deteriorate. It's a physical effect that has no plausible scientific cause. It's exactly what we call a miracle. And it points to Mary. Like at Medjugorje, God is working through Mary in it."*[1]

Concludes Faricy:

> *"Guadalupe is not over. I was there. It's still happening!! It's over at Lourdes. It's over at Fatima. It's not over at Medjugorje and its not over at Guadalupe! Guadalupe is a lot like Medjugorje. It's happening there!!"*[2]

You don't have to tell Reyes and Estela Ruiz that. The Virgin of Guadalupe was alive in Reyes life since childhood. And sometime around 7 AM on September 8, 1988, Our Lady of Guadalupe decided to talk to Reyes' wife, Estela. All the while, he just happened to be in Medjugorje experiencing what theologians like Father Faricy insist cannot be found any place on the face of the earth except at Guadalupe.

Yes, it's happening at both places. The Virgin is alive and moving powerfully. And Father Faricy will also unhesitatingly give you his opinion why: *"In both cases, Mary is here as our Mother, and we are in trouble."*

According to what Our Lady of the Americas is telling Estela Ruiz, that trouble is significant, a kind which the world has never seen before.

While a bit of research is required to understand the apparent connection between Medjugorje and Guadalupe, it's not hard to see a mystical link to the Virgin's apparitions in South Phoenix. The Guadalupe-Medjugorje-Arizona connection definitely exists, although it is not totally defined.

But it doesn't have to be. Theologians who study these types of events say that many mystical visits are linked. Some day, those who get to Heaven will perhaps see how it was all connected, how the graces, blessings and events of God's people link together one century after another, one generation to the next.

Indeed, they would have to be linked. For each generation has faced a common enemy. His name is Satan. And God's plan to help his people combat the devil has always existed and has been ongoing throughout the ages, in what the Church calls "the communion of saints."

At Guadalupe, at Medjugorje and likewise in Arizona, the Virgin immediately points her finger toward her greatest foe. In an incredibly powerful statement to Estela, Mary announced that the battle was underway. For just as the beginning of the final battle had begun at Guadalupe, it would now conclude with Medjugorje and Mary's many other manifestations throughout the world, including her visits to Arizona. As she told Estela:

"As I now become known in the Americas, I beg all of you to help me by turning to prayer. I ASK THAT YOU PRAY FOR THE SUCCESS OF MY PLAN! Today, I want the Americas to know that my Plan is the same Plan that Our Heavenly Father has had from the beginning of time, and that is that all His children be saved from evil and become His children!!!

"I come as your heavenly Mother to ask and to beg that THE AMERICAS RETURN TO THE LOVE OF OUR FATHER, SO THAT YOU MAY ONE DAY RE-JOICE WITH HIM IN HEAVEN!!!!

"My children, you are aware that Satan has a grip on many of my children on your continent at the present

time! I now come to battle the Evil One, so that he will let my children go!!!

I WILL NOT ALLOW HIM TO CONTROL MY CHILDREN ANY LONGER!" [August 19, 1989]

It was a bold statement, even more profound than many realized. In essence, Mary was saying that the millions returning home from Medjugorje were returning to a spiritual war zone, one that seemed to be central to the outcome of the coming Triumph of the Immaculate Heart announced at Fatima in 1917.

Slowly, with great care and detail, Mary revealed to Estela what Satan had done to America. Much like he had done before in ancient Mexico, Satan had a grip on society, and now the times were even more serious. The devil's reign was at hand, Mary revealed, and she had been sent by God to help bring it down.

In many messages, Mary revealed to Estela what exactly was unfolding:

"It is not an easy road you have chosen, my little ones. I know, for you must continue to struggle against the call of evil which is so strong and powerful. The Evil One has never battled so powerfully to keep souls under his dominion. He is very aware of my presence throughout the world and has gathered all his power to keep my children from turning to God. Beware my little ones, beware for he is a great deceiver. He has worked very hard to deceive many into thinking that their deeds and decisions are done for the good of man, yet these deeds are destructive, not only physically but more importantly, spiritually. The Evil One can destroy your soul in many ways and during these times is working from the most subtle way to the most visible outright evil way he can. Many of you, my faithful ones, can see it and even feel it in your own lives.

"I, as your Heavenly Mother, am here to bring you the Good News that evil cannot win over God's goodness. Our Almighty Lord will be victorious in the end. You, my faithful ones, must believe this and hold it in your heart, lest you become weak and fall under Satan's

attacks. Yes, Satan is attacking in full force, yet you, my children, must remain strong and committed to the work of God." [February 6, 1993]

Mary further explained that Satan's full force attacks on God's people have been very successful:

"I have come to you, my children, in your hour of need. I have seen your suffering as the world is devastated by evil, and I have come to help you free yourselves from this grip. Satan has done great harm to my children on earth. He has fooled many into thinking that God should have no place in their hearts, and my children in the world have designed a new golden calf to worship. That golden idol has now been made into the image of man.

"My little ones, you have allowed Satan to deceive you into thinking that power and material things will make you master and lord of all. As you all strive to be the most powerful, you go about destroying each other, and human life, which God created, is left devastated throughout the world.

You are living in an age when hate, anger and jealousy hurl brother against brother and nations against nations. Men set themselves up to be worshiped and idolized, and have forgotten their true God, their Creator." [May 18, 1991]

Likewise, the Virgin told Estela how Satan is not so easily detected:

"I want you to know that Satan is very angry because of the many souls that have been taken from his power and have been won over to Our Lord. At this time he is out prowling to tempt my children and bring them back to his evilness. You, my little ones, must be very careful that your weaknesses do not allow him to overpower you. He knows your weaknesses, and he has been able to use his evil wiles in the past to destroy your soul. He is like a

wolf in sheep's clothing working to make you believe that what is wrong is right." [June 30, 1990]

Mary told Estela that the whole world was being deceived about what was right and what was wrong:

"I am here because I want to reach out my hand to all who may take it. I want to reach out to all my children in the world because these are hard times, and as your Mother in heaven who loves you, I want to bring comfort to my children in pain. Satan is running rampant over the world and has brought his evil and darkness to the world.

"There is an ominous cloud of evil that hovers over the world, a cloud that has blinded the eyes and hearts of the children of God. You, my beloved, who are the children of God, are also my children, given to me by my beloved Son, Jesus. My children in the world, this dark cloud has caused you not to be able to see God and His words in the world. Because He is out of your sight, you have also put Him out of your minds and hearts. You have stopped acknowledging Him as your Creator and Savior. You have pushed Him out of your lives.

"All the things that keep you from the love of God have become a way of life for the world. Greed, hate, anger and viciousness against one another is the way of the world, and God's goodness is hard to find.

"I come to my children to speak to all, praying that my words reach all souls. I come to bring you the good news of God's love and mercy for His children. I come to tell you of His forgiving heart, of His generosity and goodness. I come determined to pull you out of the clutches of the Evil One, and as your Heavenly Mother return you to your rightful place, which is with our Lord, who loves you and waits longingly for you to return to Him." [September 18, 1993]

With her messages to Estela, Mary posed the challenge. Was Satan going to continue his terror or not?

"Many of God's children have been deceived by Satan and have come to believe that his evil ways lead to happiness. Hate, anger and violence rule the world, and there is no happiness in that because they are contrary to the nature of God. Greed and lust reign supreme, and discord has separated and pitted brother against brother and children against parents, and Satan has divided and conquered.

"Is Satan to remain in control, or are you, my beloved little ones, ready to reject this misery and return to your rightful inheritance, which is to be children of God? Because you were given free will, only you can answer this question; only you, each one of you, can make this decision. Will hate, anger and confusion continue to reign until humanity is destroyed and extinguished, or are you, the children that God created, ready to change hearts and souls to God's love and peaceful ways?" Only time will tell." [November 6, 1993]

Despite her wise warning, the Virgin also revealed God's coming victory over the Evil One in America, and then in the world:

"I need you to help me fight the greatest battle of all. Together we will defeat Satan..." [June 13, 1988]

The victory, she further revealed, was already unfolding:

"Satan is very angry that so many have changed their lives and turned to God. As many respond to my call and begin to make changes in their way of living, he does all he can to interfere. It angers him greatly that many are changing the direction of their lives, and he uses many ways to prevent my work. But because many who have answered are praying, fasting and taking God's love to others, my work of touching hearts for my Son is growing and becoming fruitful." [February 16, 1991]

But as Mary has repeated around the world, time is a factor. God will act at a decisive moment, and those not converted will suffer the consequences. This she made clear to Estela:

"I call on all the people of the Americas to turn to prayer so that together, we will defeat Satan and all his false promises... Help me, my children. Help me. Time grows short!" [July 1, 1989]

And Mary also implied to Estela that once Satan was conquered in America, the whole world will follow the country's example:

"It has been joyful to see you responding to my call, and to pray with you for the salvation of the world, especially the Americas. I have seen the Rosary movement grow in great strides. I have seen you, my children, fall in love with prayer, and begin to learn how to use it for your spiritual growth and for the reparation of the sins of the world.

"I see so many of you with Rosaries in hand, and your faithfulness to the use of your Scapulars. Many of you have accepted ridicule from others and, in some instances, even from the clergy because of your faithfulness in wearing your Scapulars. I want you to know that I am well pleased, that you bring me hope, hope that someday many of my children in the Americas will hold their Rosaries in hand and wear their Scapulars around their necks to show the world that the people in the Americas believe in prayers; that soon the Americas will let the world know that its people are dedicated to God, that they know Him and love Him!

"One day the Americas will let the world know that Satan REIGNS NO MORE, and that all families have chosen God as their King and Master." [November 7, 1989]

Alone with Estela, the Virgin explained many important things. She taught her about love. She taught her about children. She especially pointed out how important it is for little ones to pray, as their prayers bring many blessings to families.

Mary also said that it is important to understand that, before peace can reign in the world, it must reign in the family. To defeat Satan, families must forgive and stop hurting each other.

"Love," Mary told Estela, *"must develop within ourselves and for ourselves, and then for other people."* She assured Estela that this would then spark conversion. Indeed, whether Mary appears as Our Lady of Guadalupe, Our Lady of Medjugorje or Our Lady of the Americas, she is always Our Lady of Conversion.

On a warm spring evening in May of 1989, Mary appeared to Estela and spoke to her *"mother to daughter."* It was a long talk, serious yet light, general yet full of detail.

The Triumph of the Immaculate Heart was near, Mary said, as was the fulfillment of the prophecy in Genesis. Indeed, Mary explained to Estela that she was going to crush the head of the devil.

Late that night, Estela addressed a huge crowd gathered to hear the Virgin's words. And she explained to them what Mary had told her:

"..first of all, I should explain that earlier today, after the cleaning, I kind of tried to relax. I always try to do that, and as I was preparing to take a shower and freshen up and go to my room, I heard her (Our Blessed Mother) call me.

"She said, **I need for you to come and talk to me!**

"So I went into my bedroom and closed the door and she told me, **This evening I want you to write the message, which I will give you earlier today.**

"She must have known that we were going to have such a big crowd, and I was going to go like, Oh my goodness !! Because she gave me the message, and she asked me to write it down, and she said, **When I do talk to you throughout the prayers, it will be mostly conversation between you and me...like comadres!**

"This is what she told me, and you know what it [comadres] is ... from our culture ... it is two women that have great rapport with each other!

"So this pretty much is what happened, but she did say this evening, as we prayed here, that she wanted to welcome all the new people that are here, and for me to explain that she is here in the Americas, and that she is doing many, many things with many, many people! She's

here to stomp on the head of Lucifer, and that he will know, and that he does know, that she is here, that she is going to show him what a victory is!!!

"So, she is going to ask many people to help her, and as you come to this home, you will be asked to be part of what she wants to do!

"You do have the choice of saying, yes or no.

"She will not be angry, or anything else, if you say no.

"She will continue to love each and every one of us.

"If you do say, 'yes,' be prepared to grow very much spiritually, because that is what she is going to ask of us.

"She is here, not as one particular name. She is here in many different ways to many different people.

"For the Hispanic, she is here as Our Lady of Guadalupe. For the others that love Our Lady of Fatima, she is here in that way to touch hearts!

"...she is THE IMMACULATE HEART OF MARY, and she wants to be called OUR LADY OF THE AMERICAS, because the work that she is to do will be here in the Americas, which is North America and South America.

"There are many other things going on throughout the world that she's involved with, and the time has come for her to show her strength to Lucifer.

"He now, at this time, knows that she is here, so he will try to tempt you, try to sway you away from what you are doing, but do not let him, because she will be here protecting each and every one of us!!!

"She stresses that you wear your scapular. It's very important because that will be your protection against Satan!

"He may try to tempt you, and he may try to make you believe differently, but she is here and will protect you, so that for those of you that do not wear a scapular, get one and wear it!

"Do not be afraid to wear it!

"I'm telling you this, because I used to be [afraid]. I was embarrassed, is the word, to wear it because I thought, People are going to think I'm crazy.

"So I used to put it in my purse all the time, and I thought, well, you know, I want to be safe, but I don't want to be embarrassed!

"So I'll put it in there and see if it works!!!!

"And one day she told me, 'Put it on...NOW!!'

"She said, 'NOW!,' and boy, was I digging in my purse for it! And I was driving, by the way ... a funeral was coming right by me, a policeman was coming right at me, and I thought, O my Lord!

"I don't know why, at that moment, she wanted me to put it on, but I did ... in a hurry!!

"That's one of the things she stresses to all that come here: Put your scapulars on! So I beg of you to do it, please!

"I'm going to read the message that she gave me earlier:

"To my faithful children, I again welcome you with my Heart full of love and thank you for continuing to come and pray with me for the conversion of those that want to come to my Son, but do not know how to go about it.

"Tonight I want to talk to you about your spiritual growth. I want you, this evening, to take some time to meditate on whether you are at the point I need for you to be in your love of God and your brothers and sisters in the world. If you think that you are, or you think you are close, think about this: Today...how many occasions did you have to show your love toward my Son and me? Did someone reach out to you needing some caring and love? Did you give it? Was it your neighbor, or the man or woman in the street — those that are hard to love, like the poor, the homeless, the emotionally or physically handicapped? Or even closer to home, was it your son, your daughter, father, mother or your spouse? Did you show them unconditional love, or did you ask of them to be the way you want them to be in order for you to understand them?

" You see, my children, I know that most of you pray to Our Lord to be understood and nurtured. You all seek the Lord, so that He can feed you, but when are you go-

ing to get to the point where you finally learn to feed yourself and then turn and feed my weak and hungry spirit?

"Don't you know that this is where I need you to be? Can you, at this moment, turn to the next person, the person at your side, and say, I love you, and mean it from the heart, without hesitation or question, whether you know them or not?? That is the unconditional love that I require of you, in order for you to be ready for what we must do.

"Can you start by helping each other here to learn to love one another without condition? I beg of you that you start!!! Let our prayers here tonight be said for that intention, so that, when the day comes for you to do what I will ask, you will know how to do it. If you allow Him, the Holy Spirit will come to you and help you. He is longing for you to ask Him to come to you! Reach out to Him and ask — He will be there for you instantly! My Son, Our Lord, Jesus, and I beg you to start today. Reach out to each other, and we will teach you how to love the world. GOD, THE FATHER, IS WAITING FOR THIS LOVE....START TODAY!"

Indeed, this message and others like it have set many on the path of conversion. *Our Lady of Conversion* is piercing hearts everywhere in and through her apparitions in South Phoenix, and Estela Ruiz's hard, worldly heart was the first to feel the sting.

But there was definitely one big miracle that the Ruiz family still lacked, one family member's heart that needed to be touched.

For if anyone wondered about the validity of Mary's apparitions to Estela Ruiz, there was one thing that could quickly erase all doubt, one miracle that could come only from the hand of God. Indeed, it was generally agreed that no one on the face of the earth could change Little Rey. No one knew how.

...no one till now.

FOR THE SOUL OF THE FAMILY

CHAPTER EIGHTEEN

"LIKE JOHN THE BAPTIST"

When South Phoenix's drug coffers couldn't fill Little Rey's demand, he would often dash over to Tempe to refill. Tempe had been good to him since he was a teenager. He liked Tempe. It was like a second home. And after his folks kicked him out due to his rampant, reckless lifestyle which he vowed never to change, Tempe became even more a part of his identity.

By the late eighties, Little Rey's appearance had radically changed. Cultivating an almost freakish Mexican-rebel persona, Little Rey grew his hair and threw on some earrings. He matured to match his outward image. It was an image that defined him on the streets, something that gave him power, something which he needed and enjoyed.

The crystal meth Rey was using in 1988 was something else he enjoyed. It gave him *"weird experiences."* Translated, this meant *"unpredictable highs"* that continued to validate his pledge of experimenting with new things.

Crystal meth was also cheaper. It hit the streets not a minute too soon, as Little Rey's coke habit was destroying him financially. Without the necessary funds to supply his cravings, he often had to drop down to marijuana or even settle for tequila. Even when he broke his foot in 1987 and ended up in the hospital for six days, his friend still brought him coke.

But by 1988, the streets were getting meaner. They were meaner and much darker. They were dangerous and even more unpredictable. People were dying. In South Phoenix and in many cities around the country, the situation was bad.

While Rey's family basked in the new warmth of spiritual light, Little Rey walked the tightrope of inner city violence.

One night, as Rey and some of his gang were hanging out at a local theater, they decided to rough-up some *"white boys"* for fun.

After physically ambushing two young men and laughing it up, the prank backfired. The next thing they knew, twenty more white boys were hot on their heels. Things got out of hand quickly. A car-chase ensued. This evolved into a drive-by shooting, a shooting that found Little Rey almost dead.

By early 1989, Little Rey was converting like the rest of the family. The problem was, his conversion was a spiral downward. He was sick, sicker than he realized. He tried rehab and failed. He was down to 195 pounds, an all-time low for him. Little Rey was headed for the bottom, and he knew it.

And without a doubt, that was right where the Virgin wanted him.

Reyes Sr. had a word with his youngest son before departing for Medjugorje.

"Write a petition for me to take to Medjugorje," Reyes told Little Rey.

Without resisting, Little Rey complied. His petition stated, *"Help me, Mary, to stop doing drugs."*

God was his only hope, and he knew it. As cold and callous as he had become, Little Rey even broke down and cried. It happened the night his dad told him he didn't exist anymore. Bluntly, Reyes Sr. advised him, *"You are dead!"*

But raising the dead has always been God's greatest miracle. From Lazarus to Jesus Christ Himself, resurrection from death to life is what Christianity is all about. It's the reason Christ was born.

When Mary first appeared, Estela told her all about Little Rey. *"I can't take care of him anymore,"* said Estela. *"He's too old. He's a grown man. I can't go with him, wherever he goes. Blessed Mother, you have to take care of him!"*

After Mary informed Estela that she wanted Little Reyes to help spread her message, Estela was put in a rough position. She had to tell Mary her son's response, that Little Rey had said the Virgin would have to *"take me like I am."* It wasn't like she had to speak to a neighbor; Estela had to tell the Mother of God what was tantamount to blasphemy. But Mary's response was not surprising.

"Yes, tell him," she said to Estela, *"that's the way I want him!!"*
The Virgin's response shocked Little Rey.
"The Blessed Mother said that's the way she wants you," Estela told him.
Little Rey was dumbfounded. *"What does that mean?"* he thought. He was stunned. His heart was touched that anyone could ever accept him the way he was. *"Overwhelmed,"* he said, *"Nobody has ever loved me for who I really am."* He then fell to his knees and wept. *"Tell her,"* Rey said, *"that I will help her."*
The deal was done.
But the Virgin Mary had other things in mind. Once she received Rey's yes, it gave her the green light she needed to go after his heart...
...to perform a miracle.

That same night, Rey went back to his apartment. He set up a little altar, and placed a crucifix, some Rosaries, and some pictures of Jesus and Mary on it. Suddenly, as he stood next to his altar, he felt his heart cave in.
The big guy dropped to his knees, like a tree axed in two.
"O.K., God, here I am!," he stammered, *"I have nothing to offer You. I don't even own a home... O.K., I don't own a car. I own nothing. I have nothing in my possession All I have is this body. So, I'm going to offer that to You. All I have is this soul, so I'll offer that to You."*
With that, Little Rey waited to be struck. He didn't know by what. But somehow, he felt something was supposed to happen, but nothing did.
He spoke to God some more.
"God, all right, here I am... I'm Yours," he said again. And again, he waited.
And then, something did happen!
In a mighty tug, God grabbed Little Rey's soul and filled it. He filled it with His warmth and His love. He filled it with peace, His deep, serene peace which Little Rey had never found in drugs. It was, says Rey, a heavenly peace beyond words. *"It was like God took me into His arms and He said, O.K., O.K., My son."*
Little Rey says he heard no voices. He saw no visions. But suddenly, he knew that everything would be all right.

The next morning he rose early and went to Mass. Inside, Little Rey says he felt an awakening of who God was, who He really was. Almost impossibly, his hunger for drugs vanished. Even his beloved marijuana no longer beckoned him. Suddenly, the urge was gone. He seemed, he said, to have the will to decline the desire.

With the change on the inside came a change on the outside. Within just one short week, the drug king began saying his Rosary.

And Little Rey didn't just pray the Rosary; following his father's lead, he wore the Rosary. Although his new style began as a single Rosary draped around his neck, soon Little Rey was wearing Rosaries everywhere. Two around his neck, then four, then six, seven, eight Rosaries. These, he said, *"were only the exposed beads."* Around his wrists were more - wrapped tightly between his fingers. From his pockets, more Rosaries hung out.

Indeed, Little Rey was no longer Little Rey. In a matter of weeks, people said, he became like *"John the Baptist."*

His outwardly-religious public persona was fueled by Little Rey's new mission. He wanted, he said, to counter the signs so many wore of Satan.

"O.K., world," said Little Rey to himself, *"If you can show your insignias of Satan — skulls and crossbones, tatoos of devil symbols on your arms — then I can wear my Rosaries."*

And the world took notice. *"This guy has changed,"* Rey would hear them muttering. *"My God, he's become a Jesus freak!"*

But Rey couldn't care less what others said. He had never cared before, and nothing had changed. His same stubborn mentality was engaged, only for the other side. He made no apologies. Rey flatly confronted his inquirers:

"You know what? I don't care what you think! But since you brought it up, I'm going to tell you about God. I'm going to tell you about the Blessed Mother. I'm going to tell you about everything you never knew about the Lord!"

It was strangely powerful.

Indeed, when Little Rey walked down the street, people began to move out of the way. He was a man on a mission.

Just one month after the apparitions started, Little Rey was already working with teenagers, trying to help them to avoid what he says happened to him.

Not surprisingly, Rey's drug buddies kept expecting him to return. Those who hadn't seen him for a while would stop by to see if he had any drugs. And this often led to a big surprise and for a few, a big lesson.

"What happened to you, man?"

"What's with all these Rosaries hanging around your neck and hands?"

"You know what, buddy?" Rey would say. *"I need to talk to you..."*

With that, some would immediately flee as if they were seeing a ghost. But even then, Rey the Baptist wouldn't let them off without the last word: *"Something wonderful has happened in my life,"* he would tell them as they backpedaled in confusion, *"and something wonderful can happen in your life too!"*

"You know, God can change you, if you want it. Come here, I got something better for you!"

Remarkably, some did convert. For the grace of the Virgin's work was available, and Little Rey was spreading it.

Like with his mother Estela, an image of Our Lady in the Ruiz home struck again, converting one drug addict almost on the spot.

It happened out of nowhere. Little Rey's friend, Charlie, knocked on the door one day, looking to score some cocaine.

"Hey man," Charlie whispered to Little Rey. *"I'm looking for some coke."*

"C'mon in here," Little Rey told him, quite innocently. *"Let me talk to you."*

Like a black widow with a tight web, as soon as Charlie stepped inside, Rey poured the Virgin's words of love all over his unsuspecting victim.

"Listen, man," said Rey, *"this beautiful woman changed my life. And she can change yours."* Sounding like his dad, he then escorted Charlie across the room. *"Let me introduce her to you."*

With that Rey positioned Charlie in front of a painting of the Virgin in his living room that his dad had painted and said, *"See this beautiful lady, she'll change your life. Charlie, this is Blessed Mother. Blessed Mother, this is Charlie."*

Slowly, Rey slid back and away. And suddenly something happened to Charlie.

"I don't know what it was, but something just happened to me right then and there," Charlie later told Little Rey. *"It was just like she changed my life. She touched me..."*

A couple weeks later, Charlie was off drugs. Like Little Rey, he enlisted in the Virgin's army.

The entire notion that drug users and street gang members could accept and respond to the Virgin Mary's call, in whatever form, is a phenomenon in itself. Kristy Nabhan, in her study on the Ruiz family, noted Mary's *"gang connection."* It was a mystery which she examined in her thesis:

> *"Interviews with several Hispanic gang members high-light Mary's role as both a protecting mother and a con-quering, liberating woman of the streets.*
>
> "Arturo Weis, a forty-five year-old ex-member of the Chula Vista gang in South Phoenix, has addressed Mary quite frequently during interviews and off-hand remarks. He has specifically stated that Mary is used to cover their backs, and to protect them from other gang's bullets.
>
> *"Ruben, an ex-member of the Arizona Maravilla gang, said that the Virgin of Guadalupe is like a mother to gang members. He also mentioned that it exhibits neighborhood pride and the Mexican tradition to wear Mary on shirts or in the form of tattoos. His friend Mark, who is the nephew of Estela and who is also an ex-gang member, agreed with his sentiments and said that Mary is the ultimate mother.*
>
> *"In light of this brief discussion of another kind of Marian phenomenon in the community of South Phoenix, Mary is perceived as a mother-protectress as well as a lib-erator-conqueror. This latter image is not as conspicuous as the former; yet it is part of the gang ideology surround-ing the Madonna. She watches over gang members not as a meek, submissive mother, but as a tough mother, one that is willing to fight their battles with them."*[1]

"Little Rey" Ruiz and wife Donna

After his conversion, Rey's focus quickly shifted from himself to some of his brothers and sisters. *"They were into their own sins,"* he recalls noticing after his conversion. And they needed prayers, Little Rey's prayers.

It was ironic. Rey now worried about them, as he began to experience what his family had felt toward him for so long.

Like a snake shedding its skin, Little Rey shed his past. Eventually, he even did away with his three earrings, which forced him, he said, *"to give up his coolness, his badness."*

Yes, Little Rey died to himself. Within thirty days of the first apparition, he was on the road of conversion. Two wayward family members had now rejoined the fold. And Mary's eyes were firmly fixed on the rest.

But for Little Rey, it was more than a conversion. Little Rey's gift from Heaven was a deep inner healing, a healing from a disease that was not just destroying his mind and body, but also his soul. He had become blind to almost all right and wrong.

Indeed, Little Rey was just a small piece of the story of the rest of America, like a microcosm of the country's ills. Convinced that bad was good and wrong was right, he was one with the rest of a country which doesn't recognize sin at all. And one story in Little Rey's life especially reveals how bad it can get.

As an example of how callous he had become, Little Rey recalled the time his girlfriend became pregnant. When she told him that she was planning an abortion, Little Rey's response was downright pathological. Like the twisted opposite of a husband seeking to be near his wife during childbirth, Little Rey proclaimed that he wanted to watch the abortion in the operating room. Fortunately, he says today, God protected him from such a horror. The abortionist refused.

But Little Rey doesn't look back. He forgives himself for his past, believing that God has, too. After his heart-shaking experience at his little apartment altar when he called upon God, he went to confession. He claims that something entered his heart at that confession, and he was totally healed, and totally forgiven! Afterwards, Little Rey was told by a priest to give the aborted baby a name because that child, the priest said, was a saint in heaven praying for him. Little Rey did just that, he named the baby Mario, in honor of Mary.

But that *something* which entered Little Rey's heart also has a name. It's Jesus Christ. And according to Mary's messages to Estela, the rest of America is about to find Him, too.

CHAPTER NINETEEN

A GOLD MINE OF REVELATION

The miraculous conversion of Little Rey left the family stunned. All agreed, it was a wondrous display of God's power. It also substantiated the truth of the Virgin's words, for she promised Estela on the first apparition that she would take care of her children. And she had.

Thus, Little Rey's radical conversion removed all doubt about the Virgin's messages to Estela. But other signs manifested themselves as well.

A mentally-retarded young man blurted out that the Ruiz home was his *"Mother's house,"* as his family searched for the Ruiz residence one evening to join in the prayers. On another occasion, praying Buddhists present at the Ruiz home inquired about the significance of the aroma of roses which they smelled throughout the evening. It dumbfounded them, for no one else around them said a thing.

Others reported that tap water in the Ruiz's backyard was rose-scented, like perfume. While some reported to see Our Lady praying next to many of the pilgrims. One man said he even saw Our Lady of Guadelupe appear above the shrine.

On many nights, pilgrims to the family's chapel reported seeing beams of light descend from the sky and bathe the small shrine. Many others witnessed two paintings of the Virgin on the chapel altar come to life and smile at them. The Virgin's image, people said, looked so real that it left them stunned and in tears.

On still another occasion, a California man reported looking into the sun and seeing the Head of Jesus wearing a crown of thorns. On yet a different day, he witnessed a beautiful cross in the sky and a circular rainbow around the sun.

The Ruizs' two paintings which often are said to be miraculous

Most importantly, hundreds, if not thousands, of physical, emotional, mental and spiritual healings have been reported to the Ruiz's.

Yet, all in all, the apparitions to Estela Ruiz are primarily apparitions in the classic sense. They are not events exploding in mysticism and supernatural phenomena. Rather, they are very much in the tradition of the apparitions at Fatima and Lourdes. That is, while numerous signs are being reported, the Virgin's messages remain the primary focus.

In fact, one local reporter even commented on how downright calm and normal events were at the Ruiz home during the evening of an apparition:

> *"If you are not a believer, if you don't expect to see the Mother of God's eyes change and become real in the painting that hangs just behind the shrine of Jesus, as many claim to have seen it, it is difficult at first to understand what about these meetings so stirs the blood of the Ruizes and other visitors.*
>
> *"It is not the impassioned, mystical atmosphere that one usually equates with tales of miracles. No one in the*

audience shouts Hallelujah or collapses in an ecstatic fit. (Reyes says someone did the latter once, but the worshiper quickly regained all faculties upon hearing Reyes say that he was going to call 911 for help.) No one bursts into tongues.

"Even during the moments of the Rosary when Estela is seeing and talking to Mary, you wouldn't know unless you knew. Sequestered indoors with a few worshipers while the larger prayer group carries on outside, able to hear the crowd's Hail Marys through a speaker system that pipes every syllable into the house, Estela stops praying for a few minutes and her gaze fixates a little. That is all; in a few minutes the vision is over.

"Far from being frenzied demonstrations of belief, the Ruiz prayer meetings are occasions when common sense and the supernatural somehow combine, as when a man swooshed up to Estela after prayers were over and declared he felt the evening had cured him of cancer. How can I know that I'm cured? Do you think the Lord will send me a sign? he inquired of his prophetess.

"Aren't you about due for a checkup? Estela asked him. I think the doctor will be able to tell you whether you still have cancer or not."[1]

Indeed, the public gatherings are not a circus of the supernatural. They are intended only to share the experience of the apparitions with the public. Subsequently, much attention is placed on Mary's messages.

And, in the messages themselves we find the reason why. For the Virgin's dictations to Estela Ruiz are lengthy, instructional and profoundly theological. Their constitution is consistent, message after message. No rambling or disjointed communications are ever given. Each message is presented in a consistent pattern and in a manner that reveals a well-organized lesson on faith.

Most messages contain a theme, such as love, peace, faith, and hope. Others confront a specific need for the people of America to focus upon, such as materialism, family, power or evangelization.

Overall, Mary's messages to Estela Ruiz appear to be some of the purest and most inspiring messages ever received by a visionary, as they consistently demonstrate the Divine Author's perfect knowledge from beginning to end. Indeed, Mary's words to Estela reflect no theological ambiguity, nor do they give confusing or contradictory advice. To the contrary, they are concise and direct, presenting a concern and offering a solution. They are usually monothematic and never incite worry or fear.

In a sense, the messages reflect the purity of the Immaculate Virgin herself, thus giving the apparitions their greatest credibility.

What, concisely, is Mary's purpose under her Arizona title, Our Lady of the Americas ? When Mary appeared to Estela the third time, at Immaculate Conception Church in Phoenix, she clearly defined her role. *"I am the Immaculate Heart of Mary,"* she said. *"This is the time of my reign. I am here to bring my children back to my Son. The one who sent me is God the Father."*

With this, Mary declared her mission in America and in the world. Subsequently, her messages have confirmed this declaration. For the words Mary brings are more than beautiful and profound. As much as any messages given in the world today, they reflect God's plan for His people.

When examined in context with her revelations at Medjugorje, as well as Mary's profound dictations over the last twenty years to Father Gobbi of the Marian Movement of Priests, the messages to Estela Ruiz are found to be similarly vibrant in substance and consistency. Indeed, as noted, her revelations in South Phoenix are quite significant, surpassing mere curiosity or public show. Moreover, because of the length of each message to Estela, the total accumulation of dictations may exceed the public disclosures given at many major apparition sites.

Indeed, during the first six-year period of the apparitions, hundreds of messages have been given, each one several paragraphs in length or more, usually 500 to 600 words total. While quantity alone is not relevant, a scrupulous examination of the messages *content* clearly demonstrates the overall significance of the apparitions. Mary has not only said a lot, but none of her words have been wasted.

Each revelation contains a gold mine of truth. Thus, the sum of all of them would lead one to conclude that this apparition is very important in God's current plan for the world, a plan, once again, which was clearly spelled out in Mary's third apparition to Estela. While it would be a monumental task to study each message in detail, highlights can be excerpted by topic. Such highlights reveal the overall profound nature of the vast disclosures from God to the world through Estela Ruiz.

Following are excerpts of some of the most thought-provoking and edifying messages given to Estela, especially for America. These messages confront what Mary defines as America's greatest problems.

ON WAR AND DESTRUCTION

"The world stands in great danger during these days of great loss. The lack of love of God and of each other as children of God has brought about the possible destruction of many. Our Lord is not happy with the behavior of His children. There have been many who changed their lives and turned to prayer, but there are still so many who do not acknowledge their Creator and disregard His laws and Commandments.

"They have no respect for each other and therefore lack love for God.

"The destruction of each other can be the only outcome.

"I ask all my children who have learned how to pray, to offer your prayers and sacrifices so that all men can learn to love God, that all men can desire peace and that they can come to know that peace can only come through respect and dignity for each other and commitment to God's love.

"I have come to this earth to help men open their hearts to this love because I see the world in much danger. I have seen mankind bring suffering upon itself because of lack of respect and kindness for each other and because of the desire for power, control, and material things. Men no longer want to feel or tolerate the pain they have brought upon themselves, so they fill their bodies with substances that can deceive their souls and make their minds believe all is well." [December 1, 1990]

"When I have chosen to manifest myself in the world, it has been because I have seen a need. This time is no different. You, my children, are facing grave changes in the world. You are facing grave changes in your country. [The] Possibility, grave possibility of destruction of lives is very real.

"You who have answered my call must be very aware of this catastrophe that is possible. I ask you this evening to continue to stand firm in your commitment as you have done. Now, more than ever, your prayers must continue. You face grave tragedy because of the desires of men for control and power." [December 29, 1990]

"I ask today of those who are praying for my work that you especially pray for those who control the world, because as they have been put in positions of power, they have left God's mandates and have placed themselves as gods over people. They set up their own mandates and are leading people astray and toward perdition and destruction. Pray, my children, pray that these men and women may not be successful in their attempts to rule not only the body of people, but their minds and spirits, for surely they will drive the world to destruction and chaos.

"Is there now not enough chaos and destruction that might cause men to wonder if there is something terribly wrong going on? Is there not enough misery and despair to make men see that the world, as it is, is in great need of goodness, God's goodness? What will it take for all, every single human being, to understand that you need God? Can it not be by transforming your hearts to goodness and love, or must it be the total devastation of men?" [September 4, 1993]

"I am here to remind you of my love for you and to remind you of my Son's love for you. I also come this day to tell you that the heavens weep as the world moves ever closer to destruction and war.

"I came to this world to reach out to all my children in the world, yet many of those who have heard my voice

have not learned to commit their lives to God's love and care. There are so many who claim to love God and to love me, yet have not learned to entrust their lives to Him who created them. Many say to our Lord that they give themselves to Him, yet continue to cry and groan in their lives of turmoil. Much time is spent on asking God to change events in each life, and little time is given to God's work and to commitment to a true relationship with Him.

"He desires that each one trust in Him. If you say to Him, I trust in you, yet, continue to lead chaotic lives and then cry out because your soul is not at peace, then you are not at peace, and you are not truthful with your God. If your soul is not at peace, if this world is not at peace, it is not God's doing but yours. This world has not come to this destruction through God's hand, but through your own.

"Humanity has allowed the evil of Satan to overpower it, and his power is rampant over the whole of mankind. Chaos, destruction, hate and greed abound and there seems to be no way out.

"Yet, I come into this world to point you, to guide you to the way of peace and love. My Son came to save humanity through His death, yet the world has rejected the truth of His salvation. There is no trust in Him who is the only way out of this destruction." [March 5, 1994]

ON POWER

"A soul without God is a soul without life, and a soul without life is open to Satan's attacks, open to his power of destruction. He roams the world and he seeks souls and oh, how easy it is for him to invade a soul without God. A soul without God, lifeless, is susceptible to all his wiles and deceit. A lifeless soul does not understand that he uses his wiles in a very clever way. He implants in the soul a desire for power and lust, and the soul then falls into sins of materialism and of the flesh. Out of these two

major sins come many other sinful desires that will lead a soul to perdition, right into Satan's arms. It is his pleasure when power and lust become the gods of the children of God, because then these souls no longer desire to be children of God and to follow His Commandments.

"The children of God were created so that He could love them, not to become children of evil. What these souls fail to see is that eventually these desires of power and lust will bring them pain and suffering, because men and women were created for God's Kingdom; and when these souls turn away from God, they have turned away from their rightful inheritance. Once a soul finds no happiness from power and lust, once these desires have brought nothing but pain and suffering, this soul understands its real need. A soul really needs the peace and love that can only come from God, but that lost soul now only feels turmoil and chaos." [October 30, 1993]

"Many of my earthly children have chosen to be their own power and strength, and they do not understand that this is not enough to overtake the power of evil. It is not through your own power that you can go against the powers of evil and darkness. The power of evil is too strong for your weak nature. It is only through God's power that anyone will be able to go against this evil that seems to have overtaken the world. Once you allow the power of the Holy Spirit to take over in your life, you will have the strength to overcome the darkness. Then you will understand God, His goodness and love. Then you will have found the Kingdom of God on earth. God gave you a great gift and that gift is free will, the gift to choose what you desire. I have come to help you choose the Kingdom of God, because that is what you were created for. Let me touch your hearts, my beloved children, that the world may change its path to destruction to everlasting life with God. I love you and thank you for listening to my words." [July 31, 1993]

ON PRIDE

"The sin of pride is not good, for it sets you up to believe that you are better than others. It is a grievous sin because it robs you of compassion and true, unconditional love.

"A hard heart is full of pride, and it is the hardest sin to rid from within you. Those who profess to love God and are still full of pride are as the Pharisees putting themselves above others. They are incapable of forgiving or asking for forgiveness for they can only see the sins of others and refuse to see their own imperfections.

"You cannot love others with a heart full of pride because your love becomes conditional. You will show love only if others behave according to your will. Pride is a grievous sin against God for it keeps you away from Him. When you are full of pride you see yourself as a god and you will judge others according to your will. You cannot love God and love others if your heart is full of pride because compassion will be lacking and compassion is one of the main ingredients of love.

"To those of you who have heard my call and responded, I beg that you begin to soften your hearts by working to rid yourselves of the sin of pride, as it does not allow you to love with the love necessary to win others to God's love. Pride does not allow the love of which I speak to shine through you. The love of God in you is never prideful; it is meek and humble and good. Allow that love to shine through you."[July 4, 1992]

ON ANGER

"During these times there is much need for prayer for the salvation of men. There is great anger that dominates the world. This anger is so great that it is hard to break through. This anger lies in the hearts of men and causes much of the tribulation and chaos that has over-

taken the world. It causes men to hurt each other, and then it causes them to be unable to forgive and to ask for forgiveness. Hearts are overtaken by this anger, and it becomes very hard, almost impossible, to penetrate.

"Everyone is susceptible to this anger, even those that profess to be very close to God. When this anger takes over, bitterness and resentment become full blown, and it becomes very hard for God to touch the soul. Anger is the main ingredient of turmoil and chaos, and [it] causes men to hurt and destroy each other. It is difficult for the spirit of God to live in a heart full of anger, for in such a heart, the spirit of hatred and violence lives, and those things are not of God. Love cannot reside in a heart full of anger and bitterness, and such a heart cannot be open to God's love and will not be able to love others.

"Anger is a powerful tool of the Evil One and can cause your spirit to be lost. You must work yourselves out of all angry situations. How can you do this? You can do so by first having a forgiving heart. Forgive all who have hurt you, truly forgive them, and then ask to be forgiven by God and by those you have hurt. The Sacrament of Reconciliation can help you do this. That is why our Lord gave it to you." [June 20, 1992]

ON FEAR

"There is a fear that prevails over the world during these times. Fear of losing material things, fear of death, fear of loneliness, and oh so many other fears. But on this day I must tell you that the only fear you need have is the fear that you, all of my beloved children, will never get to understand God's love for you, for if you do not understand it, you will not understand what He is capable and willing to do for you. He sent His only Son, and mine, to die so that all men could learn to love and to hope. On this day I ask that you begin to believe in this love so that you may live in hope and in faith." [February 1, 1992]

"Fear is a tool that the Evil One uses, and it is one of his most powerful tools. Because of human frailties and weaknesses, Satan has been able to use fear in men to attempt to keep them from trusting in God. Throughout the world, man has come to believe that he can control and manipulate anything to meet his needs. During these times men think only on human terms and base everything according to physical needs. My children on earth have forgotten that the spirit is more powerful than the flesh, and it is through spiritual needs that you must base your life on. When you satisfy only your body, your spirit is weakened and you find yourselves full of doubt, anxiety and fear.

"Fear can grip your life and paralyze your spirit. Fear brings about a misery that can stop you from fully trusting in God. When you allow fear to overpower you, you are afraid to feel, to think, to live and to love. You are even afraid to die! Because your spirit is weakened, you have forgotten the words of my beloved Son, who died for all men so that they could live. He who believes and trusts in God shall not perish, but will live forever.

"My children, begin to put your fears aside and begin to trust in God. Nourish and feed your spirit through prayer, love and sacrifice, so that your human fears will not prevail and so that you can begin to think and feel on a spiritual level. You are living in times of turmoil and unrest, and these things can accelerate your fears if you allow it. But if you begin to think on a spiritual level, it will allow you to put your fears aside, and you can begin to trust God and believe in His love for you, for God truly loves you." [October 12, 1991]

ON MATERIALISM

"You do not yet understand the seriousness of the state of the world, especially you, my children in the Americas. The Evil One has so many concerned with mundane and material things that you fail to see the cri-

sis in which the world stands. You are on the brink of great destruction, that you are still focused on whether you want to acknowledge God's power and might. Many of my earthly children refuse to acknowledge His existence and sadly will never do so until it is too late.

"My beloved children of the Americas, I call on you this evening to let go of your grand and material life which leads you to worry about your flesh and does not allow you to concern yourselves about your soul. Money and material things will not save your soul if you use them to concern yourself over them so much that you forget to honor your Creator, trust in Him and know and understand that it is Him, whom you need in your life. The vision of my children in the Americas at the present time is limited to worldly pleasures and material things whether you possess them or desire them. I am here to help you refocus on what is really important, and that is your soul."

[September 22, 1990]

STRONG EMOTIONS

"I want to encourage you on to the next step, which is beginning the work of detaching yourselves from emotions that are not good for your soul. These are the feelings in you of greed, hate, selfishness and lack of charity and hope.

"If your priority in life is still material goods and not God, then there is greed in your heart. If your anger causes you to burst out and hurt others, then you have not done away with that emotion and it may cause you to hate. If you cannot share your God with all that come into your life, by showing God's love through you, then selfishness still remains in your heart. If you have not yet learned to reach out with great love to help your brothers and sisters in need, the charity of which I speak about is not present in you. And if you continue to try to manipulate and control all things around you, believ-

ing only you can change them, then the faith and hope in God that should be ever-present in you does not exist." [March 16, 1991]

"*Tonight I visit to speak to you, as your Heavenly Mother, about learning to detach yourself from those things that keep you away from total commitment to God. Anger, selfishness and envy can keep you from truly learning to love your brothers and sisters in the world. These things cloud your eyes and keep you from seeing my Son, Jesus, in others. If you have committed to prayer but you have not worked to detach yourself from these traits if these things still linger in your heart then your prayer is not totally coming from the heart. If these things are still a part of who you are, then you have not truly understood my messages.*

"*If others around you can see anger, selfishness and envy in you, then my Son is not visible in you, and no matter how much you claim that you love me and my Son, you will not be believed. If you have not found total peace in you, it is because you have not and will not detach yourselves from these traits that do not allow you to obtain it. How can you ever expect the world to obtain peace if you as individuals cannot find it in yourselves?*

"*Evil pervades the world because men have allowed it to happen. When each of you, my little ones, begins to strive to do away with these traits that are not from God, you will begin to defeat the evil that surrounds you. Listen to my words, my children, because I am guiding you to your true peace.*" [April 6, 1991]

CRISIS AND CATASTROPHES

"*I have spoken to you about the catastrophes that would occur through the world. You are experiencing these catastrophes at present, yet many still do not understand God's power. Your eyes and ears are closed to the tremendous sufferings of humanity throughout the world. This is especially true of my children in the Americas. Within your own country many lives are being lost because of the evil that pervades. In your country men want to control each other and use many means to try to do so. The financially and physically strong want to overpower the poor and the weak. There is no compassion, kindness and love for each other, and many lives are being lost because of this greed that comes from the evil side. Many of you walk around without feeling the suffering and pain of others in the world. All of this happens because men have put God aside, no longer believe in Him or acknowledge His existence.*

"I come to remind you, my beloved children, that your eyes and ears need to open up to this truth, that God exists, that He loves you and wants your love. The Heavens tremble and weep at the total disregard of men for each other, and the disregard of men for their God.

"You, the children of God, are in great crisis. You are suffering from lack of love, love of God and love for each other. God's Spirit is no longer present in the hearts of men, and the spirit of evil reigns. If God is not present in your hearts, you cannot love each other because God is love. With His love He brings into your souls compassion, kindness, humility and mercy. Yet during these times what reigns throughout the world is anger, hatred, greed and unmerciful pride. Many times even those who profess to love God carry pride and lack humility and are always ready to lash out at those whom they do not agree with. Indeed, your world, your hearts and souls are in great crisis." [October 3, 1993]

TURMOIL AND CONFLICT

"I come to you during these times to pray with you and for you, during these days of great need. There is great need in America, for the spirits of my children. All

my children need to be healed and transformed. It is a time when my children need to open up to my Son, Our Lord Jesus, so that He may come into each heart and through His love renew and refresh each heart. These are times when souls are in great despair, so full of conflict and confusion that they can no longer keep the peace and love of God present in them.

"The turmoil and conflict in the Americas is not much different than the turmoil and conflict that is occurring all over the world. The only difference is that the strife and the conflict occurs from within your souls and manifests itself as hatred and anger for each other, and you see yourselves, brothers and sisters, as enemies. You are all brothers and sisters, because all of you are children of God, regardless of any physical differences.

"This conflict and despair is implanted by Satan himself as he comes trying to snare souls and take them unto himself. He causes confusion so that you may not understand what God wants from you. He causes despair so that you cannot understand God's immense love for you, His children. I come to bring words which will encourage you to transform your lives, that when you feel this despair and confusion, you may learn to turn to God. Our Lord God is not a God of anger and hate. If anger and hate has entered your hearts, it is not from God that you have received this; rather, you have allowed evil to enter your soul." [October 16, 1993]

"The world you live in does not make it easy for you to do so. The confusion and turmoil throughout your world makes it very hard for you to follow Him. Much of that confusion is because you have not yet learned to trust in our Lord who can see beyond those things that you cannot see. Your spirits struggle to belong to God, yet the world and its ways still pull you to it. I understand, my little ones, the struggles you face. I know that it is not easy. Yet, I continue to call you to God's love because I know that He is your only salvation. I continue to ask

you to trust in Him, even when you do not understand or when it is hard. I am your Mother, and I would never lead you astray. I love you and want what is best for your soul. As your spiritual Mother, I know that God in your life is what will provide your spirit with what it needs for everlasting life.

"Yes, my children, I come to ask you to trust in God, even when you don't understand His ways, even when it seems difficult. If you do, and you continue to persevere in this trust, even in your confusion and turmoil, the day will come when you will understand God's great love for you. Do not give up! Walk your journey to God in trust and love, for you will surely find Him there." [November 16, 1991]

The Virgin's words to her American children do not beat around the bush. Week after week, Mary makes her point, clearly and directly. Indeed, she has to, for as she tells us, time is of the essence.

Often Estela and Reyes are on the road when Mary appears to Estela with her message. Consequently, some of her messages are especially designed and formulated for the people whom they are visiting in a specific state or country.

Usually, Mary blesses the area and often thanks her devoted workers. Like a good mother, the Virgin always shows positive reinforcement, and expresses her appreciation to those who are listening to her. Our Lady also accepts the special acts of consecration that Reyes and Estela offer at each state or country they visit.

But the Virgin's thrust is especially aimed at those who haven't yet responded. Again, motherly and concerned, Mary focuses her attention on her children who most need her attention, those who seem to be straying from the fold. For like her Son, she says she's come for everyone.

Indeed, Heaven's Queen is very concerned over those who seem to be lost, especially unbelievers. Because for these souls, Mary says, the fate of all eternity is at stake.

CHAPTER TWENTY

PEARL HUNTING

I t was De Montfort who did it, Saint Louis de Montfort. Few before or since this miracle-worker of the Eighteenth Century can lay rights to defining the Virgin Mary's power as well as he did. De Montfort spelled it out for everyone. The closer one moves toward Mary, the closer he draws to God.

The critics wailed. De Montfort wanted people to be slaves of Mary! Not quite, De Montfort corrected them. Rather, they were to be slaves of Jesus, through Mary.

Indeed, De Montfort was all for holy slavery. And the Rosary, the saint declared, was to be the chain that shackled the slave. While to many, the Rosary was a simple prayer that was elementary and repetitious, De Montfort moved to expose its power and wisdom. Sent by God, De Montfort was a man on a mission.

Eddie Doherty, in his book *Wisdom's Fool*, explains De Montfort's theory on the Rosary:

> "*Louis believed that if he could put a Rosary around a sinner's neck, the fellow would never get away. He believed that if you say the Rosary faithfully every day until your death, you will receive an eternal crown of glory, in spite of your sins.*
>
> "*To him the Rosary was the Book of Wisdom translated into beads of wood or bone or glass, which even a blind man could read. It was a trysting place where the good Lord met His children and gave them a share in His sorrows, His joys, and His glories. It was a fence around a garden of holy mysteries. It was a long, long caravan, heavily laden with graces. A Christian should prize it as a duchess prizes her necklace of fine pearls. He usually*

had a Rosary around his neck, another dangling at his
side, and maybe a dozen more in his pockets, for some-
body always needed or wanted one. And he wore a chain
around his waist as a sign of his loving slavery to Jesus
through Mary."[1]

Sound familiar? Little Rey didn't know it, but his approach to the Virgin's call had been previously executed. Indeed, what both men were showing to the world was not their slavery, but their devotion — their true devotion!

What made De Montfort so unique and extraordinary was his open, ardent love for Mary. Like Little Rey, he publicly pronounced his faith in God and his love for the Virgin to the point that it scared people. De Montfort was a *"Jesus Freak,"* years before the term ever existed.

Perhaps even worse than the above label, many felt De Montfort was a *"Mary Freak,"* which was borderline heresy. People suspected that the priest loved Mary more than God.

Unfortunately, his critics never realized that the driving motivation behind his love for Mary was the intimacy which it brought him with God. Indeed, meditation on Mary's life of holiness, her perfect surrender and perfect trust, gave De Montfort great insight into the Eternal Perfect Wisdom, the wisdom he so longed to possess.

His poetry reflected his intimacy with God, and his search for that Wisdom:

> *Divine Wisdom, I love You unto folly.*
> *I am Your lover.*
> *You alone in this world I seek,*
> > *You alone I desire.*
> *I am a man gone mad with love,*
> *Forever chasing You.*
>
> *Tell me who You are*
> *For I'm half blind.*
> *I can discern only*
> *That You are a secret I must fathom.*

Show Yourself fully to my soul
Which dies for love of You.

Where do You live,
Wisdom Divine?
Must I cross continents or seas
To find You,
Or fly across the skies?
I'm ready to go wherever You are,
Not counting the costs, to possess You.[2]

Saint Louis de Montfort lived during a period of the Seventeenth Century in which religious philosophers and thinkers emphasized Christ's Incarnation more than His Passion, Death and Resurrection. His education was the product of a French school of thought which believed that God's greatness was most evident when hidden. One of the greatest examples of God's hidden power, according to this school of thought, was the Lord's prenatal Reign in Mary's virginal womb.

Through loyal dedication and persistence, De Montfort expounded upon this belief and extrapolated a deeper meaning, that of the Virgin's special role as Mother of God.

Doherty again presents insight into De Montfort's thinking:

"*What is the glory of Solomon compared to the glory of God? What is the glory of a flower compared to the glory of Mary? The flower has lifted a boy toward his Creator. Mary will lift him higher - as high as he desires to go. The flower is more than a flower. It is a proof of God's presence, of His might, of His love. Mary is more than a woman; and she is still alive!*

"*Wasn't she assumed bodily into heaven? God lifted her up as easily as the boy the flower. And God gave her to us not only as a proof of His love, but also as an all-powerful mother. She transmits His love. She radiates it. We transmit our love of God through her.*

"*The flower is perfect? Mary is the one perfect creation of the Most High, and dearer to Him than all the rest*

173

of His miracles of perfection. Who does not love her does not love God.

"Mary was, to Saint Louis, not only the gate to the Way to Paradise; she was an earthly paradise herself: The true paradise of the new Adam...filled with untold riches, with beauty, with delights, with all sorts of good things the new Adam left there.

" In this Eden, he wrote, this weedless garden...one may find trees which were planted by God and maintained by His grace. There is the tree of life which bore Jesus as its fruit. And there is the tree of the knowledge of good and evil, whose fruit was Incarnate Wisdom, the light of the world. There are, in this most beautiful place, flowers of virtue whose fragrance thrills the angels. There are fields of flowers, meadows of hope, towers of strength, and mansions of simplicity and trust...

" The air is pure. Day reigns here. Day without night. A beautiful day, the day of the Sacred Humanity. The sun does not cast a shadow. It is the sun of the Divinity.

" The Holy Spirit speaks of Mary as the sanctuary of the Divinity, the resting place of the Trinity, the throne of God, the city of God, the altar of God, the temple of God, and the world of God."

"De Montfort could not write anything about Mary without also writing of Father, Son and Holy Ghost."[3]

Thus, for De Montfort, the surest road to Wisdom was through Mary. De Montfort gave himself entirely to Mary, believing that the more truly a soul is consecrated to Mary, the more truly it is consecrated to Jesus.

Wrote De Montfort:

"True Devotion to Mary is an easy, short, perfect, and safe road to perfection, which means union with Christ. To a Christian, perfection is nothing else than such a union. It is an easy road. It was opened by Jesus when he came to us. The road of Mary is gentle, peaceful. One finds there, it is true, great difficulties and fierce battles. But our mother

is ever near, to light the darkness, to clear away doubts, to give strength, to banish fear, to help in every way. The Virgin road to Jesus, in comparison with all others, is a stretch of roses and bee-trees packed with wild honey. There have been a few, not many, saints who have walked that way — Ephrem, John Damascene, Bernard, Bernardine, Bonaventure, Francis de Sales. The Holy Ghost, Mary's Spouse, had revealed it to them... The road is a perfect one by which to reach Christ and be united to Him. Mary is the most perfect creature, the purest and holiest.

"The Most High, the One Beyond All Understanding, the Untouchable God, He Who Is, came down, perfectly and divinely, to us mean little worms, through the humble Mary. He came without losing anything of His divinity. Therefore, it is through Mary that we little ones must, perfectly and divinely, and without fear, ascend to Him."[4]

Indeed, Mary's perfect reflection of Divine Wisdom is eternal. And the Seventeenth Century path to truth outlined by De Montfort is confirmed today by Mary's many apparitions and manifestations.

Most of all, it is confirmed by Mary's words. Mary's perfect words are just that because they are allowed and inspired by God, they are communications from I AM to His people through a most perfect, devoted messenger, the Blessed Virgin Mary. The Virgin's messages throughout the world today, including those given to Estela Ruiz, confirm what De Montfort knew so very well. Mary brings the wisdom that God wishes to give as nourishment for souls.

While many visionaries over time purport messages from Heaven, the Virgin's words to Estela Ruiz are special. Like hidden pearls in oysters deep within the sea, each message seems to contain a profound seed of wisdom, nestled perfectly at its core. These pearls can be difficult to find, unless one takes time to hunt for them. But like true gems, they are wonderful when discovered and illuminated, for they can be treasured and appreciated for all time.

Indeed, against the backdrop of time and history, it shall not be surprising if Mary's messages to Estela Ruiz form the basis of serious study by future Marian and theological archaeologists.

The Twentieth Century has probaly showered the world with more private revelation than any other time in history. Unlike most revelations which have occurred over the centuries, modern visionaries are reporting incredibly lengthy theological discourses from Jesus and Mary. And while all of this is not to be confused with Divine Revelation, some of this era's revelations may one day emerge as significant contributions to the better understanding of God's mysteries. Of particular emphasis in many of the world's private revelations is God's desire that mankind comprehend His great love, from which emanates all mercy and justice.

Undoubtedly, the revelations to Estela Ruiz significantly add to this chest of wisdom. In fact, they may fill an entire chest or two themselves for they remind one of the wisdom and teachings found in the Book of Psalms and the Book of Proverbs.

The following excerpted messages of the Blessed Virgin to Estela Ruiz give further insight into the Divine Wisdom so sought by De Montfort, and also illustrate the importance of Mary's messages in the completion of God's current plan for humanity.

1990

"War comes about because of the desire of men to have power and because of greed and hate." [December 29, 1990]

"I do not come to ask you to come to me for salvation, but ask you to walk with me as I guide you to Him who awaits you to show you His love and mercy." [January 5, 1990]

"We will not win this war without disasters and catastrophes because the Evil One is powerful and has many who follow him." [January 27, 1990]

"Love and prayer will conquer this world." [January 27, 1990]

"You make a concerted effort to remember each offense and who made it so that, given a chance, you can

strike to hurt that person. However, I need to remind you that once you do strike back, this action does not bring satisfaction and peace to your life." [February 10, 1990]

"If you meet a man or woman that, according to human category, seems to be of higher social and financial status, you tend to dignify and respect them because world standards impose this behavior on you. If you meet a person whose state in life seems to fall on low social or financial levels, you deny them the same dignity and respect. This is a terrible error on your part, my children. You must begin to understand the true meaning of respect and dignity. You dignify a person by loving and showing respect no matter what their social or financial standing is.

"Dignify them simply because you see the Christ in them. Take away the covers from your eyes that blind you to what true human respect and dignity are all about. They are about kindness, love and humility. Not one of you, my children, is greater than the other, because Our Lord created all with the same love. That each one of you falls on different social and financial levels is not God's doing, but man's own doing. In Our Lord's eyes, not one of you is greater than the other. My Son died for all, regardless of what or who you are. Remove those blinders from your eyes so you may see with Our Lord's eyes and not measure how much love and respect you will give according to man's standards." [February 17, 1990]

"The kind of love understood in the world now is not love, it is lust. Lust of the flesh, of material things, and of sinful power. Or it is a misunderstood love. A love for kindness is shown only when those others are the same as you — the same color or social level. Or maybe that other has something that you want from him, and so you treat them kindly or show them a false love. No, my children, if that is the way you understand love, then you are in error. The love I speak about is not selfish or self-serving. It is unconditional, and given freely and abundantly to everyone that comes in contact with you. Yes,

even those that are not like you or act like you, those that are hard to love, and each one of you knows who that is in your own life." [February 24, 1990]

"Understand that if you are not willing to live the messages, make the necessary changes in your life, your prayer cannot be strong. You must first apply my words to your life and your heart and work toward your conversion before your prayers can be used for others. Otherwise, your prayers have to be for your conversion and are not much use for others in the world." [March 10, 1990]

"My children, when will you finally learn that this faith you have — believing that earthly materials will bring peace and happiness or that other people are responsible for your well-being — is false? These are your false gods and idols whom you have come to worship and believe in. These things are not bad in themselves, except when you have made them the source of happiness in your life." [March 31, 1990]

"If your path ever takes a different direction that is not toward God, it will never be because He has abandoned you." [April 14, 1990]

"When our God is not your King, when you are the controller and manipulator, when you want to be king over all, then God is far away from your life." [May 5, 1990]

1991

"If you cannot share your God with all who come into your life, by showing God's love through you, then selfishness still remains in your heart." [March 16, 1991]

"Men take for granted God's gifts to the world." [March 23, 1991]

"Anger, selfishness, and envy can keep you from truly learning to love your brothers and sisters in the world. These things cloud your eyes and keep you from seeing my Son, Jesus, in others. If you have committed to prayer but you have not worked to detach yourself from these traits, if these things still linger in your heart, then your prayer is not coming totally from the heart." [April 6, 1991]

"Many innocents are dying because of the need of some to have power over all." [April 13, 1991]

"Each one of you, individually, must bring order into your own life." [April 20, 1991]

"If there is no order in your own home, do not expect your countries and nations to have order." [April 20, 1991]

"I ask that you do not get discouraged in your life of prayer. I see that it is so easy for you to get discouraged because your human weaknesses do not allow you to understand the great power of prayer. If you don't feel gratification immediately, then you are prone to stop communicating with your God. You want Our Lord to speak to you and to make you aware of His presence in you every moment, yet you are not willing to listen. It is through prayer that He will speak to you. Slow down and listen to His words to you. It is possible to hear Him, to feel Him, to feel His presence in you at every moment, but you must be willing to listen."

"Sometimes you do not listen because you do not want to know what He has to say to you. You are afraid that He might say what you do not want to hear. You are afraid that He might ask you to give up things that you are not able or willing to give up. I want to tell you that He will never ask you to give up anything that is good for your soul. He wants nothing else but for you to be happy. The things that the world offers you are not what will bring true happiness into your life. The things of the world bring

you instant gratification, then turn around and bring you misery and unhappiness. This gratification does not last because it is not your true happiness. It is God's love which is your true happiness, yet many cannot find it because they are not willing to put their trust in God. Many prefer the misery and turmoil of the world, and then cry out in pain as they blame God for this unhappiness." [July 6, 1991]

"*It has never been easy for men to trust in God because man is not moved by the spirit, rather he is moved more by the flesh. It seems to be much easier for men to focus on physical and material needs than on the needs of the spirit. But you, my little ones, have forgotten that the physical and material things will end for you one day, but your spirit will go on for eternity.*

"*If you can understand this, even to a small degree, then why can you not understand that you must focus on your spiritual well-being? Most of you have found that focusing on the material things has not brought you true happiness. Most of you have catered to your physical comfort and yet have found that it does not truly fulfill you. You sense there is something missing in your life. This is because for most, the spiritual needs have not been met. To meet the needs of the spirit you must open your hearts to God. You must develop a true relationship of trust and faith in Him and believe that He loves you. You must have faith that He will nurture and feed your spirit with love and believe that He wants to be part of your life.*

"*You cannot get totally away from your physical being, but you must begin to understand that your spiritual being is more important and that it must grow in love and faith in God so that you can have the peace that God intended for you. Therefore, you must learn to trust God. But it is difficult for you, my children, because you focus so much on your physical needs.*" [October 19, 1991]

"Your heart continues to be empty, always desiring more. This is because it is your spirit that must be nourished fully instead of your bodies." [November 23, 1991]

"If anger, greed and hate continue to dominate, the world cannot, will not see peace, but will destroy itself." [November 30, 1991]

"The harsh events happening throughout the world are not God's doing, but men's inhumanity for each other." [November 30, 1991]

"Doubts cause you to lose faith." [December 7, 1991]

"Fear keeps you focused on your physical well-being and does not allow you to see the needs of your spirit!" [December 7, 1991]

1992

"The kind of love that is understood in the world is controlling and lustful." [January 11, 1992]

"The Evil One has deceived many of my children into believing that treating others with contempt and disrespect and unkindness is a sign of power and intelligence." [January 11, 1992]

"Gratification of the body comes from the Evil One and cannot give you everlasting peace." [January 25, 1992]

"If your world is to change, if there is to be any hope for God's Kingdom to reign in your hearts, you must open them up to let His love for you penetrate. It is only through His love for you and your love for Him that you can be open to love your brothers and sisters in the world without reservation. It is only through His love that you will

stop focusing on your differences, which many times cause you to hate and bicker; it will allow you to see your common bond, which is that all of you are children of God. God, our Father, desires to love you and wants to have your love in return. You cannot love God if you continue to close your lives and your hearts to the Spirit of God, Who wants to be in you and work in your life. And you will not be able to understand God's love for you if you continue to ignore what God, Our Lord Jesus, and my beloved Son, did for you on the cross. For God so loved the world, that He gave His only beloved Son so that all His earthly children might live, and He continues to give you His Son, so that He may be your salvation. This is the Good News, my children, that I lay at your feet. Please listen to my words, for I love you and do not wish to see you lost." [February 8, 1992]

"There will be a few who will turn away from you, but most will listen to your message of hope." [February 22, 1992]

"Allow God's Spirit to flow through you in your strongest moments and in your weakest moments, for He can do great things in you either way." [February 22, 1992]

"I have been speaking to you on faith because many of you continue to be weak in the way you believe. Many of you believe that the ways of the world are more natural than following the ways of God. If someone shows anger toward you, you respond with anger. If someone speaks ill of you, you respond by speaking ill of them. If they are spiteful and disrespectful toward you, you retaliate by behaving the same way toward them. This has become a way of life for most of humanity, and this behavior has brought about turmoil and chaos in your world. Humanity wants peace, but cannot find it in the midst of this anger and hate. Vengeance and retaliation are what rule mankind. Men have come to believe that this is the natu-

ral way of life. Men no longer believe that the love Mm Son came to teach you should be the governing force." [March 14, 1992]

"If there are still some in your families who are resisting or fighting against God's love because they cannot understand it, do not despair. If you despair, you may be lead to treat them in anger or impatience, and they would not be able to see God's light through you. Rather, treat them as my Son has treated you and taught you — with kindness and love and patience. It is only in this way that my Son can radiate in you. Continue to remember that my Son is your hope and that these are times of His great mercy. Even as we pray on this day, we move ever forward to the Triumph of my Immaculate Heart over the world, when we will see all of God's children finally come together in love, respect and dignity for each other, and when all will bow down to God's love and greatness." [March 28, 1992]

"It is not the destruction of temples of stone which is my utmost concern, but the destruction of the temples of flesh, for you are God's creation and He created you so that you could be His dwelling place." [May 9, 1992]

"Humans categorize each other and separate themselves based on how they look, how they believe, and what material things they possess." [May 30, 1992]

"Never has the Holy Spirit been more powerful than now." [June 13, 1992]

1993

"This world will end. Your body will end, but your soul will go on forever... The Evil One who has brought this darkness upon the world has brought many to believe that there is no soul and that it is only your body you must

satisfy. I come into the world to tell you that it is your soul you must concern yourself with." [January 9, 1993]

"Examine what it is that controls your life. Is it anger and hatred, or is it love, compassion and goodness?" [January 16, 1993]

"I come to guide you to your true joy and peace which is my Son, Jesus. During these times everyone in the world seeks peace, yet I come to tell you that there will not be peace until there is peace in the hearts of men.

"God created you as a unique human being, with self-will, with the capacity to reach great heights both mentally as well as physically, but much more importantly, spiritually. He created you that you might reach an understanding of His great love for you. He created you with free will, that this will might move you to unite with Him in His great love for all men. Yet, evil has entered into the hearts of men, and this has caused the destruction of men's souls — where anger and hatred live and there is very little love or compassion for one another. This destruction in men's souls is also bringing about the destruction of your world. Every action done or word said to one another brings about anger or mistrust, and so brings about misunderstanding and division. As you divide, the evil forces become more powerful and, during these times you are living in, [they] have become so powerful that hatred and violence abound throughout your world.

"It is only if men turn their lives to God's truths that this world will be saved. It is only if men begin to open their hearts to God's goodness that your world will turn from the road to destruction it is headed for. It must begin in each heart. I come to ask that each one of you, my beloved children, look into your own hearts. Examine what it is that controls your life. Is it anger and hatred, or is it love, compassion and goodness? Your heart and soul cannot belong to God's realm if there is hatred and anger, for God is love, compassion and goodness. And if

you are united with Him, love, compassion and goodness must reign in your own heart." [January 16, 1993]

"The Evil One can destroy your soul in many ways and during these times is working from the most subtle way to the most visible outright evil way he can." [February 6, 1993]

"Man destroys life for no reason and believes that this gives him control and power." [February 27, 1993]

"The great deceiver has done his work well, and now men believe that what is wrong is right. Humanity has been deceived into believing that sin does not exist, that it is not wrong to destroy, and so during these times men destroy each other. Not only does man destroy the body, but [he] is destroying the mind and the soul. The mind and the soul are what God wishes to use in order to help you understand compassion, respect for each other and, most importantly, love. Yet the great deceiver has deceived even the most learned, the most knowledgeable minds, and these men who have been able to penetrate the highest level of the mind cannot begin to understand the level of the soul, which is where God desires to reside." [March 13, 1993]

"Your faith and love for God must grow greatly in times when your spirit is strong and healthy so when your spirit is weak and troubled your faith will carry you through." [April 24, 1993]

"Even the great minds, the most learned of men, cannot understand the cause of this chaos and turmoil in the world. The truth is simple, my beloved children. Man has forgotten God, or has chosen to put Him aside and therefore cannot remember what God's love is about. I come to remind you, my children, that God's love is about giving and sacrifice." [May 29, 1993]

"God is first merciful, before He is just and punishing." [June 5, 1993]

"Humanity has evolved from men who could see and believe in the miracle of life, to men who do not believe in any kind of miracle; therefore, they cannot see the miracle of their own lives." [July 24, 1993]

"There is no horror, no despair so great that Our Lord cannot conquer for you." [September 11, 1993]

"I cannot and will not stop calling you until I can do it no longer." [July 2, 1994]

"Open up your eyes, my children, and see what a world without God looks like. It is a world whose inhabitants are full anger, hate, pride, jealousy and envy, all those things that are evil and totally against God's ways. Humanity cries out the equality of all men, yet destroys itself because of differences in race and creed. Men pronounce God's name as they speak, yet deny His very existence with their acts, and the Heavens weep to see the state of the world.

"As this country and all countries who honor my Son enter into the season of His life, there is little focus on Him, who brought salvation into the world. The true meaning of His birth has become lost in the desires of men and what men see as important in their lives. It is no longer God who is the focus, but the ways of the world that are important to men and women.

"Oh, my beloved children, I have come to warn you that what you sow will be what you reap. What will be your harvest, my children, your earthly goods, your earthly ways? Or will you heed my call, turn your eyes on your God and reap the love, peace and joy which only He can bring? Again I tell you, your free will, your freedom of choice will bring into your life what you seek. Will you focus your eyes on God, who brings life to the

spirit, or will you focus your eyes on the ways of the world, which bring satisfaction to your body but destroy the soul?" [December 11, 1993]

As one can see, Our Lady's words are pearls, an endless string that God is sending the world through the Virgin Mary. But the Virgin's messages to Estela Ruiz contain a serious side, too, a side that is urgent and prophetic, especially for America.

Indee, by 1994, the Virgin's words to Estela began to profoundly shift in tone. And this change reflected a Mother who was, Mary emphasized, running out of *"time..."*

FOR THE SOUL OF THE FAMILY

CHAPTER TWENTY-ONE

ABORTION AND THE RETURN OF QUETZALCOATL

America – the Land of the Free. But when one considers the over thirty million babies who have been aborted in America since 1973, that title seems grossly in error. Indeed, any explanation is impossible, particularly to the unborn victims of that guaranteed freedom.

Like the peasant Aztecs in Mexico, the innocent lives of these aborted children have been rationalized away as unnecessary or inconvenient, for one reason or another. In essence, the rationale behind America's staggering abortion rate is the same as that behind the Aztecs bloody rituals. According to surveys, in most situations, the sacrifices were undertaken to uphold the "quality of life."

But behind the scenes, in the dimension of the invisible yet very real world of the spirits, exists another factor. There, looming in the darkness, is Satan. His control and his influence have incited this guilt-free holocaust. And if a nation as noble, as powerful and as great as America openly defends such a slaughter, it seems logical that a titanic struggle between the Virgin and the Evil One is really occurring in America and is headed towards a climax.

Historically the bastion of freedom and defender of the innocent, America has become the supreme battlefield of a spiritual Armageddon.

And by the mid-1990's, the evil one's deplorable grip on America could be most clearly recognized every second of the day, especially through the modern world's great idol-television. It is reportedly the idol, the Virgin Mary has revealed, foretold in the Book of Revelation which the world would come to worship.

In America, even the politicians are now admitting that this worship has led to great bloodshed, as endlessly disgraceful television programming has reached new lows. And we do not need to be spiritual to understand the evil that has entered into our house through television. For as early as 1939, Congress, and the country were being warned about the effects of television.

After television was first demonstrated by RCA at the New York World's Fair in 1939, E.B. White, writing for *Harper's* magazine wrote, *"We shall stand or fall by television...a new and unbearable disturbance of the modern peace or a saving radiance in the sky."*[1] In 1952, A Senate subcommittee headed by Estes Kefauver warned against the effects of televised violence, especially on *"children."*[2]

Indeed, perpetually disgraceful TV programming has reached new lows, as every form of blasphemy and contempt oozes from television sets into people's living rooms. And as we know today, violence has not been the only damaging effect. With significant help from television, a total collapse of morality has occurred, with materialism and sensuality emerging as the new gods of our society and times. Thus, on our streets, people are mirroring offensive behaviors. Perverted sex and the occult are nearly mainstream. Few magazines or newspapers are morally acceptable, while billboards and shop windows alike shamelessly promote Satan's agenda.

Michael Brown, in *Prayer of the Warrior*, describes America of the mid-1990's as swallowed by, and absorbed in, every kind of evil. It is an evil, Brown says, which Mary predicted at Rue Du Bac in 1830 and then defined at La Salette sixteen years later. Brown writes:

> *"All justice would be trampled underfoot and **only homicides, hate, jealousy, lies, and dissension,** would be seen, said the La Salette Madonna, correctly anticipating a crime rate that now includes 25,000 homicides or cases of non-negligent manslaughter a year. In one New York neighborhood, the 75th precinct in Brooklyn, a murder occurs on average every 63 hours!"*

Brown continued:

"Such was the fruit of a society that, as the Blessed Mother forecast, had gone cold and secular. It was a result of demons rising from the hellfire as a test and punishment for all of mankind."[3]

The peasant Indians of the Aztec culture knew nothing of Satan and demons, as the disguised agenda of the evil one relied on fear, greed, weak-mindedness and hate to fulfill its mission in middle-age Mexico. This has always been Satan's methodical and pathetic strategy. But he was there, Mary's image on Juan Diego's tilma confirms this, as she is revealed to be crushing the head of the serpent.

According to experts on the Tilma of Guadalupe, this is symbolized by the darkened crescent moon which the Virgin Mary is seen to be standing upon. The darkened crescent moon was the symbol of Quetzacoatl, the celestial serpent to whom the Aztecs offered their human sacrifices. Thus, the image on the tilma fulfills the words of Genesis 3:15, in which the woman *"crushes the proud head of the serpent,"* Satan.[4]

Of course, misery, suffering, blood, and death are always evidence of Satan's presence. Yet, as he offered Christ the kingdoms of the world, the enticements of Satan are often camouflaged by worldly glitter, sensual satisfaction, and sub rosa unaccountability.

Indeed, examples of his conflicting presence abound. In Rome, beautiful marble edifices lined the Roman forum just a short distance from the Colosseum, where bloody rituals served as public spectator sports. And Sixteenth Century Mexico City, so full of technological advancement, architectural grace and innocent bloodshed, was believed to be the crown jewel of the world's great cities, an observation that again reflects the devil's wily ways.

Late Twentieth Century America holds the same twisted honor. The United States as a nation and as a civilized society is perhaps the greatest in the history of the world. From engineering to architecture, medicine to education, entertainment to transportation, Twentieth Century America is unsurpassed. Even the poorest of families owns a television, telephone, refrigerator and automobile. Collectively, Twentieth Century Western society has reached an unprecedented level of human technological achievement in almost every professional field and endeavor.

Yet, like Rome and Mexico City, America is now totally oppressed, and possessed, by the spirit of the world. Consumption is the goal of the majority, while sacrifice, love, respect and morality are consistently diminishing. Pride has replaced shame. The laws of God are calously ignored, ridiculed, repressed, intentionally misinterpreted and legislatively removed. The pattern of evil in every part of society is flagrant and without explanation. While a supposedly advanced American society finds itself spiritually paralyzed, the Prince of Darkness gloats with lustful satisfaction upon his temporary throne.

The poor Aztec peasants had no idea who the stone gods really were, or whose image they represented. Likewise, most Americans today are just as blind to their own gods of money, flesh, and power. But a common denominator which exists between the cultures is the mutual sign of innocent blood. This similarity has always existed, as not only the Mayans, but many other civilizations as well, have sacrificed innocent people to idols.

From Kali in India to the volcano god in Polynesia to the Canaanite's sacrificing of children to the god Molech, history records a malicious legacy of innocent bloodshed.

These less-impassioned civilizations, controlled and manipulated by Satan through false religious systems, used idolatry as their excuse for bloodshed.

But prominent civilizations have also raised up idols. These idols are human ones, that also mysteriously extract blood from the innocent. From ancient Rome to Twentieth Century Soviet Union and China, and even to modern-day Iraq, the enormous and abundant portraits and statues of human leaders are no different than the idols of stone or fire in the past.

The images of Caesar, Stalin, Lenin, Mao, Hitler, Sanger and even Sadaam Hussein have been worshipped by citizens who somehow or in some way ignore the bloodthirsty legacy of genocide which they represent. Many of these rulers have even overtly practiced the occult or followed Satan himself.

Today, Satan's mysterious and unquenchable thirst for blood is gruesomely manifesting itself in America in monstrous proportions. The pending widespread legalization of euthanasia and the exportation of abortion worldwide is swiftly advancing the devil's dangerous plan. Likewise, by 1996 in America, the upholding of partial-birth abortion as legal and the pending approval by the government of RU486, the chemically-induced abortion pill, are both actions which will accelerate the coming of God's justice. Yet, all the while, few blame Satan, as most are blind to the spiritually demonic connection between the civilizations of the past and present.

Charles Baudelaire, a French poet of the Nineteenth Century, is credited with the often quoted observation that *"the devil's cleverest wile is to convince us that he does not exist."* Since Baudelaire's cavalier yet poignant remark, numerous Popes and Church leaders have echoed this assertion. As Pope John Paul II stated,

"It is in his [Satan's] interest to make himself 'unknown.' Satan has the skill in the world to induce people to deny his existence in the name of rationalism and of every other system of thought which seeks all possible means to avoid recognizing his activity." (August 13, 1988)

But Mary reports that Satan's pride is now so brazen that he is smugly flaunting his existence in our very faces. Indeed, the Vatican reports that Satanic submission is at an all-time high in Italy. And one only need visit America to experience his influence everywhere. From the lyrics of rock music to the explosion of Black Masses, from Satanic consecrations to human and animal sacrifices, the Evil One has become the inescapable companion to many souls in desperate need of repentance and God's grace.

Father Randall Paine, ORC, in his book, *His Time Is Short; the Devil and His Agenda,* noted this unfolding phenomenon of Satan's highly visible presence.

"You see," wrote Fr. Paine, *"we have reason to be grateful that the devil is beginning to show his face more openly as the Twentieth Century grinds to a close. We have grown so jaded in the*

face of any supernatural prospect as to greet the real thing."[5]

Likewise, the Virgin Mary confirmed to Estela this exact scenario,

> *"The great battle of good against evil is upon you and evil has raised its power and Satan can be seen clearly throughout the world. Where before he was working subtly, almost hidden, now he is evident, manifesting himself outwardly, destroying everything he can that is in his path. The souls of humanity, men, women and children, are his main targets and there is nothing he will not do to devour them. He manifests himself in many ways, through children, who have given themselves to evil and also moves to work within those places that are dedicated to God and His work. Satan has unleashed all his power to gain souls and many have fallen to his wiles."* (June 1, 1996)

Ah yes, old Beelzebub now wants to be recognized, and publicly too. In ancient Mexico, Lucifer slapped his image on stone. Now he's interacting with modern society via the media and entertainment industries. His arrogance is unshakable. Indeed, the devil has gone beyond all imaginative bounds and in the ultimate insult to Twentieth Century society, Satan has maneuvered to resurrect his most deadly image: the blood-hungry image of the god Quetzalcoatl.

In the city of San Jose, California, the Aztec serpent god of Quetzalcoatl has symbolically resurfaced. Described by some City Council members as having *"beautiful attributes"* and being *"a giver of life,"* a new $500,000 monument to Quetzalcoatl will be erected. Three-stories tall, and wide enough to walk through, this bronze statue will be of a loving, benevolent *"god,"* according to its supporters. It is also being judiciously represented as a tribute to the city's ancient Hispanics.

Indeed, under the prevailing trend of thought sweeping America, Quetzalcoatl is coming back to life. Through the misdirected argument of *freedom of choice* and *protection* of *personal liberty*, supporters of the Quetzalcoatl project in San Jose say the monument will be a source of spiritual help.

Not surprisingly, the reemergence of the blood-hungry god of sacrifice may not be restricted to San Jose. For with media assistance, his image may quickly spread.

While the return of Quetzalcoatl to one city may not be a significant concern of true merit, in reality, it does represent a *"sign of the times."* Thousands are dying in the streets. And the blood of thirty million children was sacrificed to the Evil One in America from 1973 to 1994 alone. It is a sacrifice that has been made in almost every family, although secretly and without the knowledge of most members. In Mexico City it was through (witch) doctors, today it is again executed by those with a similar title. Indeed, abortion is, most of all in America today, the key sign of Satan's dominance of the family and our society, a deadly dominance Mary warned of at LaSallette and at Fatima through words and visions.

Most significantly, by September, 1996, the urgency of the danger surrounding the right to life issues is seen in itself to be directly related to Mary's pleas that time is running out. Even the Holy Father warned on September 1, 1996, that *"a nation who kills its own children is a nation without hope."*

Indeed, Our Lady told Estela on February 3, 1996,

"I have been sent into the world for a very special purpose. As the destruction of the children of God continues because of hate and anger, the heavens cry to see how lightly God's children have taken the gift of life that God creates. The purpose of My coming is that I may come to touch hearts, to call all souls to come back to God's ways. It is only if God's children return to the ways of God that you, My children in the world, can begin to stop the destruction of mankind on earth.

"In my love for you and in my great love for God, I come to tell you, to warn you that time is running short. As man disregards man and they destroy each other, the

life that God created on earth diminishes. This is offen-
sive to our God. It is offensive to our Lord to see men and
women hate each other. It is offensive to our God to see
that peace does not prevail in the hearts of men. Peace is
a gift from Him, yet men have turned to chaos and ha-
tred instead of receiving the gift of peace which was meant
for the world."

For the Ruiz's, especially Papa Reyes, the Virgin's arrival at
Medjugorje could not have come too soon. How Mary could help
a family with so many deep problems was a miracle. Undoubtedly,
it will take another such miracle to help the entire country.

But the Virgin had not come to surrender. Indeed, Scripture
promised quite the opposite. And with the time remaining, it is
clear. As Mary had begun with the Ruizs, all families are now
being called to conversion and reconciliation. It is an urgent call.
For the conversion of the family appears to be the key to Mary's
coming triumph!

CHAPTER TWENTY-TWO

FOR THE SOUL OF THE FAMILY

Yes, time is a factor, an important factor. Exactly how and why, no one knows for sure. But a message received by Estela on September 15, 1990, provides a clue of why Mary regularly declares the urgency of the times:

> *"I come to warn you, my little ones, that the world is at a crossroad. It will either cross into the path of destruction, or allow Our Lord to reign in the hearts of men. Time is running short. I am here to beg all that will listen to turn to God."* [September 15, 1990]

Approximately one year later, the Virgin delivered to Estela an ominous warning that deepened this mystery:

> *"You have no more time to lose. As the world moves more and more toward self-destruction, you cannot stand by the sidelines and watch without deciding one way or the other. I come to invite all my children in the world to decide for God...*
>
> *"Allow your eyes, hearts and minds to see and understand the gravity of the state of the world in which you live. Do not continue to close your minds to that truths that I bring you."* [November 9, 1991]

And on August 3, 1996, Mary's words were filled with an ominous question:

> *"How far will you, all of my earthly children, let it go – until it is too late to turn back?"*

In the early 1980's, Mary unveiled two significant facts at Medjugorje. First, she revealed that her present apparitions would be the end of her appearances in the world. Second, she declared that the end of Satan's reign of evil and destruction in the world would come soon.

While unique, these messages flatly confirm her messages to Estela, as well as agree with what many theologians and biblical scholars have already suspected about the present times: Satan and the Virgin are now engaged in a major struggle, a spiritual struggle that will be decisive. In the end, only one will triumph.

There were messages from visionaries the world over that concurred with these revelations. In addition, mariologists and lay experts in apparitions also agree. Something big is about to happen. The times are near fulfillment, all agree. And that fulfillment will bring a new era of peace and renewal into the world.

Probably the best confirmation of this fact comes from the only surviving visionary of Fatima, Sister Lucia. In a famous interview conducted by Father Fuentes on December 26, 1957, Sister Lucia explained what Mary told her about the present times:

> *"Father, the Most Holy Virgin did not tell me that we are in the last times of the world, but she made me understand this for three reasons:*
>
> *"The first reason is because she told me that the devil is in the mood for engaging in a decisive battle against the Virgin. And a decisive battle is the final battle where one side will suffer defeat. Also, from now on, we must choose sides. Either we are for God or we are for the devil. There is no other possibility.*
>
> *"The second reason is because she said to my cousins (Francisco and Jacinta) as well as to myself, that God is giving two last remedies to the world. These are the Holy Rosary and Devotion to the Immaculate Heart of Mary. These are the last two remedies which signify that there will be no others.*
>
> *"The third reason is because, in the plans of Divine Providence, God always before He is about to chastise the*

world, exhausts all other remedies. Now, when He sees that the world pays no attention whatsoever, then...He offers us with certain fear the last means of salvation, His Most Holy Mother. It is with certain fear because if you despise and repulse this ultimate means, we will not have any more forgiveness from Heaven because we will have committed a sin which the Gospel calls the sin against the Holy Ghost. "[1]

Sr. Lucia's concise explanation added credible confirmation to the urgency of the times and also outlined the work which the Virgin was attempting to complete. God had sent Mary because world circumstances were spinning out of control, dangerously out of control. With the total loss of respect for human life, mankind was obviously on the verge of destroying itself.

Indeed, the Virgin's words to Estela Ruiz say no less. And in Medjugorje in 1981, Mary immediately addressed this scenario when she began appearing to the six young visionaries, saying, *"It is necessary for the world to be saved while there is still time."* [November 29, 1981]

The following year, Mary explained to Medjugorje visionary Mirjana Dragicevic Soldo what was happening in the Twentieth Century, and what was left to fulfill. Mary stressed to Mirjana:

"You must realize that Satan exists. One day he appeared before the throne of God and asked permission to submit the Church to a period of trial. God gave him permission to try the Church for one century. This century is under the power of the devil, but when the secrets confided to you come to pass, his power will be destroyed. Even now he is beginning to lose his power and has become aggressive. He is destroying marriages, creating division among priests, and is responsible for obsessions and murder." [1982][2]

In this message, Mary's reference to the destruction of marriages is most significant, as it reveals the primary thrust of Satan's modern-day attack. Satan is forcefully and relentlessly attempting to destroy families, Mary says, as they are the foundation for all human life.

Indeed, as the center and basis of all civilization, the traditional family is under massive attack. Mary says that Satan is acutely aware of the family's importance in perpetuating life. She also indicated that if the family, God's greatest gift, can be so assaulted, the gift of life itself will severly suffer with it.

Indeed, modern statistics speak for themselves concerning Satan's war on the American family:[3]

In 1965 the divorce rate was 2.5 per 1,000 population. By 1976 it had doubled. By 1994, sociologists predicted that 60% of all marriages would end in divorce.

In 1970, 40% of all American households contained a married couple with young children. By 1990, it was down to 26%.

In 1988, of the 57.9 million U.S. women who were 15-44 years of age, 60% practiced contraception.

There are an estimated 12 million cases of sexually transmitted diseases a year.

In 1989, there were 1,396,658 legal abortions in America alone, as reported by the Center for Disease Control.

U.S. teenagers have one of the highest pregnancy rates in the world. America's rate is twice as high as England, France, and Canada. Each year, 1 million teenagers become pregnant. Only 58% end in births.

In 1990, marriage occurred at an average age of 26.1 years for men (22.5 in 1956) and 23.9 years of age for women (20.2 in 1956).

In 1991, there were an estimated 2.9 million unmarried couples living together, an 80% increase from 1980.

The number of working mothers rose from 32.8 percent in 1948 to 66.6 percent by 1990.

A 1995 study from the National Center for Education Statistics shows that 45% of children who have not yet reached their first birthday now regularly spend portions of their day with someone other than parents.

24% are being cared for by a relative;

17% by a non-relative;

7% at a center.

Thus, the data presented here overwhelmingly suggests that the traditional family is undergoing radical change. It is also common knowledge that numerous forces are openly seeking to legitimize and redefine those changes.

Margaret O'Brien Steinfels, in her study *"Taking the Measure of the Family,"* objectively concludes what she sees happening in America:

> *"These efforts to legitimize different forms of the family may be a tribute to the power of the idea of the family and part of a compassionate impulse to make room for non-nuclear forms of the family, but they may also too easily celebrate forms of the family that can have a detrimental effect on children, especially if they are accompanied, as they often are in single-parent families, by economic and social marginalization. And after nearly two decades of so-called no-fault divorce laws, it is becoming increasingly clear that women and children pay a steep price for family break-up and marital termination. Even in two-parent families where women have to work in order to sustain a middle-class income, children may pay a price for our new economic and social arrangements. When people argue in favor of 'family values,' then, they may be talking about very different, even conflicting ideas about the family and about values that turn out to undermine rather than support family solidarity."*[4]

The attack on the family and its disintegration is obviously a very complicated issue. But in spiritual terms, the picture is quite simple. It is a direct result of Satan's ageless cry, *"I will not serve."*

Seeking to stand alone, seeking to compete with God, the devil's prideful statement is clearly echoed in America's ever-pervasive trend toward individualism. Simply put, individual choice, guaranteed and protected by law, has taken over the country. Everyone wants to *"do their own thing,"* no matter how much it hurts or destroys their neighbor. This means no strings, no commitments, no permanent responsibilities, and no consequences — and so called choices which are very much opposed to the freedoms of respect and personal liberty which they claim to uphold.

This trend of haphazard personal freedom at all cost is clearly illustrated in the entertainment industry. While claiming to imitate societal trends, many destructive elements within the field actually create, teach and encourage negative cultural values. Edward DeBerri, in his report *"Popular Culture,"* reflects on this frightening reality:

"According to traditional codes, the level or morality in the United States is low. Lying, cheating, or stealing are practices in which many, if not most, Americans engage. In many instances, these practices are not critically examined in the various public media.

" Greed is good. Michael Douglas's words in the movie Wall Street epitomize the erosion of traditional moral values in the United States during the past three decades. In both the public and private realms, America has lost its moral consensus.

"On prime time, Doogie Howser loses his virginity and Murphy Brown becomes pregnant without benefit of a husband. Knots Landing and Falcon Crest have replaced Ozzie and Harriet and Father Knows Best as staples of American life. Sam Malone has succeeded Ward Cleaver as America's television hero.

"In this instance, television only mirrors reality. Recent best sellers include Final Exit, the how-to suicide manual, and Cheating 101, a guide to academic guile. (A) Baseball superstar serves... six months in prison for income tax evasion and is issued a lifetime ban from his sport for gambling on his team. His fellow criminals include financial hall-of-famers... of whom were convicted of financial fraud and other misdeeds. Their individual improprieties echo more systemic transgressions, such as the Savings and Loan fiasco or the BCCI scandal. Religious leaders have not been exempt from indecorum...Clergymen whose ministries have been targeted by sexual allegations.

"The decline in morality is perhaps most evident in the political realm. Senators... are forced to withdraw from recent presidential bids... for alleged womanizing and... for alleged plagiarism. Watergate and the forced presiden-

tial resignation of Richard Nixon is only the most obvious example of skimpy public morality.

"The increase in individualism has resulted in the individual becoming the preeminent moral authority. The decline in a sense of community has diluted the sense of responsibility for a common good. Both factors have contributed to an alarmingly low level of morality in U.S. popular culture and life."[5]

Indeed, the great moral decay which modern society faces has not escaped the notice of numerous religious and political leaders around the globe. Since his first moments as pontiff, Pope John Paul II has struggled courageously to defend the family, and has indicated that the serious moral decline of the entertainment industry presents a grave danger to the world.

A prophet in his own right, John Paul II has repeatedly and heroically beseeched his flock to preserve the integrity of the family. Well-aware of the ominous contents of the Third Secret of Fatima, his exhortations and actions seem to support the theory that this Secret is actually a great chastisement that is quickly approaching, just as Mary has hinted. Thus, like Mary, the Holy Father is waging a war that is *for the soul of the family.*

The height of the Pope's heroic defense of life and the family was best illustrated at the United Nations International Conference on Population and Development, held in Cairo during September of 1994. On that occasion, John Paul II outlined the scene on the world stage, and declared that the future of civilization and humanity was at stake.

Abortion, under the guise of "human reproduction services," was at the heart of the agenda in Cairo. And America, through its eroding moral leadership, sought to impose upon the world its anti-family philosophy in the name of population control. Pope John Paul II, as if led by Mary herself, defended life and the family step by step, and exposed the deceit and danger of the conference.

For Catholics, this danger is understandable in a precise yet simple theological explanation. Dr. Scott Hahn, a reformed protestant minister who teaches at Franciscan University in Steubenville, Ohio, writes emphatically that birth control directly interferes with

God's covenant with His people, a covenant based on the family. In their book *Rome Sweet Home*, Dr. Scott and Kimberly Hahn expressed this understanding:

> *"...marriage is not a contract, involving merely an exchange of goods and services. Rather, marriage is a covenant, involving an exchange of persons.*
>
> *"...every covenant has an act whereby the covenant is enacted and renewed and that the marital act is a covenant act. When the marriage covenant is renewed, God uses it to give new life. To renew the marital covenant and use birth control to destroy the potential for new life is tantamount to receiving the Eucharist and spitting it on the ground.*
>
> *"...the marital act demonstrates the powerful life-giving love of the covenant in a unique way. All the other covenants show God's love and transmit God's love, but it is only in the marital covenant that the love is so real and powerful that it communicates life.*
>
> *"When God made man, male and female, the first command he gave them was to be fruitful and multiply. This was to image God-Father, Son and Holy Spirit, three in one, the Divine Family. So when 'the two become one' in the covenant of marriage, the 'one' they become is so real that nine months later they might have to give it a name! The child emobodies their covenant oneness.*
>
> *"I began to see that every time Kimberly and I performed the marital act we were doing something sacred. And every time we thwarted the life-giving power of love through contraception, we were doing something profane. (Treating something sacred in a merely common way profanes it, by definition.)"*[6]

But this danger, in its purest form, should be seen through the eyes of the Virgin. When considered in context with her many messages around the globe, it is frighteningly obvious that the world must mend its ways. If not, our Lady consistently warns us, a time of suffering and woe is on the horizon.

While numerous, Mary's messages are seldom very different. In essence, most of her legitimate messages confirm and continue her urgent words of Fatima. Those words, Marian experts insist, clearly outlined the destruction of the family as the key blow which would bring the world to the verge of destruction.

On the final day of the Fatima apparitions on October 13, 1917, Mary fulfilled a promise. As officials and crowds humanly clamored for proof that the young Fatima visionaries were truly communicating with a heavenly visitor, Mary promised to grant them a sign.

Shortly after noon, Lucia pointed to the sun, and 70,000 heads looked up. Suddenly the sun swirled and sputtered, and then to the horror of all, it plunged toward the earth. According to witnesses, the sun appeared as a giant ball of fire, one which they assumed would consume the planet and bring the end of the world.

However, while thousands witnessed this horrific vision, the three Fatima visionaries were privileged to see something else. It was a vision of the Holy Family. In the sky above, Mary, Saint Joseph and the Child Jesus appeared, united in familial love.

According to some Marian experts, the two simultaneous visions at Fatima that day were probably connected, and possibly signified the urgent message of mankind's future in relation to the family. That is, it is possible to infer from this vision that through our very own actions, God was showing that people can choose family and life, or fire and death.

In upholding and preserving the family, God gives us the means to stop ourselves from destroying the planet. By defending the family, God shows us how to bring peace, real peace. As Pope John Paul II said on January 1, 1994:

> *"An enduring peaceful order needs institutions which express and consolidate the values of peace. The institution which most immediately responds to the nature of the human being is the family. It alone ensures the continuity and the future of society.*
>
> *"The family is therefore called to become an active agent for peace, through the values which it expresses and*

transmits within itself, and through the participation of each of its members in the life of society.

"In the face of increasing pressure nowadays to consider, as legally equivalent to the union of spouses, forms of union which by their very nature of their intentional lack of permanence are in no way capable of expressing the meaning and ensuring the good of the family, it is the duty of the State to encourage and protect the authentic institution of the family, respecting its natural structure and its innate and inalienable rights.

"Among these, the fundamental one is the right of parents to decide, freely and responsibly, on the basis of their moral and religious convictions and with properly formed consciences, when to have a child and then to educate that child in accordance with those convictions.

"The State also has an important role in creating the conditions in which families can provide for the primary needs in a way befitting human dignity. Peace will always be at risk so long as individuals and families are forced to fight for their very survival.

"The family, as the fundamental and essential educating community, is the privileged means for transmitting the religious and cultural values which help the person to acquire his or her own identity.

"Founded on love and open to the gift of life, the family contains in itself the very future of society; its most special task is to contribute effectively to a future of peace...

"The family which lives this love, even though imperfectly, and opens itself generously to the rest of society, is the primary agent of a future of peace.

"A civilization of peace is not possible if love is lacking."

Besides revealing Satan's global effort to destroy life, the events at the 1994 Cairo Conference on World Population also exposed in greater detail why America is so important to Mary's plan. Particularly after this meeting it became obvious that few nations in the world allow such an open attack on the family and on human life. Even in Germany, where only 19% of the people believe in Heaven, abortion is regulated and controlled much more stringently than it is in America.

America, through international organizations, currently seeks to export its "culture of death" to the entire world. Thus, it's no wonder the words of Our Lady of the Americas to Estela Ruiz are so direct and powerful, as some of the values now protected by, and upheld in America are dangerous to the world at large.

And the danger is not difficult to pinpoint. While some may attempt to rationalize the problems away in the name of progress or personal freedom, in his heart of hearts, each person knows the truth.

The more human life is openly opposed and destroyed, the more man sins. This total accumulation of sin, according to Mary, is a threat to world peace. For with greater sin, each individual's mind becomes darker and less able to think clearly. Thus, world leaders are bringing the planet perilously close to self-annihilation through mankind's own actions.

Since World War II, the dangerous scenario brought about by nuclear weapons has existed. As Mother Teresa of Calcultta, India has warned, *"the fruit of abortion is nuclear war."* And the Virgins says that as sin mounts, the world moves closer to a serious error. As she told Estela on September 4, 1993:

"I ask today of those who are praying for my work that you especially pray for those who control the world, because as they have been put in positions of power, they have left God's mandates and have placed themselves as gods over people. They set up their own mandates and are leading people astray and toward perdition and destruction. Pray, my children, pray that these men and women may not be successful in their attempts to rule not only the body of people, but their minds and spirits, for surely they will drive the world to destruction and chaos.

Is there now not enough chaos and destruction that might cause men to wonder if there is something terribly wrong going on? Is there not enough misery and despair to make men see that the world, as it is, is in great need of goodness, God's goodness? What will it take for all, every single human being, to understand that you need God? Can it not be by transforming your hearts to goodness and love, or must it be the total devastation of men?"

In Mary's messages to Estela Ruiz, the Virgin makes it clear: Satan has won the hearts of many people, and America is a nation in serious trouble. In November of 1993, the Virgin spelled this out even more vividly:

"Many of God's children have been deceived by Satan and have come to believe that his evil ways lead to happiness. Hate, anger and violence rule the world, and there is no happiness in that because they are contrary to the nature of God. Greed and lust reign supreme, and discord has separated and pitted brother against brother and children against parents, and Satan has divided and conquered.

"Is Satan to remain in control, or are you, my beloved little ones, ready to reject this misery and return to your rightful inheritance, which is to be children of God? Because you were given free will, only you can answer this question, only you, each one of you, can make this decision. Will hate, anger and confusion continue to reign until humanity is destroyed and extinguished, or are you, the children that God created, ready to change hearts and souls to God's love and peaceful ways? Only time will tell." [November 6, 1993]

Seven months later, the Virgin indicated to Estela that America was falling even deeper into the abyss. Just two months before the Cairo Conference, Mary declared that America had no respect for life. The country was traveling on a course, she said, which would lead to destruction:

"And so today I speak again of God's love for you. I remind you that present times in the world are times of pain and destruction. The signs of the times tell you that the world is in crisis. The greatest offense against God is the lack of respect for life. Yet that is the greatest offense going on in the world. Never before has man destroyed life so much as during these times. This is done

cruelly and without conscience. How can God bless you, His children, if there is no regard for that which He created — life?

"During these times, because of His great love for you, and because my Son died for all of you, He can only pour His mercy on you, that you may repent and change the course of destruction to which you in the world are headed.

"Listen to my words, my children. Hear me! God loves you and does not want to see the destruction of that which He created — you, His children. Allow Him to enter your hearts, that He may teach you to love, that He may take the hatred from your hearts. He loves you and desires to live in you. I love you and desire that you open your hearts to His love." [July 2, 1994]

The Ruiz family understood completely what the Virgin was saying. Before God had allowed her to intervene in their lives, the family had lost respect for life, for each other and for God.

The truth of their self-portrait was especially painful for the Ruizes due to their Mexican-American heritage. Part of a culture which places great importance on life and the family, which emphasizes solidarity and the subjection of individual interests to the needs of the family as a whole, the Ruizes were a sorry example of that ideal. Instead of the traditional Mexican-American value of looking out for and supporting fellow family members, the Ruizes had often turned their backs on each other in order to "live their own lives."

Again, the Ruizes were the perfect example of an American family in need of the Virgin's wake-up call. A family steeped in sin, upon which Satan had wreaked havoc, the Ruizes sorely needed to fast from the diet of hate and materialism which society was feeding them.

Indeed, Estela's son Armando Ruiz could now see it all and frankly exposed his family for what it had become, and why Mary chose it: *"God needed to take a family,"* said Armando, *"that had obvious warts and pimples — big ugly ones that cannot hide. He picked our family because there is not a sin that we have not com-mitted ... short of murder."*[7]

Around America, if every family were to look into the mirror, much of the same could probably be said, for many. The signs of the times are at hand.

America is just refusing to look.

CHAPTER TWENTY-THREE

ARMANDO AND FERNANDO COME HOME

After the apparitions began, the Ruiz family's small, unassuming residence in the heart of South Central Phoenix quickly became a different place. While Estela and Reyes had for years contemplated moving to a new location, all that changed once the Virgin began appearing. They were back to square one. Crime or no crime in their own backyard, South Phoenix was where they believed the Madonna wanted them.

But there was one problem: space. How could they accommodate the hundreds of pilgrims who made 30 East Cody Street their destination each weekend?

Indeed, every Saturday, with Rosaries in hand, the faithful began to come — young and old, Anglos and Hispanics, men and women alike.   The Ruizes even erected a huge bilingual sign proclaiming the family's mission: *"Please enter and visit the shrine. The Ruiz family meets with pilgrims after the Rosary."*

The pilgrims all had one thing in common — a strong belief that Mary was truly appearing and speaking to Estela Ruiz. Dozens, then hundreds, and even as many as a thousand squeezed into the little grass-covered backyard. They stood. They sat. Some knelt under the Palo Verde trees or paced about the yard. Many learned quickly and would remember to bring fold-up lawn chairs or little carpet remnants on subsequent visits, thus claiming permanent turf.

Whether under the sun or the stars, prayer was always the order of the day. Lots of prayer. After all, this was the home of Reyes Ruiz. Like a poverty-stricken man hitting the jackpot, Reyes had arrived at his moment of glory. Now shifting his prayer diet from bread to steak, the gathering for the apparitions each Saturday was, under his direction, a prayer smorgasbord. With bilingual Scripture readings, an occasional Biblical skit, a little singing, and always an emphasis on the Rosary, there was something for everyone to spiritually indulge in.

But the highlight of Saturday evening remains the apparition and the message from the Virgin Mary, Heaven's Messenger. For the Queen of Peace's words are aimed at the hearts and minds of all who are there to listen. Nothing is placed above this.

While the pilgrims pray outside, Mary usually appears to Estela a little after 7 p.m., as the Joyful Mysteries of the Rosary gradually progress into the Sorrowful. The Virgin's primary reason for coming in the evening is the same as the pilgrims: she's there to pray. And besides these important prayers, Mary also blesses her children, and brings them heavenly graces and gifts, or as Estela calls them, *"candy kisses."*

The actual moments of the apparition are always a paradox. While Hail Marys resound over and over on speakers inside and outside of the house, one must stare very, very closely at Estela as the apparition begins. For at a certain point, she almost invisibly goes into ecstasy while kneeling or sitting in her living room before a small shrine of religious pictures, paintings, crucifixes and statues.

A small cluster of pilgrims are usually invited into the Ruiz living room to witness the apparition. The room can only hold about twenty people, and half of that space is often filled by the sick or those in wheelchairs. The room is usually dimly lit, as both Spanish and English voices can often be heard in the crowd.

Like outside, some kneel, while others sit or stand depending on the space. Reyes himself always kneels on a little wooden kneeler to Estela's left, as if guarding her. His presence is so intense that one cannot help but wonder if he, also, is seeing the Virgin.

Estela, too, is quite motionless during the apparition. As if frozen solid, not a hair on her head sways for the five to ten minutes Mary is with her. The best clue that the apparition has begun, says Reyes, is that Estela's fingers stop tracing the Rosary beads in her hands.

According to experts, it's a classic apparition, as it contains many of the elements associated with such phenomena: the visionary's strong, unwavering stare and transfixed eyes; her motionless body; the inaudible conversing between her and some invisible entity; the total oblivion to her surroundings; the slight nodding of the head in nonverbal response to the Virgin's conversation; and the complete ecstasy and joy which the visionary exudes, as her eyes seem to come to life like nothing in this world could cause. According to eye witnesses, it is as if she is *"out of this world."*

Indeed, this is what has been observed in the past.

In France a man names Jean-Baptiste Estrade journeyed to the then-unknown grotto of Lourdes to scoff and jeer at the child visionary, Bernadette Soubirous. But instead of heckling, Estrade witnessed an incredible event. According to his own words:

> *"Suddenly, as though a flash of lightning had struck her, she gave a start of amazement, and seemed to be born into another life. Her eyes lighted up and sparkled; seraphic smiles played on her lips; an indefinable grace spread over her whole being. From within the narrow prison of the flesh, the visionary's soul seemed to be striving to show itself outwardly and proclaim its jubilation. Bernadette was no longer Bernadette!...*
>
> *"Spontaneously, we men who were present uncovered our heads and bent our knees like the humblest woman. The time for argument was past, and we, like all those present at this heavenly scene, were gazing from the ecstatic girl to the rock, and from the rock to the ecstatic. We saw nothing, we heard nothing, needless to say; but what we could see and comprehend was that a conversation had begun between the mysterious Lady and the child whom we had before our eyes."*[1]

Just as in Lourdes, the events of South Phoenix have a strong impact on the onlookers. Five to seven minutes after beginning her encounter with the "invisible Lady," Estela's head drops, which serves as a sign to others that the Virgin has departed.

Shortly thereafter, she journeys outside into the candle-lit yard to read Mary's weekly message to the pilgrims. As it's usually her second apparition of the day, Estela has already prepared Mary's message in advance in both English and Spanish to read to the crowd.

But before going outdoors, hugs and kisses are distributed inside, as a smiling Reyes and Estela always initiate a celebration of joy when Mary visits their home. It's a powerful moment, often accompanied by the flow of tears.

Finally, after the *Oh Maria* but before departure, the pilgrims stand and face Reyes. With arms stretched and fingers twirling, they must all give themselves a great big hug by wrapping their arms completely around their back and squeezing tight. All the while, Reyes chuckles with delight over his successful ploy to induce more love into each one's life, starting with one's self.

Over and over, the Saturday night apparition leaves people filled with this joy and love. Indeed, the special event is designed to touch all. And the Ruizes spread their love generously and sincerely, leaving no one out. In fact, they will hug you to death, if you let them! Little Rey can often be seen swallowing up two or three bodies at a time, as he and his brothers and sisters reach for everyone in sight.

Yes, it's a special time, and it's the family that makes it such a success. For not long after Estela and Little Rey's conversions, the Virgin's work with the rest of the family began, too. Indeed, just as the Immaculate Conception Novena had petitioned, Mary was working to mold the entire family to God's design, with her focus also being placed upon twins Armando and Fernando.

Her powerful influence did not take long to affect them.

In short, the powerful brothers became the prayerful brothers, as Mary's love and grace soon embraced their hearts. *"Our Lady is kind of sneaky,"* says Estela. *She has a way of stealing hearts."*

For State Senator Armando Ruiz, the change was gradual. But eventually, his heart was completely stolen, as totally and permanently as Little Rey's.

By the early 1990's, Armando knew he was through with politics. While Washington could have been his, he chose East Cody Drive, where both he and brother Fernando own homes on opposite sides of their folks.

His political exit left the pros aghast. No one could understand how, at the peak of his career, Armando could just walk away. Peter Rios, President of the Arizona State Senate and a Democratic party leader, almost took it personally. Armando's decision, he railed, radically affected a district realignment that was in the works. Yet it wasn't an easy decision for Armando. He heard no voices. He saw no visions. He didn't even receive a message from Mary to his mother which could have hinted to him to quit.

At first, after the apparitions began, Armando rationalized that they were a confirmation that God was leading him to higher and higher political goals. The road to Washington, he began to believe, was paved with God's grace.

But soon Armando saw the light. *"God wanted me to walk away from politics,"* says Armando, *"and do work that was really going to help Him."*

To friends and colleagues, the change which occurred in Armando appeared almost as radical as Little Rey's. Former State Senator Alfredo Gutierrez, who knew the hard-driven, ambitious Armando, couldn't believe what he observed. Gutierrez commented,*"Now he [Armando] has a very different view of the world; he is open and appears to be happy."*[2]

Instead of the fancy suits, ties and expensive dinners that once occupied Armando's daily life, he began working with the youth at the Y.M.C.A., many of whom were former gang members or just street kids.

As Program Director for the Y's South Phoenix branch, Armando dealt with the kids everyday worries, but also tried to be their friend and a spiritual lantern in the darkness. Often, he helps kids leave gangs and drugs for God, guidance and strength. Indeed, such direction is important to Armando, as he believes that the only thing that will change these young people's lives drastically is the realization that *"God is alive."* In 1995, Armando began a new job as one of the Governor's assistants for the development of neighborhood revitalization.

On weekends though, the former politician still gets to "press the flesh." At the Saturday night prayer vigil, Armando successfully warms up the crowd, and draws upon his years of public-speaking experience in the Arizona State Legislature and the public spotlight. The fifteen minutes of persuasive witnessing for the Lord, he says, leaves him just as high.

After his moment in the spotlight, Armando hurries back to his role as event manager and full-time baby-sitter for his daughter, Natalie. It is a role which Armando believes God has chosen for him. In fact, Armando can see God's Will everywhere now, especially in Our Lady's coming to South Phoenix. It was, he says, a very deliberate part of God's plan.

Armando and Peggy Ruiz with children
Natalie, Elias and Armando (4 months)

States Armando:

"I was watching a program about the Blessed Mother, and it was said that historically she has appeared in places that have been difficult to reach. You have to make a pilgrimage to get to those places. I was thinking at the time, that doesn't necessarily apply here, but it does. It's not Paradise Valley — it's not a pleasant trip for folks to make. It's not an easy one because you're going into an area that has a reputation for being a rough part of town, and there are occasions when, during praying, you hear gunshots. It is a pilgrimage to get here."[3]

The Virgin's persistent yet gentle calling of Armando to holiness was also a radical change for his wife, Peggy. A native of South Phoenix's affluent neighbor, Scottsdale, Peggy was comfortable with the powerful, important lifestyle of a Senator's wife. The changes which began to take place in her husband, and then later in herself, were in many ways grueling.

For years Peggy had enjoyed a fast-track lifestyle that left her lacking very little. Used to playing and gaming with the "rich and famous," she admits that she came full-force from the "My" generation of the eighties. Peggy's dreams involved being a lawyer and marrying a lawyer. She was a self-proclaimed super-Yuppie, with no shame and no excuses attached.

Indeed, Peggy's view of her life and dreams for the future had nothing to do with heavenly apparitions. But as the events surrounding her mother-in-law began to increase in frequency, attention and urgency, Peggy was forced to take a long, hard look at herself and her values. She soon decided that changes were in order.

With a new realization of the Truth, Peggy quickly abandoned her Yuppie cravings. Before long, she had become a Reyes Ruiz clone, dutifully marching to the beat of Hail Mary full of grace ! Exchanging her Gucci jewelry for a plastic Rosary, she began to keep her precious beads in or near her hands at all times, just like her father-in-law.

Indeed, her internal metamorphosis was significant, and she is now proud of her new, humbled focus. The change has been so great, in fact, that she no longer jumps at the sound of gunshots which so often pervade the surroundings of the Ruiz home. Even when her car was stolen from in front of her house, Peggy says she barely blinked.

Rather than escape South Phoenix in search of six-figure mansions and plush comforts, Peggy is now drawn to help the neighborhood. Her prior preoccupation with recreation and entertainment has been replaced with feeding the homeless. And she now admits that she was selfish. The world, says Peggy, had sucked her into its terrible grasp.

"Evil sneaks into our lives in so many ways," she says, *"I now realize I was a terrible, terrible person."*

Certainly the hardest part of Peggy and Armando's new life in God, though, was their marriage itself. For although they both began to bathe in the grace of conversion, both were also previously divorced. Consequently, according to Church Law, they were not permitted to receive Holy Communion, as their marriage was not officially consecrated in the Catholic faith.

Once enlightened by the reality of Christ's presence in the Eucharist, neither could bear the thought of doing without the precious gift. So, while their annulment proceedings were unfolding, they attempted celibacy in their marriage in order to remain in a state of grace, which consequently allowed them to receive the crucial sacrament.

Thus, while the road of conversion has been a challenge, the silver lining in the cloud has appeared. Armando now marvels at his own self-discipline, especially at his transformed view of women, relationships and people.

"Sex was always the first priority in my relationships," recalls Armando. *"So my relationships were hollow."*[4]

Now, the former Senator asserts, he knows how to focus on the person. He knows how to look beyond the shell, and discover the heart inside. Armando says he has a new awareness of who his wife really is, and he sees as never before a person of great thoughtfulness, love and concern.

Sex, he now advises, is no basis for any strong relationship.

"I was the typical, Latin-American chauvinist," Armando admits. *"Now here is a woman the Virgin Mary who is calling me for the first time in my life to an understanding of values and purity. I am not used to that."*[5]

And just as Peggy has overcome her fears of the "bad neighborhood," Armando is not afraid of the "craziness" of South Phoenix. It's home — home sweet home!

...And twin brother Fernando concurs, as his life has also taken a 180 degree turn. Although not as obviously as Armando, Mary's touch has changed him greatly. The difference was, while Armando's life took a big turn on the outside, Fernando's change occurred more gradually on the inside.

Struggling in a marriage that was blessed by four children, Fernando and his wife, Letitia, were headed for divorce. Though college sweethearts, they had become tired of each other. While money and political success had come easily, Fernando and Letitia's relationship slowly became something each abhorred.

This discontentment, coupled with his feelings of guilt and failure over not becoming a priest, left Fernando feeling low and empty. He wasn't sure what he wanted anymore, and he didn't really have the energy, or the grace, to care.

Although Fernando was present on the night of the first apparition, he didn't necessarily believe in it. But the change in his family and the Virgin's messages continued to work on him. Gradually, he says, he began to see the light. He was able to forgive himself. This personal transformation then transformed his marriage, a marriage that — according to both Fernando and Letitia — has grown tremendously.

Like Estela, Little Rey, and twin brother Armando, Fernando credits the Virgin with his conversion. *" I knew that there was somebody who loved me. I always had hope,"* he says.

On their thirteenth wedding anniversary, the couple renewed their vows in church. And like her sister-in-law Peggy, Letitia now feels there's no place like home in the center of South Phoenix's war zone. While there have been three gang-related murders in four years just a block away, and a thriving "crack" house sits just down the street from their home, Letitia insists it's where God wants them to be. Like Armando, Fernando has come home in more ways than one. Again, the Virgin's words echoed in their minds:

> *"I came to South Phoenix because you cannot run away from this world. You've got to help the world change. This is where I need you."*

And this is where they have decided to stay.

Indeed, by 1997, the Virgin's plans for the Ruizes — this once destroyed and lifeless family that was totally rebuilt by her — could be seen.

In their misery, they had become a microcosm of America at large. And now, in their rebirth, all indications are they may be so once again.

The Fernando Ruiz Family
(backrow) Teofilo, Leticia (with Fernando Jr.) Fernando and Jose Luis
(front row) Xochitli, Tepili, Rafael, and Cesar

CHAPTER TWENTY-FOUR

TONALI

It sounded like the cry of a baby. For Liborio, the young man who often cleaned around the Ruizes' shrine, it didn't make sense. He had never heard anything like it there before.

But on that particular day, as Liborio worked around the large statue of Our Lady of Guadalupe, he clearly and distinctly heard a baby cry. After thinking it over, he decided to tell Reyes Ruiz Sr. about his puzzling experience.

Upon hearing the details of Liborio's strange encounter, Reyes swallowed hard and fought to hold back his tears. In his heart of hearts, Reyes realized immediately what it had to be. He believed he knew the answer.

Like many answers he had received throughout his life, this one was mystical in nature, one which connected the natural with the supernatural. Nonetheless, it was an answer, and for Reyes Ruiz, there was nothing illogical about it.

The baby's cry, he surmised, must have been ... *"Tonali."*

By the fall of 1993, almost four years after the apparitions of the Virgin Mary to Estela began, the Ruiz family had experienced much spiritual growth, both as individuals and as a family. Each member of the family was proceeding along his own personal process of conversion. They had all come back to God. Each had given his individual *"yes"* to Mary.

But for Fernando, there still remained some hesitation, some holding back. While he and twin brother Armando had, indeed, converted their lives to God, Fernando was still clinging to a few of his old ways. His activities were not sinful ones, but they were worldly enough to indicate that he still was not totally trusting in Our Lady and in God.

In the fall of 1993, the Ruizes began a new endeavor. The family started taking courses which were part of Evangelization 2000, a new effort in Catholic evangelization that had been sanctioned by Pope John Paul II.

As Fernando sat in the classroom one evening, he listened as his instructor, Lope Hernandez, began to talk about a unique flower found just below the black sash on the Virgin Mary's dress in her manifestation as Our Lady of Guadalupe. The sash signified pregnacy while the flower, Lope explained, was a symbol of diety and is found only once on the tilma. A white flower with four petals, it was traditionally recognized by the Aztecs as a sign of a pregnant woman.

But when the flower appeared on the Virgin Mary's dress on Juan Diego's tilma, it took on additional meaning. According to Aztec tradition, when a woman became pregnant, she was given this flower. This symbolized that she was united with the Virgin and that the child she carried was of God.

Then, after the Aztecs studied the image of Mary on the Guadalupe tilma, they understood how the Virgin Mary was in *"front of the sun and over the moon."* To them this meant that she was *"of the God of all gods."* This fact caused conversion in many of them; thus, the flower became known as the *"flower of conversion."*

And Aztec indians had a special name for this flower. They called it *"TONALI,"* meaning *"divinity."*

For Fernando Ruiz, the instructor's words blended nicely into his daydreaming thoughts, ones which centered around the news that his wife Leticia was pregnant with their sixth child. As the instructor delved deeper into the subject, Fernando's wheels began turning. He had started out thinking, *"O.K., God, I guess You know what You're doing with another child here,"* but soon progressed to, *"Wow! That's going to be the name of our child! Whether it's a boy or a girl, we'll name him or her "Tonali de Guadalupe!'"*

That evening Fernando told Leticia the exciting news. For Leticia, the name generated some much-needed enthusiasm over the prospect of another child. After all, she was, according to

Fernando, no *"spring chicken"* anymore, and the thoughts of another grueling nine-month pregnancy and then delivery were not exactly music to her ears. Indeed, it would be a difficult pregnancy. Leticia felt tired and too old to be having more babies. The five other children were already a lot of work, and she also struggled to hold down her job. But although the pregnancy slowed her down, it was a healthy one. All the medical check-ups were excellent, and the entire family grew in its excitement over the coming of Tonali.

Tonali! The baby's name took on a life of its own. It became a divine name in more that just meaning. The faceless child soon became part of everything the family planned or did. Though still in the womb, Tonali swept into the family in a way no one could have imagined; as mere mention of the child's name brought hope and life to all.

Tests revealed the baby was to be a girl and Ruiz family meetings and gatherings soon began to acknowledge her regularly. Her place and name were never forgotten, especially among the children who would invoke her constantly. *"Tonali will be there, too,"* the kids reminded the elders as long-range plans were being reviewed. Likewise, Leticia's belly would receive many a pat or rub as everyone liked to touch and talk to Tonali.

Tonali de Guadalupe Ruiz was, by her seventh month in Leticia's womb, as alive and real as anyone else in the Ruiz family.

For Fernando, the child assumed an even greater significance.

He could feel something happening in his own heart after Tonali's conception, something which left him feeling that, finally, he was completely converting to God. With Tonali, Fernando became *"firm and strong"* in his convictions. This child, though unborn became a "turning point" in his spiritual life. Just as had happened with Aztec indians, Fernando's *"Tonali"* brought him to a deep and true conversion.

On June 24, 1994, two busloads of youth drove in from California to the Ruiz home. It was the Church feast day of the great evangelist himself, Saint John the Baptist. It was also the anniversary of the first apparition of the Virgin Mary at Medjugorje in

1981. At the Ruiz home, it promised to be a special day, a day of planned talks, fun, and even a play in which Fernando Ruiz played the role of Jesus Christ.

But as Fernando appeared and began to act out his portrayal of Christ, the audience began to notice that his emotions were extremely passionate and real. Almost immediately his family grew concerned.

Indeed, as he burst into tears speaking Christ's words, his sorrow reflected a deep anguish and pain. It was a suffering that was above and beyond what anyone expected from him in his role. To all, it seemed too real.

And it was.

Soon it was discovered, Fernando's life-like portrayal of Christ's own anguish was stemming from a painfully real source. For just moments before the play was to begin, Fernando received shocking news: the doctors could not find Tonali's heartbeat during Letticia's prenatal check-up that day. And further tests soon confirmed...Tonali had died in her mother's womb.

The Ruiz family crumbled upon hearing the news. One by one, they slowly whispered to each other, *"Tonali is dead."* Indeed, she was gone, never to be welcomed to the family that had come to love her so much.

"It was a dagger," Fernando would later say, to his heart. Tonali, his beloved flower of conversion, his conversion, was gone.

While the adults grieved, the pain was especially difficult for the Ruiz children to bear. This unborn sister or niece, had become so loved by them. Now, they found themselves lost and bewildered. Their emptiness exploded into tears of sorrow and pain as each one sought to cope with what had happened to Tonali. If only it weren't true...

But there would be no more Tonali to talk to and touch, no more Tonali to love so much.

A quick meeting of the family was called, as the stunned visitors from California were left wondering. The family prayed and said good-bye to Tonali, and then decided it was time for a celebration. Indeed, a celebration in Christ was in order, for one of their own was now in Heaven.

Outside, the Ruiz family heroically paraded. They announced to all what had happened, and then began a joyous celebration. In honor of the feast of Saint John the Baptist, they covered each with water, and let the day's pain give way to the joys of Tonali's eternal life in Christ.

But for Fernando and Leticia, the hard part was still to come. That evening, Leticia was admitted to the hospital. The doctors induced labor and Tonali was born. A medical investigation revealed that a "*one in a million*" torquing of the umbilical cord had occured, choking off her life around her neck. Much like St. John the Baptist who was martyred by beheading, Tonali's fate seemed similar to the great saint on this his feast day.

After the delivery, Fernando and Leticia dressed Tonali. The tiny baby looked beautiful! They then held her and kept her with them until it was time to leave the hospital.

But as they were about to depart, Fernando and Leticia received shocking news.

The hospital told them that they could not have Tonali. Her little body would be "disposed of," they explained, much like what occurs after an abortion. Definitely not a "baby," and far from a "human being," Tonali was, the hospital insisted, a "fetus"! In fact, they even asked for the right to remove Tonali's brain for purposes of scientific experiments on patients with Parkinson's disease. This removal of "fetal brain tissue," as they called it, was a routine procedure regularly practioned on aborted children of late-term pregnancies.

Shocked and angered, Fernando protested! Tonali's body would not be used in such a fashion. She was not a "fetus"! She was their child, and she deserved to be buried in a Christian manner.

But the hospital would not budge. In order to bury Tonali, Fernando and Leticia were told that they needed a birth certificate or a death certificate, neither of which the hospital would provide.

An ethical question arose, and the hospital quickly found itself in an uncomfortable position. While Leticia was admitted for the purpose of delivering a baby, which she had done, the hospital was now saying that Tonali was not a baby. The question of "*when does a human being become a human being"* became apparent. The hospital soon realized that a potential public controversy loomed, as religious, moral and ethical issues were at stake.

Fearing negative exposure, the hospital relented. Tonali was permitted to go home with her family, although no certificate of any kind was ever issued. Says Fernando, *"Technically speaking, she really doesn't exist to this day."*

But the Ruiz's know she existed! And as far as they are concerned, questions over Tonali's existence are neither complicated nor political. To them, she not only "existed," but she lived and died, she gave love, life and hope, and the family loved her as one of their own.

After Fernando and Leticia brought Tonali home, the family prepared to bury her. Fernando built and Little Rey decorated a coffin. A tiny dress from a doll clothed her, and then the family said their good-byes. Each of her brothers and sisters, as well as the entire family, gave her their love in a beautiful farewell.

Finally, the Ruiz family gathered at the shrine in the backyard. They prayed the Rosary, held a memorial service, and then buried Tonali beneath the statue of Our Lady of Guadalupe. Indeed, she was now truly *"Tonali de Guadalupe,"* as she was entombed at the Queen of the Americas' feet. The family then planted a Zunicorn in her memory. The corn, long an indian ritual, symbolized that there is no death — only life! And for the Ruizes, that meant eternal life in Jesus Christ for Tonali.

Soon after, the Blessed Virgin gave Estela a message for Fernando and Leticia:

"My beloved ones, I first want to tell you how much I love you. You have lost your beloved child, but Heaven has gained a new soul. Thank you for freely giving back to God what He had given you — a little soul. That little soul was not meant for this world, but Our Lord had a different purpose for that soul. One day you will fully understand.

"Know that God gave you the strength to accept His will, but that your fidelity to Him was pleasing to Him. I

am always a part of this family, and so I was with you at all times of you pain and joy — for your little one brought pain and joy to you, and you have learned yet one more thing about your journey with and towards God. The road to sanctity is both joyful and painful.

"Grieve no more, my little ones, for there is a soul in heaven that you produced for the greater glory of God. I love you for your faithfulness and obedience to our Lord, and I thank you for your love for me, your Heavenly Mother."

Amazingly, the story didn't end there.

Fernando and Leticia grieved over Tonali's death for quite a while. but on the 25th anniversary of their diocese, approximately six months after Tonali's death, they took a retreat trip together to the Shrine of Our Lady of Guadalupe in Mexico City in order to pray and become renewed.

During the trip, Fernando and Leticia were finally able to put their grief behind them. Together they fell to their knees. They decided that it was time to move on with their lives. The couple rededicated their marriage and their lives to God, and they returned with a large and unique portrait of Our Lady of Guadalupe. This portrait, they were told, would never be allowed to leave Mexico, but somehow they pulled it off. It's a painting they now take with them wherever they speak.

Likewise, when Fernando and Leticia returned home from Mexico City and their visit with Our Lady of Guadalupe, they brought with them another gift — a new baby. Conceived in Mexico City while visiting the Shrine, It was another surprise from God that was to mark His touch in their lives. A touch, few can arque after Tonali, that is divine.

Was it Tonali who Liborio heard crying that day almost exactly one year after her burial?

Reyes Ruiz, with tears in his eyes, can't help but smile as he recalls the Virgin's words, *"One day you will fully understand..."*

Oldest son, Isidoro Ruiz with wife Luisa and children.

CHAPTER TWENTY-FIVE

SIGNS OF THE TRIUMPH

The amazing events surrounding the Ruiz family moved ahead, as Mary intensified her work through the apparitions. By 1993, one obstacle had been overcome. The Ruizes had graduated from a quick course on spiritual survival for the nineties, one loaded with care, guidelines and loving advice.

From conversion to evangelization, the Virgin left very little out. The course had been so thorough and so detailed, that the family's spiritual understanding proved tremendous.

Trained for the harvest by the best of teachers, the Ruiz family was then sent out into the fields to begin their mission. To thirty-five different states they traveled, as well as to Mexico, Honduras, Canada, Belize, Europe and Russia. The Virgin's message was clear: she was urgently calling God's children to salvation and announcing to them that the Triumph of the Immaculate Heart was close at hand.

Indeed, she had come for everyone; as God's faithful messenger, she had come *"for their souls."*

This mission, she said, was made possible by God's great love. The world was currently being flooded by the mercy of Jesus Christ, an element which was crucial to its salvation. She further indicated that preparations were underway for the advent of a new era, an era of evangelization. Mary repeated, however, that Satan's anger had *"exploded"* and that time was *"running out."*

But things were not hopeless, she stressed, for the intensity of the approaching events would depend on the world's response.

By 1997, Estela had received hundreds of messages from Mary. These heavenly directives were for herself, for her family, for the people of America and for the world. They were for anyone who would listen.

Estela and Reyes speak at a church in Pittsburgh.

While instructional and informative, Mary's directions were extremely concise and specific. She repeatedly asked for a change of heart and a return to God. These were essential, she said, in order to prevent *"destruction."*

The Blessed Mother further indicated that this period — the end of the Twentieth Century — was marked by an increase in emphasis on the *"signs of the times,"* Biblical signs which are sent as warnings to the faithful to take stock of the world's situation.

THE SIGNS!
Yes, the signs are what it is supposed to be all about. In order to understand these times, one must know the signs. The period of the tribulation, the current era in which we are living in, had been prophesied as a complicated period with much unrest. According to visionaries and scriptural references, the world would virtually be turned upside-down, and by recognizing "certain signs," the faithful would realize that the prophesied time had arrived.

During the last crucial moments, peace in the world would be hard to find. It would be absent from the hearts of men, from nations, and even from nature.

Scripture specifically advises us that these signs fall into five definitive categories:

1. The spread of theological errors, which leads to the loss of faith and to apostasy;
2. The outbreak of wars and fratricidal struggles along with an increase in natural catastrophes;
3. The persecution of those who remain faithful to Jesus Christ and His Apostolic Church;
4. The horrible sacrilege perpetrated by the one who will enter into the Holy Temple of God and will sit on His throne;
5. The extraordinary phenomena which will occur in the skies.

Almost as if trying to send her a "wake-up call," the Virgin urgently advised Estela in late 1991 that these signs were now everywhere. And like a concerned mother whose child is sleeping late, she repeatedly pointed out this fact in her messages:

"These are the times when you must truly open your hearts to God's love and mercy. You must begin to under-

stand that my manifestations throughout the world are serious SIGNS, that you must choose to open your hearts to His love. How long must you hear my call and why do you choose to ignore it? I know you can see the SIGNS of chaos and destruction in your world, yet you continue to ignore them and continue walking your path without thinking about the salvation of your soul." [June 29, 1991]

While the signs at hand were already serious and deserved attention, Mary pointed out that many people still desired even greater proof:

"But because of God's great love for you, He will not abandon you. I have come to the world to remind you that my Son is Hope and Love and Mercy. That He is alive with you during these times in His Spirit. I come to remind you that all you have to do is begin to acknowledge Him in your life. Open your heart to Him so that He can fill your lives. Do not wait for visible SIGNS of His power, as by then it may be too late. Open your hearts now so that you can begin to feel His love in you. Love in the world can come about if each one of you opens your heart to God's love, receives it and then allows it to overflow to others. The love in you for others is the greatest SIGN that you can hope for, because that is the SIGN that God finally lives in you." [October 26, 1991]

While these signs could be helpful to speed up individual conversions, the Virgin said, they were not to be focused on, and they most certainly were not necessary for strong faith:

"It is necessary to believe in God's love for you every day and every moment of your life. Many of you have a tendency to believe in God's power only when you see external SIGNS of His work. You respond to God's love only when you can see a sign and [you] believe in God's power for a period of time, but as you lose sight of His

handiwork, you forget His love for you. This, my little one, is not deep faith.

"The deep faith that will sustain you strong throughout your life should not come from external signs; rather, it should come from within your very soul. The path to God's Kingdom is not the one so many follow, which is going from place to place seeking SIGNS of God's love and power. The path to your peace and joy must begin from within your being. You must develop a deep conviction in your understanding that God truly loves you and that He is with you always, in good times as well as the bad times in your life. God will never leave anyone; rather, it is yourselves that push God aside.

"You are living in dark and hard times, and you need to believe in God's love for you more than ever. He is not the one who has brought the darkness into the world. This darkness has been brought about by evil, and it is impossible for you not to be affected by this turmoil that is occurring around you.

"Therefore, allow the light of God to illuminate your life. For this to occur, you must believe and be fully convinced of God's love for you at every moment of your life, not just when you see the external signs of God's power. Open your hearts to the deep knowledge and understanding of His love for you, for this is what will lead you to God's Kingdom which will bring about peace and harmony into your very soul. This is the deep faith of which I speak about." [February 29, 1992]

Mary taught Estela that in America, people are overlooking the signs because they are too focused on themselves:

"You continue to concern yourselves and worry too much about your own personal needs and comforts and barely see the concerns and worries of the world around you. You see the devastation of humanity, yet you continue to focus on yourselves, your physical comforts and

*well-being. My children, when are you going to under-
stand what I am here to tell you? Are your eyes so intent
on yourselves that you are incapable of focusing on the
SIGNS that are occurring around you?"* [May 2, 1992]

In the following week's message, Mary continued her pleas:

*"I have come to call you, all of my children in the
world, with all the love of my heart; I do not want you to
continue to destroy each other as you are doing. Many of
you continue to ask for signs, yet you ignore the signs
around you. The SIGNS of your times are all around
you, yet you are so blinded by the hatred, greed and anger, [that] you cannot see and you will not see as long as
you refuse to let those hearts of stone melt. I plead with
all my children today to allow God in so He can help you
to soften your hearts. You must or you will continue to
destroy each other. It is not the destruction of the temples
of stone which is my utmost concern, but the destruction
of the temples of flesh, for you are God's creation and
He created you so that you could be His dwelling place.
Those of you who have heard my call, I ask that you pray
and love with God's love more than ever. I depend on you
to help me win this war. Ask Michael the Archangel to
share His strength with you so that you may do what you
need to do with courage and love."* [May 9, 1992]

Mary also told Estela that the time of these great signs as warnings to the world would not last forever. Indeed, the world had to
change, and soon:

*"Many ask for signs from God so that they may be-
lieve; yet, they fail to see the events of the world as
SIGNS that mankind must change their ways if your
world is to survive. I am your Mother, and I am grieved
to see the destruction of many of my beloved children
in the world as they hurt each other knowingly and will-
ingly."* [June 27, 1992]

Indeed, Mary frequently warned of impending destruction, and pleaded with her children to understand:

"It should not be surprising to anyone that I am very evident in the world during these times. These are desperate times, and as your Heavenly Mother, I come to call all humanity to return to God's love. My little ones, you can no longer continue to disregard the SIGNS of chaos and destruction around you. These are signs that you must heed. Let the signs be a warning that all my little ones must return to God. Every human being on this earth is my child, and I don't want to lose even one soul." [November 7, 1992]

By early 1993, Mary's emphasis on the signs increased further. Her news, however, became more grave: she began to tell Estela that, while some were turning their lives around, too many were ignoring all of God's efforts to save them:

"My children, do you not see the seriousness of the state of men in the world? You, who continually seek God's SIGNS to believe, cannot see the signs of destruction that are evident all over the world. Humanity has allowed Satan to dominate their hearts and, through this, Satan will destroy humanity. He is doing it by planting seeds of hatred and anger in men's hearts, and so man destroys each other." [May 22, 1993]

By February of 1993, Mary sounded almost desperate:

"My children, why will you, all of you in the world, not listen to my call? Why can't your hearts understand the signs of the times, the SIGNS that are crying out for men's repentance and transformation of hearts? Listen, my children, please listen as I come to call you out of harm's way and to the peace and love of Our Lord and Redeemer." [February 14, 1993]

Indeed, harm's way was very serious:

"Which words must I use to make you understand that you, all of humanity, are living in serious and grave times? What other way can I make you understand that change of hearts must come about if humanity is to be saved from destruction? So many of you wait for signs, and it is only then that you might turn your attention to my words. Yet, I tell you that you must not continue to ask for any signs of God's great power, for if God were to show His Mighty Hand, you, His children, would not be able to handle it. This is not the time for our God to show you His power but to show you His great mercy and love. These are times when God is pouring tremendous graces upon the world so that His children may receive them and make the changes necessary to enter the Kingdom of God. He is a loving and merciful God, but He is also a just God. Can you not see the SIGNS of the times? Has anger, hate, and other sin blinded your eyes?" [October 2, 1993]

By July 1994, the Virgin had made it clear. The greatest danger lay in America's view of life itself:

"And so today I speak again of God's love for you. I remind you that present times in the world are times of pain and destruction. The SIGNS of the times tell you that the world is in crisis. The greatest offense against God is the lack of respect for life. Yet that is the greatest offense going on in the world. Never before has man destroyed life so much as during these times. This is done cruelly and without conscience. How can God bless you, His children, if there is no regard for that which He created life?" [July 2, 1994]

Yes, the world was in a crisis, Mary said, especially America. And that crisis involved life itself.

Despite the warnings, though, Mary's primary message is, and always has been, one of hope. Indeed, hope was the essence of her message at Fatima, as it was there that she promised God's victory. And she referred to that ultimate moment of glory as the *"Triumph of the (Mary's) Immaculate Heart"* in the world.

That Triumph, according to Marian experts, will come from Mary's work as God's messenger during these times, a work which includes her many apparitions and messages from God, numerous weeping statues and icons, and thousands of other miracles. The world will be saved. Mary, as Christ's greatest apostle, will triumph in God's name. But God will be the Victor. And because this victory will come through Mary's powerful intercession as ordained and willed by God, it will be known as the Triumph of the Immaculate Heart.

At Fatima, Mary foretold: On July 13, 1917 to the three children:

> *"In the end, my Immaculate Heart will triumph, the Holy Father will consecrate Russia to me, Russia will be converted, and a certain period of peace will be granted to the world."*

This triumph, the Virgin assured Estela, was now approaching. And according to Mary's words, it would be the triumph of love in each person's heart. This love would then spread from individuals to families, and from families throughout nations and to all corners of the world.

On March 28, 1992, Mary explained more of this mystery to Estela:

> *"If there are still some in your families that are resisting or fighting against God's love because they cannot understand it, do not despair. If you despair, you may be lead to treat them in anger or impatience, and they would not be able to see God's light through you. Rather, treat them as my Son has treated you and taught you — with kindness and love and patience. It is only in this way that my Son can radiate in you. Continue to remember that my Son is your hope and that these are times of His*

great mercy. Even as we pray on this day, we move ever forward to the Triumph of my Immaculate Heart over the world, when we will see all of God's children finally come together in love, respect and dignity for each other, and when all will bow down to God's love and greatness."

In October of 1992, a special event of historical significance occurred. The Virgin Mary's army invaded Russia, a country which had long been Satan's stronghold, in the form of a tremendous pilgrimage, arranged and heavenly guided by Dr. Rosalie Turton and the 101 Foundation. Not surprisingly, Estela Ruiz was destined to be on this historic journey of almost one thousand pilgrims from around the world, this pilgrimage of tremendous spiritual significance which was characterized by many blessed events.

While in Paris on the first leg of the trip, Estela received a prophetic message concerning the importance of the unique journey, and the approaching Triumph of Mary's Immaculate Heart in the world. The joyful Virgin announced that her triumph of love was now closer than ever:

"I wish to speak to you, my little ones, who are embarked on this mission of great importance. Many still do not understand that you are living in the reign of my Immaculate Heart, and this journey is part of my plan to bring many souls to God. Many have understood that this mission you are on is of historic importance, but even the most learned of all of you cannot begin to understand the impact it will have on the world.

"In a very appropriate and significant way, you are traveling and making the necessary stops, and strengthening yourselves through prayer, as you, my warriors, accompany me to embrace and welcome my lost child into my arms and my love. My heart rejoices as you, my instruments of peace, come with me to greet with love and compassion, your sister Russia, into our fold.

"I have used many of my devoted instruments to bring this about, and you may never understand my deep gratitude for your work.

"This journey to Russia has dealt the Evil One a great blow, and this is indeed a glorious victory. The Evil One has tried to stop this mission from the beginning and has caused much disturbance and created many hurdles. Even now, he continues to attempt to stop us, but we will not fail! Believe and understand that I am with you, every moment, every step of the way. Michael, the Archangel, is in the forefront leading this important mission of love. Go forth, my children, armed with prayer, faith, hope and love. March together in great love for each other, allowing that love to multiply and increase so that you may have an abundance as you reach your destination.

"On this day, I, your mother, your Lady of the Americas, ask all my beloved children in the Americas to support your brothers and sisters on this journey with great prayer and sacrifice. Offer all you can for the success of this mission. You are an important part of this plan that welcomes your sister Russia into the folds of the faithful. Your eyes and ears have yet to see and hear the fruits of your prayers. Unite your hearts to the Peace Flight pilgrims in prayer and love. I ask the support of all who will hear my request.

"I want all the faithful to know that my Son, in His Most Sacred Heart, and united with my Immaculate Heart, is pouring forth tremendous graces upon you and this great event of love." [October 10, 1992]

Indeed, true to the Virgin's words, the pilgrimage was history in the making. The beginning of the end for the Red Dragon — or according to Mary, atheistic communism — was taking place. Indeed, Revelation's symbolic description of Satan's power in the end times under this title was beginning to break down.

As the Virgin's army of pilgrims traveled through Lourdes, Fatima, Rue du Bac, Prague, Lisieux, Rome, Czestochowa and Moscow, they seemed to march in fulfillment of legendary prophecies given decades ago by Saint Catherine Labouré, Saint Maximillian Kolbe, and Pope Pius XII. Some of these prophecies specifically foretold the Queen of Heaven's Triumph over Russia and then the entire

world. And according to the prophecies, this triumph would be sig-
nalled by the very events the pilgrims were engaging in.

Undoubtedly, a climactic moment soon arrived.

In Moscow, marching past the Kremlin, the blue-clad soldiers
of Christ crowned their Heavenly Queen at a midnight ceremony
in Red Square outside the tomb of Lenin, as a host of armed Russian militia looked on.

Almost on cue, the unrelenting rain miraculously halted over
the pilgrim statue of Our Lady of Fatima during the crowning, as
some pilgrims claimed to see immense flashes of light over Red
Square, and then the Queen of Heaven herself.

Later, while still in Russia, Mary revealed to Estela the significance of the events:

*"Rejoice with me on this day, for we have arrived at
our destination full of hope and faith! The journey has
not been without sacrifice. It has not been a journey without some suffering, but you must know that the sacrifice
has made it possible that this event not be mediocre, but
great indeed.*

*"I have told you, my little ones, that any great deed
meant to glorify Our Lord must include not only prayer,
but sacrifice must be an integral part of it if it is to be of
value. I want you to know that all the sacrifice endured
by all has not gone unnoticed, and has endeared you even
more to me. Even as your human weaknesses have shown
through, so has your spirit of faith and strength been evident. I have seen it, our Lord has seen it, the whole court
of Heaven has seen it, and the Heavens rejoice at the courage you have shown on the battleground, my faithful warriors. Come to me in your weariness and let my love en-
fold you, that I may continue to give you the strength necessary to continue your mission to completion.*

*"As you move on to the final events, you must know
and understand that they are really a beginning of other
significant events that will allow the world to see the great
love with which my Immaculate Heart will Triumph!*

"Rejoice, my little ones, for indeed we have dealt Satan a great blow! We have arrived at our destination somewhat weak but victorious. Now open your hearts and arms to your brothers and sisters in Russia, showing them the love of God, letting them know that Our Lord never forgot them or abandoned them. Spread throughout, your love and mine by means of the gifts you have brought and let them know that God lives in the world and wants to show them His love through you. They await you, my little ones, hungry for God's love. Know that your gifts have been blessed by me in a very special way, for these gifts you bring are nourishment for their souls.

"To those throughout the world who have prayed for this triumphant event, I give my thanks with great love for your commitment to my work and to my requests. You may never understand what your prayers of support have done for the success of this historical event."
[October 17, 1992]

And so, according to Mary's own words to Estela, her Triumph was near. And like a good mother, she repeated herself. Just one week later, on October 24, 1992, the Virgin confirmed to Estela that the events underway were historical. Once again, the Queen of Peace promised the American visionary, *"My Immaculate Heart will Triumph throughout the world, not just Russia.* Mary told Estela:

"My beloved little ones, you must begin to understand the significance of the event you have been involved in. This event is the spark that ignited the fire that will become a blaze throughout the world of the love of my Immaculate Heart. It is through Russia's conversion that the world will know that these times are truly the reign of my heart and that my love for God and for my earthly children will triumph over evil, so that all nations will know and acknowledge that my Son, Our Lord Jesus, is the King of the World and the hope and salvation of all."

241

This Triumph of the Virgin's love, according to her promises at Fatima and her words everywhere, will take hold with the conversion of atheist Russia. And from all observations, this conversion is now clearly underway.

Indeed, the communist empire of the Red Dragon is in fragments, shattered to pieces. Leningrad is now St. Petersburg, Stalin statues have been turned upside-down, and just one month before this historic pilgrimage, on September 8, 1992 (the Church recognized birthday of Mary), the last Soviet flag was hauled down from the MIR (Peace) spacecraft.

And, unbeknownst to all, it was also the fourth anniversary of the day that Reyes Ruiz departed for Medjugorje.

CHAPTER TWENTY-SIX

THE GREATNESS OF GOD

After countless visits with the Blessed Virgin Mary, one might well assume that Estela Ruiz knows Mary like a real mother. In this chapter, in Estela's own words, their relationship is exposed in clear, fascinating detail.

Indeed, that relationship is an intimate one. The following pages reveal it to be a loving, ongoing association between a mother and child. It's a story that brings great joy, for through Estela's words we come to understand that Mary, our spiritual Heavenly Mother, loves each one of us with equal intensity.

Q. Tell us how you receive the messages. Do you write them all down?

A. *Yes, I do now. But at that time (i.e., initially) I wasn't writing them down. We were recording them. When I would come out, they would turn on the recorder, and we would record everything. At that time she was appearing to me almost daily.*

Q. So, Our Lady was appearing to you every day, in the beginning of 1989, with messages.

A. *Yes, every day in the bedroom. In 1989 I began to come home during my lunch time, because I would want to talk to her. She would appear and speak to me, and then I would go on to work. She would give me messages for my children. One day I stayed home from work, and I was busy doing something when I heard her call me. And so I went immediately, and I knelt down and she appeared. And Our Lady said,* **I want you to take a pencil and a paper, and I want you to write what I am going to say.** *So, I got a paper and pencil, and then she began to dictate. Our Lady said,* **Write as I tell you.** *And so she said,* **My dear children,** *and I wrote, My dear children and then* *she'd dictate it, and I wrote it. All of a sudden, you know, I looked at it and there was a whole message from Our Blessed Mother! It was a Tuesday night and so people came that evening, and I told them, You know, today I'm going to be able to read you the whole message because Our Blessed Mother gave it to me, and she told me to write it down. So everybody got everything that she had said. I thought, How wonderful, this way I don't have to try to remember everything. So, during that week I went to her and I said, Could we do this from now on — could you dictate the message to me? And she said,* **Yes, that's the way we are going to do it from now on.** *Presently, during apparitions Our Lady gives me the message in the morning. She dictates the message, and I take it. She appears again in the evening, and at that time she prays with us. Sometimes Our Lady just prays with us, sometimes she'll give me something to add, a short thing to add to the one she's given me in the morning. Usually I go straight to the computer, and I put it into the computer and I translate it into Spanish, and then I send it to a friend of mine who corrects my Spanish. He's from Mexico, and he does a real good job. So it takes almost a whole day, as we prepare to fax it around the country and to Mexico and Canada.*

Q. Tell us a little of how Our Lady looks. What does her face look like?

A. *She doesn't have a long face, she has a little round face.*

Q. Are her eyes brown or blue?

A. *Blue —it's kind of like a deep, dark blue.*

Q. Is she always dressed the same?

A. *She is always dressed the same, except for Christmas and Easter of the first year, 1989. On those days she was dressed in brilliant gold.*

Q. Do Angels ever come with her?

A. *I have never seen any angels. I would certainly like to see angels! I have not. One time I saw her with baby Jesus in her arms.*

Q. Does she gradually appear, or does she appear all together at once?

A. *She suddenly appears all together at once.*

Q. Tell us about the messages. Has Our Lady spoken about fasting?

A. *She spoke in the beginning about fasting. She said,* **I'm not going to ask you to fast. For those that are already fasting, that's fine. But those that are beginning to fast, I'm going to ask that you offer up one meal a week — one meal a week for peace in the world — because Americans are not ready for sacrifice. The American people do not know how to sacrifice. And if I asked, it would not happen.** *She said,* **I will speak (later) to you about fasting.** *And as you now know, she has asked us again.*

Q. How much does she want us to fast?

A. *Twice a week.*

Q. Does it matter what day?

A. *In Medjugorje she said Wednesdays and Fridays. So many people are choosing those days.*

Q. What has Our Lady said about conversion?

A. *Our Lady said that* **conversions will be the biggest miracles that we will see.**

Q. Our Lady appeared to you also at Immaculate Heart Church in Phoenix. Tell us about that.

A. *She appeared right over the top of the altar inside the church. It was the Diocesan Feast of Our Lady of Guadalupe. Our Lady appeared and I spoke to her, and at the time I asked her who she was, what she was doing and who had sent her. She said,* **I am the Immaculate Heart of Mary.** *She then said,* **This is my reign — this is the time of my reign. I am here to bring my children back to my Son. The one who sent me is God, Our Father.** *And so I said, All right, I'll tell Reyes. I said, I'm sorry, but my husband asked me to ask you these questions. And she said,* **That's all right.** *She said,* **It is all right for you to ask me these things.** *Also, when I asked her who she was, she said,* **I am the Immaculate Heart of Mary — but, I am the same one that has appeared all over the world.** *She told me,* **Look around this church and see all the different forms in which I have appeared.** *In this church they have Our Lady of Sorrows, Our Lady of Guadalupe, Our Lady of Fatima. Our Lady said,* **I am the Mother of God, and I have appeared in different places.** *She said,* **There is only one, and that is** *me and I am all of these. But I come today, at this time, as the Immaculate Heart of Mary, as this is the reign of my Immaculate Heart. And I've come to call my children back to God. And then I begged her. I said, You know, Blessed Mother, the Bishop isn't going to believe this. You know that he's not going to believe what I say. If it ever gets out, and I'm sure it's going to get out, Blessed Mother, he's not going to believe me. And she said, Don't worry about the Bishop. Don't worry about my son. I will take care of him. And I said, Would you give him a blessing so that maybe through that blessing, one day he will believe? And she said, Yes.*

Q. So has there been any ruling by this Bishop?

A. *Yes. He set up a committee to investigate. The committee was comprised of three people — a priest, a psychologist and a nun. They came here. They were here on a Saturday and then later they came and spoke to me, for many hours, several times. They spoke to others in my family.*

Afterward, they stated that they found they could not call it miraculous because there were no visible findings of a miracle. The Church could not say that it was miraculous. But they found no problem in that there was anything out of order on the teachings of the Church. We spoke to the Bishop, and he told us about the report before it was published. He also said that we should get a spiritual director, and we now have one.

Q. In summation, can you tell us more about the essence of her messages?

A. *The messages talk about treating each other, whoever it is in your life, with **LOVE**. The basic message is this: she wants us all to be saved and the road to salvation is through Jesus Christ and by following the commandments of God — the two greatest of which are loving God above all else and loving your brothers and sisters in the world. And that is essentially her message. Learn to love each other. She says, **Even the ones that you think you cannot — those that you look down on, like the homeless, the mentally ill or those that have hurt you. Those are my children, too. I want you to learn to love each other.** And in Our Lady's messages, she tells us how to do it. That's what the messages are for.*

Q. What has Our Lady taught you about yourself?

A. *She's always made me very aware that all of this has nothing to do with my being great. It's the fact that God is great. And she (Blessed Virgin Mary) says never, never, doubt the greatness of God who can work in you and through you. It has nothing to do with me because, of course, I am just a child of God who is very little — really nothing. I am not capable or worthy of anything, let alone this work. It's totally God's choice. The more you understand the great work of God, the more you understand that there's nothing you have done to deserve this. I'll never be worthy. I have come to understand totally this in my heart. I will never be worthy of the work of God. Never...never. I'll reach my death and even then, I'll be struggling to say, You know, Lord, I'm not worthy of the cross. I'm not even worthy of going to Heaven, but You're so kind and so good and that's why I'm going to go.*

Q. Why does God use us?

A. *It's mind-boggling to me. But, I think what it has done for me is it has really made me grateful to God. You know, that He would even consider to choose His unworthy children on this earth. I many times tell Our Blessed Mother, Boy, Our Lord must really be desperate if He lowers Himself to a point where He has to use me. But that's the way He works. And that to me just tells me the greatness of Our God. How he chooses to show us, you know, His greatness. It's mind-boggling that God would even consider us. He doesn't have to, He could wave His mighty arm and it would get done. Yet, He doesn't work that way. He works through you and me, and that is really something.*

Q. Is there a spiritual war going on?

A. *It is amazing. You know, one time when Our Blessed Mother spoke, I'm not sure if it was a general message or if it was a message to the family, she spoke about the spiritual warfare that's going on. She said, **You cannot begin to understand the spiritual warfare that is going on — that angels are all around you.** So yes, there is a war going on.*

Q. Many visionaries say this spiritual warfare is part of what Scripture refers to as the Great Tribulation. What do you think?

A. *You know, it seems to me that... I think there will be something that will happen. As far as the tribulation and all that, I person-*

ally believe that we are in the middle of it. I really do. I believe that we are in the middle of it, and we don't recognize it because it all seems so normal. You know, you look outside and buildings are still, and the earth isn't moving. People are walking about. So, things seem to be almost normal. Except when you focus with the eyes of God. When you focus with the eyes of God, if you allow Him into your life and into your heart, then God begins to allow you to see through His eyes. Then you begin to see the real times. The Book of Revelation talks about the "beast." I believe that the beast is here. I believe that we're living in those times. All you have to do is turn that television on and put on "MTV" and you can see the "beast."

Q. Mary reportedly said to Father Gobbi that the "beast" is all the forms of mass communication in the world right now that deny God, whereas the "Red Dragon" was Communism which denies God on a state level. Tell us how Satan, or the "Beast," is working.

A. *Satan's works, you know, are what is swallowing us up: greed, lust, hate, anger, violence. Those are the quakes that are swallowing us. And we're going to see it get worse. We're going to see all of that stuff, especially in this country, that is going to happen. We already see people killing each other — people hating each other so much, they're willing to end a life. The way people take lives anymore, they don't even call it taking a life. You know, you shoot somebody else and its considered a clean thing for some reason or another.*

Q. Does our society see the signs of the times in all of this evil?

A. *You see, we're still waiting for these signs. We're waiting for thunder in the sky and all that. But the Evil One (Satan) is laughing in our faces. He really is. I can see this with my heart. The Evil One is laughing. He is saying, Ha! They think that this is going to happen...that's not what is going to happen. It's going to come right through here! (Estela points to television.) You know, the Evil One is saying he's going to come and take over these people. And they are not going to see or know the power of that evil. They're going to get caught up in looking for other signs.*

Q. Have you seen the astrology, witchcraft, and everything that is now on T.V.?

A. *Yes, these people sit there as if everything is normal. Meanwhile, millions and millions are watching it.*

Q. So, what are we to do?

A. *Well, there's nowhere to go because evil is everywhere you go, even if you left and went up to the hills and became a hermit. Maybe, you know, that would help. But that's not what God is calling us to do. One day, I remember thinking, I don't want to be a part of this. It's uncomfortable, it's ugly... and I was thinking, I want to go into the hills and hide. And then on the next visit from Our Blessed Mother, do you know what she said?* **But I don't want you to go, [to] go to the hills and hide. I want you to stay here, and I want you to do my work.**

Q. She asked you to stay right here?

A. **Because it is only,** *and she keeps repeating this in her messages,* **It is only through the work of people like you that I have chosen, [that] this country will have a chance of surviving the horror that has overtaken the world.**

Q. What kind of work does God want us to be doing?

A. *We must plant the seed. People have their own wills, they will either be converted or say No, I don't really want to hear about this. But what people are doing is going to have a tremendous impact on the world! Tremendous!*

Q. Do you have a spiritual director?

A. *Yes. Father Doug Nohava, of Saint Catherine's Church.*

Q. Can you tell me what Our Lady has said about family in her messages to you?

A. *She has talked a lot about families from the very beginning. I think she is here to help families to heal, because there are so many broken families, because we have hurt each other so much in so many different ways. She has come now to bring these families healing. I think that has to happen. Before a family can become functional and become a true family again, a family of God, the healing has to occur.*

Then the family can come back with love, that unconditional love that Our Blessed Mother speaks about. She has spoken about how we should treat each other as family. She speaks about the reinstitution of families based on God's love, and families dedicated to God.

I think that our Blessed Mother picked a family — and we [the Ruiz family] all work together in this ministry — because we believe with all our hearts that she picked the family as a whole, and not just Estela Ruiz to tell the world that healing can occur in a family. Our family has gone through a lot of healings, and because of those healings, [it] has been able to come back to God and to believe in His love and in His mercy and in the fact that God forgives. As family now we have to learn to forgive each other and to respect each other.

Our Blessed Mother has said to love all our brothers and sisters, with respect and dignity. She has always said it starts with your own family. That is something that has really been missing in our families. We have not been loving each other with respect, and so we insult each other, and we hurt each other, and we do things to each other that break families apart. She is coming to teach us how to function as families and how to be able to make families that are dedicated to God.[1]

Q. Would you say that Our Lady has had a central theme or that her messages revolve around a theme? Is family the main theme?

A. *No. She has different themes. She is here for different reasons, not just family; family is a major part of it. But she has said that she is here for families, that she is also here for the youth. Right now our youth are in a lot of pain. Because they are in a lot of pain, they are getting into things that will destroy them, like drugs and alcohol and gangs. She is here also for the youth. She is calling the youth to come to her. Sometimes you really have to go to her as a mother before you can make your peace with God and with your family, so she has brought a lot of healing to the young people.*

She is also here, she has said, for priests, for the brokenness of the priests. There is a lot of brokenness in our church, and a lot of it has to do with the fact that priests are no different from anybody else. They are human beings, and they, too, have gone through a lot of pain. When they become priests, they bring this pain with them. They have to heal, to come to a healing within their own lives, so that they can become more functional in the Church. I think also she comes to bring her love to the priests, so that their own pain, which they carry with them — and believe me, they do — can be healed.

I guess we can say she is here to heal the problems that exist in this world by bringing us her Son. Because He is the Great Healer, and so who would know better how to do it than His own Mother? So she comes as a mother, not only as His Mother, but ours too, because she loves Him and she loves us. She knows that if we come together with Our Lord Jesus, then the healing will occur.[2]

Q. Has she said anything to you about unity, particularly unity of the church (the various denominations)?

A. *Yes, she has, in the sense that she has said that we must love each other. She has also said that God did not divide people into different religions; man did that. So God does not come to the world and say I come for Catholics, or I come for Protestants, or I come for... God comes for all His people, which includes the people in all faiths, all religions. Every single person that exists is a child of God. The divisions have evolved because man has divided himself, not just by religion. We have also divided ourselves by color and race and in many other ways, rich, poor. We have economic status lower economic, higher economic so many things by which we divide ourselves: different cultures, different countries. Even in our own country, we have categorized ourselves into so many different groups that one of these days we are going to categorize ourselves into so many groups that there are going to be groups of one person. That's going to be awfully lonely. Unless we learn to love each other; no matter who we are, what we are, what we do, what we believe in, and that [unless we learn] God loves us, we will not be able to love each other no matter what.*[3]

Q. Has she said anything about unity within the Catholic Church?

A. *I think a lot of it has to do with the fact that she is coming to bring about healing for priests. Through that healing...will also come about the unity of the church. Within the Catholic faith, the parish and the priest must be united. If these are not united, then people divide also within the parish or within our own great Catholic Church. We have divided ourselves there, also.*

So, she has come also to bring the healing of her Son to our own Church that we may unite, that we may love each other. The greatest word in that is love. A lot of times we won't love people if they won't believe the same as we do. That is conditional love. I love you on the condition that you do this. And if you don't behave that way or do this, then I won't love you. That is conditional love, and as human beings, we have brought that into the world. Our Blessed Mother has said God does not love you with conditions. He loves you, and I love you, and you have to learn that love has to be unconditional.

...As much as we want to get away from it, with the world the way it is, we have dysfunction going on in every family. There is no family that has been exempted from dysfunction in some form or another. The pain and hurts of those things happening around us and within our own families have caused our families to be dysfunctional.

The reason [our families] are dysfunctional is that we have forgotten to love one another the way God intended us to love each other. It is so easy to go out on the street and to say to someone, Oh, I love you. But [it is different] to come back into our own homes and to tell each other within the family, I love you and mean it with all your heart, which means you have to give up trying to control that person.

That is what it means, and that includes parents. When your kids are old enough to start making decisions for themselves and learning to live, then you've got to let them control their own lives. As parents, we still want to control them. We still want to tell them, You should be doing this, and you shouldn't be doing that.

I have seen women come here — forty and fifty years-old —and tell me that their mother is telling them, You should do this and you shouldn't do that. We've tried to control each other in this world. It is hard enough to control yourself, but to control someone else — that is an awful responsibility. We [my husband Reyes and I] say, Allow them to make their own mistakes. I believe that if you love them with all your heart, they are going to make mistakes — the same way you made them — but that the love you have given them and nurtured them with will hold them, and that they will come out of the pain and that they will be better people for it if we just leave them alone.

Power is an important thing in this country. Everyone wants to have power, and that begins all the way at the top from our president on down to the lower levels, to our own job sites. [People begin to] believe that their way is the only way. This is the country we are living in, and because of that, we have a lot of pain. A lot of pain.

We have traveled throughout the country — we have been in twenty-eight states already — and there has not been one place that we have gone where we have not had people come and tell us the tremendous pain [they are in]. There is so much pain, and that pain comes from within the family.

We have heard it all. We have had little kids — little seven year-old kids — come and say, Could you pray for my mother because she is on drugs, or My mom is an alcoholic, or My dad is hitting my mom — would you pray for them? or My dad left us and my mom is by herself. There is tremendous pain, and then we wonder why our kids are on drugs and all these things that are going on.[4]

Q.   Has she said anything about the title of Mediatrix of All Graces or Co-Redemptrix?

A.   *She has never mentioned [those titles] to me. We were in Seattle last week, and a gentleman stood up. We learned later that he was not Catholic. He had a hard time believing all these things and that we call Mary the Blessed Mother of our Church. He got up and said, Do you believe that all the graces that come to man come from the Blessed Mother, that she is the Mediatrix of Graces, and that it doesn't come from God? He was looking to see if I was going to say that she is greater than God.*

I told him the first one who would tell him that she is not greater than God is Our Blessed Mother. She has told me that. I understand it perfectly. I do not love her because I think she is my Savior. I love her because she is my Mother, and she loves me, and that is very special. But Our Lord is the only one who gives us graces.

If Our Lord wants to say to his mother, Here, I trust that you are going to give the graces to your children because I gave them to you, then I am not going to concern myself with where they came from. If He gives them to us straight-out, hey,

*I am open. And if He wants to give them to His Mother to give to me, I still am open. I don't care where they come from. I just know that they come. We can argue about issues and about all these things. And that is what has come to separate us. Because we can't agree on anything. I don't care who gives me the graces. I'm just thankful that someone does. I understand totally and perfectly when our Blessed Mother says, **I am not God. I am not your Savior. My Son Jesus is your only Savior, and that is the only way you can get to Heaven. You can only get to Heaven through Our Lord Jesus Christ. That is the only way you are saved.***

I tell people, If you don't want to hold on to her hand, because Our Lord Jesus gave her to us so that she could help us, and if you want to turn away God's gift of His Mother, then that is your prerogative. I choose to hold onto her hand, because I know where she is going to take me. We can argue about what her titles should be, and we get lost in the issues and then we forget to love God, to really open up to Him and to His Mother.[5]

Q. Wasn't that exhausting for you to see her on a daily basis?

A. *No. Our Blessed Mother is the smartest, wisest woman I have ever met. You know, when you first get married, the honeymoon period? You can't get enough of this wonderful man that you married? You think, I want to be with him every second. That is the way it was. I wanted to be with her every second. I would go to work (because I worked for six months after she came, to finish my contract year) and I couldn't wait. I never [used to] come home for lunch. But [after she started appearing] I used to come home for lunch and pray. She just swept me off my feet.*

She stripped me of all that garbage that I carried, those facades, the conditions I put on life and on the world, the self pride, the feeling that I was the one that controlled my life. There was a lot of work that she had to do with me. Our Blessed Mother, being the perfect and gentle Mother, did it gently. Her presence is a very powerful thing, and so I wanted to be with her every day.

Not only myself, my kids got swept up in that love. Everybody used to come home and huddle at noon, and we would talk about her and her love and God. Then in the evening we would come back, and we would pray together, so we grew a lot in that time.

That is what was intended for us — to grow. We were going to be called to a ministry. We did not know it at that time; we were just enjoying the fruits of her love. Now knowing what our Blessed Mother is like, I tell people to watch out, that she is very sneaky! She steals your heart and then she puts you to work! That is what she did. Every day was the most wonderful thing. It was wonderful.

Saturday we totally dedicate to our Blessed Mother — the whole day. We get up in the morning and I receive the message, then we go on to Mass, and we come back and we begin to work in the yard so that we can get it beautiful, so that people can come here and feel beautiful and know the beauty of our Blessed Mother.

A lot of the work my husband and my sons have done — it's constant. It's always. Now she is really pushing us not only to that, but in our own lives to do things. It is the work of God, because there is such great need, and so she is bringing us to do many other things.

Reyes and I go throughout the country at least once a month, sometimes twice, to speak about Our Blessed Mother's love and about what she is here for, which of course is to bring God back to us. That is also something Our Blessed Mother has started us with. Now that we are hers and she knows it, now she has put us to work.[6]

Q. How does Our Lady come to you? Do you pray at a certain time, or does she call you? Do you know when she is coming?

A. *I can often hear her audibly. You could call it an exterior phenomenon, because I could hear her speaking to me. She would call my name. I could hear her, even if I couldn't see her at the moment, even if I was doing something else. Several times I heard her say, **Come to me. I need to speak to you.** Then I would go into prayer, and she would appear.*

She would give me the directions that she wanted, whatever she wanted to tell me. I got a lot of direction from her, a lot at the beginning.[7]

Q. Did you ever see flashes of light before she appeared?

A. *What happens is, I see the room light up, as if it had been dark and then the sun had come out —that kind of feeling or vision or seeing. I see the room, the light become brighter and brighter, and then the room becomes very bright, especially around the area where she is going to appear. And then I see a misty cloud form at the bottom, and then I see her standing there, on the cloud. She stands on a cloud.*[8]

Q. I read that she comes out of the picture.

A. *I don't think she comes out of the picture. We use that picture and it is very special, and a lot of people have said it seems as if Our Blessed Mother comes out of the picture of the Immaculate Heart of Mary, as well as the other picture [that Reyes painted].*

   I would say probably that she just appears in front of it. Why a lot of people see the other phenomena, I don't know. She touches hearts in many ways through this picture. Hundreds of people have told us that they have seen something from the picture.[9]

Q. Has she been giving you secrets also?

A. *The message that I would like to give is a positive message, and that message is that we have to live in hope because God is still alive in this world, and He is hope and He is love, and that is the message I prefer to give. We do have hope. God loves us and He wants us to love Him in return; these are the words our Blessed Mother says to me. There is still hope in this world, and we cannot give up.*

   If we learn to love each other, one by one, peace will come — to you, to me, and then because this peace comes, we learn to love each other, and then we can go out and learn to love others.

Q. Tell us about the time you heard Mary singing.

A. *We were in Philadelphia. I began to pray and almost immediately started to hear singing. I closed my eyes because I knew the singing to be of heavenly origin. As I closed my eyes the singing became louder. Our Blessed Mother was singing praises to God. As she sang the praises, I could hear other voices in the background joining in praise of God. The words sounded like the Psalms in Sacred Scripture. Our Lady sang in a beau-*

tiful voice about God's greatness, His majesty and His good-ness. This went on for about five minutes, then it stopped and I opened my eyes — Our Lady was there. She proceeded to give me the message for the day. Afterward she asked me to relay a message to the prayer group praying in the other room.

Q. Should people concern themselves with the Evil One?

A. *The Evil One wants to stop the work. He brings false visionar-ies, especially right now, which is such a big thing. But what people are doing — spreading the messages — that is very important. Visionaries don't even come close to that kind of work.*

Q. One time the devil appeared to you instead of Our Lady. How did you know what was happening?

A. *I began to feel the difference. There was a tremendous differ-ence. The first part of the apparition was fast paced and con-fusing and loud. The voice at first was very soft and beautiful and then it got really low and ugly. Then, I knew it was Satan that was there. The Blessed Mother then appeared and I asked her why did this happen. And the Blessed Mother said, "It was allowed so you would always understand."*

Reyes: *Did we mention there was another time where he showed himself. This was at the time when Our Lady was ap-pearing every Saturday. This time, Our Lady told Estela, "I want you to take a message after everybody's gone. It's a spe-cial message that I'm giving to the family." That evening, when Estela went into prayer, I was in my bedroom and I started falling asleep. Then I heard a voice and the voice told me: "Get up and protect her." The voice just came out the same way I'm saying it. But I started falling asleep again. Again I heard the voice: "Get up and protect her." So I realized some-thing was trying to guide me to do this. So when Estela was in the other room, I just kneeled down and I went into heavy duty prayer. When the apparition was over, which was after about an hour, and this was roughly about midnight or so, Estela saw me and I was still in prayer. She looked at me and said, "What are you doing?" And I said "I was just praying." I didn't tell her what had happened. But then we laid down we started talking. And then she asked me, "What were you really doing?" And I said, "Something told me to get up and protect you." She then told me that she had heard footsteps.*

Estela: *I told him [Reyes] that Satan was trying to disrupt me. And he was! But, by that time Our Blessed Mother had already taught me about Satan. She taught me about Satan very well. She told me he will harass you. He will try to give you a bad time. But always remember if you have followed my teachings, he cannot hurt you. Don't ever be afraid of him she said...ever! But be aware that he is around you. He will always try to interfere in the work that I'm doing. So I've stopped being afraid of him, because I know that She can step on his head and he's gone. He's afraid of her. But I know he is there. See, I never believed in Satan before. Our Lady had to teach me right away that there is a Satan. That there is evil. And that we people don't believe that there is. You know, we are under a great delusion, because he is there. And Satan has manifested himself to us several times. But I no longer am afraid of him. Because I know that there is a greater power than he could ever be. But he is there. There's no doubt about it.*

Q. When you say "manifested himself" did you have any visual sightings of him?

A. *No, but he was in a dream one time. It was after Our Blessed Mother had told me never be afraid of him. I dreamt I had gone through the back of our house where we have that big room we use for meetings. I had gone into the office. When I opened the door to the office he was there. He was ugly. And he came at me, with a beastlike noise.*

*He came at me and he was trying to scare me. He made a tremendous sound an ugly sound. He came towards me. I felt my heart, you know...beat. I was scared for a second. Then I heard Our Blessed Mother's voice saying, "**Never be afraid of him.**" So I said to myself, "I have Our Blessed Mother on my side. See, there's nothing he can do to me,"*

Q. You said Mary taught you about the Holy Trinity. Can you tell what she has told you?

A. *Our Blessed Mother is a true Trinitarian. If anybody has studied the messages (the Virgin Mary's messages to Estela), they will see that Our Blessed Mother never finishes, or very rarely finishes, her messages without mentioning the Father, the Son and the Holy Spirit.*

One time I saw her praying. It was during a time when one of our grandchildren was born. We were praying and she appeared. She spoke about the life that had just come into the world and she said that the heavens rejoiced when a soul came into the world. Then she began to praise God in her own way. And when she began to praise God, she began to praise the Trinity. When she prayed to the Trinity, it was as if she went into her own world filled with God and she would praise the Father and the Son and the Holy Spirit. Ever since then I have always known the great love she has for the Three. Since then, I have in my heart come to understand how she's related to all Three in a very special way.

Q. Mary has taught you how much God loves you and in essence loves all of us. Explain the insight you have been given about God's love for His children.

A. *Yes, I think that for me, and I say it openly and publicly to anybody who is going to listen, that the amazing thing for me is not so much that I love God but how much God loves me. What Our Lady has taught me has been so profound, the depth of how Our Lord loves each soul on this earth. That is what she taught me. When she first came to me, she never asked me,* **"How much do you love God?"** *Even though I know that when she came to me I was very limited in the things that I did for God. I did everything, only to the point where I thought this is only what He wants I don't have to do any more than this. I was limited...everything else was done for me.*

But when the Blessed Mother came into my life, she never asked me, **"I came to find out how much you love God,"** *but what She came to say to me is* **"I came to tell you how much God loves you."** *For me that was and has been the greatest, the most profound thing that she has done in my life. Because from then on, I realized the tremendous love that God has for each and every one of us here on earth. And so how could I not answer that love in return? That's how I fell in love with God. Because She came to tell me how much He loved me!*

Q. Was she talking about an unconditional love?

A.   *Yes, an unconditional love. God loved me and Our Lady even says, **"Even sinners that you are."** I knew then that I was totally ignoring Him. Yet, He never ignored me. Never! And neither did she! Even when I was the one that rejected her. Never once does she reject me. I think that if all the world could understand the profound love God has for each and every one of us, there would be just no way that we couldn't respond to that love. There would be no way. Because there is no greater love than the love that God has for us. It's a tremendous love, incomprehensible love. We cannot even begin to understand it. It's so great. That's very special for me. You would think that God would love those who show love for Him. I mean in human terms, that's the way we do it. If they love, we love. If they don't love us, well we kind of strike back. But God doesn't do that. He loves us in our sinfulness, in our rejection against Him and in everything else. He continues to love us in all of that. That is the unconditional love that we as human beings find it very hard to understand. Because we as human beings love conditionally. If people do something for us, then we kind of like him or love him, if they don't behave the way we want them to behave, then we have this thing against them. But that's not how God loves. He loves us. Sinners every sinner that is on this earth, He loves.*

CHAPTER TWENTY-SEVEN

PREPARING HEARTS

In 1830 at Rue du Bac, Paris, the Virgin Mary instructed Saint Catherine Labouré to have a medal struck with the Hearts of Jesus and Mary engraved upon it. Since that time, Heaven has been leading the world to a mystical understanding of the Hearts of Jesus and Mary, their unity, their importance, and how we — with our own hearts — are to imitate and become one with theirs.

For those who are not Catholic, spiritual discussions concerning the Hearts of Jesus and Mary are rare, as outside the Catholic Church, knowledge of the history and significance of this mystery is scarce.

Yet the mystery is not lacking in spiritual and historical reference. A brief examination of the issue provides much edifying insight into the interesting and important concept.

The heart, as a focal point, has always existed in human and spiritual matters. Throughout the centuries, the heart has been used to describe emotions, affections, attitudes, feelings, or the lack thereof. Phrases such as, *"Have a heart, He is all heart,* or *Put your heart into your work* are common. Men are called *"hard-hearted," "tender-hearted," "big-hearted," "warm-hearted," "cold-hearted," "chicken-hearted"* and *"heartless,"* all evidence of the great importance attributed to the human heart in everyday affairs.[1]

In Scripture, the word heart is frequently used to refer to the *"higher part of the soul,"* or the *"interior perfection."* Jesus Christ began His public career by saying that He had come to heal the broken-hearted: ***"The spirit of the Lord is upon me...to heal the broken hearted"*** (Lk 4:18). And when the word heart is used in reference to Mary, it refers to her Immaculate Conception, her fullness of grace and blessedness (cf. Lk 1:28, 42).

Webster's dictionary takes into account the full range of meanings applied to the heart: *"a muscular organ; the emotional, as distinguished from the intellectual nature, as heart and head often disagree ; courage, spirit; a conscience, a moral sensibility; temperament; mood; a man; a person; the inmost character; sincerity."*[2]

Therefore, to understand the heart is to understand the character and personality of a person.

Likewise, the history of referring to the Hearts of Jesus and Mary is certainly well-rooted in Scripture. God's love for man is the essence of His being. Scripture tells us that this love comes from *"the heart of God."* In return, God asks us to love Him with all our hearts.

However, recognizing that our hearts are not capable or worthy of such love, God tells us He will give us a new heart and a new spirit to complete the task. This new heart is the Heart of His Son, Jesus Christ, and it is the fulfillment of a prophecy given in the Old Testament: *"I will give you a new heart, and I will put a new spirit within you"* (Ez 36:26)

Saint John Eudes (d. 1680) explains that, in order that we might know what kind of a new heart and new spirit God promised, He added, *"I will put my spirit, which is my own heart, in the midst of you."*

According to the wise saint:

> *"It is only the heart and spirit of a God that is worthy to love and praise a God, and which is capable of praising and blessing Him to the degree He deserves. That is why, dear Lord, you have given us Your heart, which is the heart of Your Son, Jesus, as also the heart of Your Holy Mother, and the hearts of all the angels and saints who, together, are but one heart, as head and members have only one body."* (Acts 4:32)[3]

Theologians explain that, as God sowed His words into the hearts of His prophets and people and gave them His own heart and spirit, likewise did He sow The Word, His only begotten Son, into the heart and womb of the Virgin Mary. Again, this fulfilled the prophecies of the Lord's coming in the Old Testament: *"Let the earth open and bud forth a saviour."* (Is 45:8) Thus, it was in the heart of this earth — in the good heart of a virginal woman — that the Lord came down from Heaven to save mankind.

From Mary's heart came the purity, faith, humility, love and charity that made her worthy to be the Mother of the Son of God. These same virtues made her worthy to be the Mother of all mankind.

The angel's declaration to Mary that *"the power of the Most High shall overshadow you"* (Lk 1:15) referred to the power to conceive the Son of God, both in her heart and in her womb. This power then gave her the ability to form Him and make Him grow.

In her womb, the two hearts were united in the flesh. Because she was to be the Mother of all God's children, she was also united forever to the children of Adam and Eve, thus making them members of the Body of Jesus Christ.

Over the centuries, as the mysteries of the Christian faith unfolded, Christ's Heart came to be recognized as the symbol of His love for His people. That love was so great that on Calvary, He opened His Heart for them.

As time passed, more and more saints and mystics began to speak of the Heart of Jesus in conjunction with the great mystery of His love. Moreover, they also began to write and speak not only of Jesus' Heart, but also of Mary's Heart, and the union of these Two Hearts with ours.

In 14th Century revelations to Saint Bridget, Mary revealed, *"Jesus and I loved each other so tenderly on earth that we were one Heart."* And concerning a vision of the Passion and Crucifixion, Mary also told her, *"...I boldly assert that His suffering became my suffering, because His Heart was mine. And just as Adam and Eve sold the world for an apple, so in a certain sense my Son and I redeemed the world with one Heart..."*[4]

By the Seventeenth Century, the Lord was ready to manifest His plan that the world might better understand the mysteries of His Sacred Heart and the Immaculate Heart of Mary.

Two saints, Saint John Eudes (1601-1680) and Saint Margaret Mary Alacoque (1647-1690), were two of God's special envoys who helped reveal to the world the love and mercy available to all souls through the Hearts of Jesus and Mary. Since then, many other saints followed suit by writing of the Hearts of Jesus and Mary, such as Saint Francis De Sales, Saint (Louis) Grignon de Montfort, Saint Alphonsus Liguori and Saint Maximillian Kolbe.

From the Nineteenth Century apparitions of Mary, it became understood that, just as Mary brought us closer to Jesus on the natural plane, through her tender heart we are also most easily led to Jesus on the supernatural plane. Likewise, it became evident that, just as Jesus came through Mary the first time, the Lord would now also come through her again, to reign with her as King and Queen of all Hearts.

"These Two Hearts are formed together," said the inner voice to Saint Catherine Labouré in reference to the Two Hearts Mary wanted placed on the back of the Miraculous Medal.[5] But the mystery involved more than just these Two hearts on the medal. There was also an empty space between them, and according to theologians, that space signifies something the Lord told Saint John Eudes:

> *"I have given you this admirable Heart of My dearest Mother, which is but One with Mine, to be truly your Heart also, so that her children may have but one Heart with their Mother... so that you may adore, serve and love God with a Heart worthy of His infinite greatness."*[6]

After Paris, the Nineteenth and Twentieth Century manifestations of Jesus and Mary increasingly emphasized the Sacred Heart of Jesus and the Immaculate Heart of Mary. It became obvious from these revelations that God wanted our hearts to be joined to Theirs in order to truly receive the many graces He wished to give us. Numerous revelations focused on the heart as the key to a deep and true relationship between God and men.

And later, with the revelations at Medjugorje, Mary began to teach us how to achieve this intimate relationship with God. Since 1981, the Virgin Mary has continually called her children to join their hearts with hers and her Son's.

From the very beginning of her apparitions at Medjugorje, the Virgin called for prayer from the heart. And within just a short period of time, numerous Church authorities were proclaiming that Medjugorje, indeed, was the fulfillment of Fatima, where Mary had declared that her "Immaculate Heart would triumph." Stated Cardinal Frantizek Tomasek of Czechoslovakia in 1988:

"I am convinced that Medjugorje is a continuation of Lourdes and Fatima. Step by step, the Immaculate Heart will Triumph."[7]

If, indeed, the Immaculate Heart will triumph "step by step," that same Triumph will happen gradually, "step by step," in each person's heart. And when each heart is united to the Hearts of Jesus and Mary, peace will reign in the world.

At Medjugorje, the call to place our hearts between the Hearts of Jesus and Mary is clear. While Mary's messages there define the moment of Satan's reign and involve secrets of what the future may hold, the majority of the messages are for her children's spiritual growth and welfare. Most consistently, the messages have pointed to the heart — to our hearts and to the Hearts of Jesus and Mary.

Among the messages Mary has given at Medjugorje concerning the heart are the following:

November 22, 1981:
"The heart is a sign of mercy."

March 30, 1984:
"I wish that your hearts would be united to mine, like my Heart is united to that of my Son."

April 21, 1984:
"Raise your hands, yearn for Jesus, because in His Resurrection He wants to fill you with graces. Be enthusiastic about the Resurrection. All of us in Heaven are happy, but we seek the joy of your hearts."

May 23, 1985:
"Open your hearts to the Holy Spirit. Especially during these days, the Holy Spirit is working through you. Open your hearts and surrender your life to Jesus so that He works through your hearts."

December 4, 1986:

"Prepare your hearts for these days when the Lord particularly desires to purify you from all the sins of your past... Prepare your hearts in penance and fasting."

By giving our hearts to God, we are led to consecration. And through consecration, Mary tells us our heart is then side by side with her Son's. Our heart, as we can vividly infer from the Miraculous Medal, is between Their Hearts and is therefore protected. Our heart then joins with Theirs to produce the River of Peace which God wants to flow throughout the world.

Since the call at Medjugorje to change our hearts in order to become more like the Hearts of Jesus and Mary, numerous visionaries and mystics in the last two decades have received the same understanding. We especially see this in the Virgin's messages to Estela Ruiz: In fact, perhaps as much as any visionary, the messages to Estela Ruiz specifically focus on God's call for conversion of the heart. Here are some of those messages given to her:

"This evening I want to ask all of the world, and especially you, my children in the Americas, to help me in the work that I am doing by learning to pray with me to Our Dear and Beloved Lord so that all hearts who want to turn to Him shall find the strength and courage to do so. Those who are already praying to full capacity, continue to do so. But remember, there is always room for one extra prayer. To those who are beginning to learn, I ask that you move forward as fast as possible to learn to pray from the heart. And for those who have not started, begin without any more hesitation, as there is no more time for you to flounder around in doubts and excuses. You must begin to pray with the heart and the faith of a child." [June 16, 1990]

"Open your hearts to love and prayer. Learn to love God over everything else and then learn to love your brothers and sisters around you, starting with your own families mothers, fathers, sisters and brothers. Honor each other and treat each other with dignity and respect.

If you learn to understand that love will win over all evil, and that prayer is the basis to grow in love, and learn to pray, then you will hep me in the work I am doing." [October 6, 1990]

"I have come to guide you not only back to God's love, but to commitment for each other as children of God. I desire to guide you, my earthly children, to understand how important it is to love each other with God's love. It is of great importance for you, all my children in the world, to stop looking at physical differences and to begin to see that God made you of one heart, and that the heart keeps not only your physical body alive, but also your spirit.

"These are times when I come to call all my earthly children to love one another, to become one heart. It is only through love for one another that your world will change and will survive. The holocaust that does away with humanity is anger, hate and greed, and it causes your hearts and spirits to die. Without hearts and spirits that live, you will not find God's peace and love in your lives, and you will continue to hate and hurt each other because it is only through the heart and the spirit that God's love can live in you.

"On this day I ask you to put your differences aside. You have no time to squander seeing each other with hate, jealousy and envy. You have no time to waste on categorizing yourselves at different levels of behavior and existence so that you may judge each other on those terms. You must become one heart in love, respect and dignity for each other, regardless of your differences. If you can become one heart you will learn to understand how God loves all His children. He does not separate you or love one more than the other. You are His creations and each one is special in His love. Open your hearts to God's love and let Him teach you the beauty and greatness of His love." [July 18, 1992]

"It is during these days that many celebrate the coming of my Son into the world, but I come to tell you that,

more importantly, my Son wants to live in your hearts. He wants to dwell in each heart, that each one of His children know and understand the great love He has for them. Many in the world have forgotten His love and suffer, because, not knowing His love, [they] do not know how to turn over the worries and concerns of each day to Him. At present, the world suffers greatly in brokenness and despair because of the pain man inflicts upon each other. Faith and hope do not live in men's hearts; therefore, neither can love, the true love of God, abide in those hearts.

"Our God is a God of peace, and if there is no peace in the world, it is because God has been put aside, is no longer acknowledged and no longer allowed to dwell in the hearts of His creations.

"I come as your Mother, especially during these times when I see you suffer, to remind you, to call you back to faith in your Savior. As the songs of peace and love ring out throughout the world, let them remind you of God's love for you. As you scurry around, remembering my Son in a materialistic and worldly way, I ask that you take moments out to remember Him as He would prefer. Open your hearts to His love. Let not your songs of peace, hope and joy be lost in the wind; rather, use the moments to allow God to enter into your heart and truly abide in you. Then you will understand the reason for His coming into the world, and as you begin to understand that reason, you will also understand why I am manifesting myself throughout the world during these times. It all has to do with Our love for you." [December 19, 1992]

"It is only if men turn their lives to God's truths that this world will be saved. It is only if men begin to open their hearts to God's goodness that your world will turn from the road to destruction it is headed for. It must begin in each heart. I come to ask that each one of you, my beloved children, look into your own hearts. Examine what it is that controls your life. Is it anger and hatred, or is it love, compassion and goodness? Your heart and

soul cannot belong to God's realm if there is hatred and anger, for God is love, compassion and goodness. And if you are united with Him, love, compassion and goodness must reign in your own heart." [January 16, 1993]

"It is today, then, that I come to call you, my beloved children in Washington, to become soldiers, to help me in the work I am doing. If you allow me into your hearts, there is no way you will not become totally aware of my Son's love for you, because as I brought Him into the world that men might have salvation, I come into the world again to remind all my children that there can only be salvation through Him, who has loved all men without limits.

"My children throughout the Americas and through the world, you cannot wait any longer to acknowledge God and His love. You have put Him aside for too long, and now your world sits in darkness and in pain. You, my children, are on the verge of destruction as you suffer in the arms of Satan and his evil that has overtaken your world. I come to invite you to open your hearts and souls with God's love. Allow Him to touch your souls that you may learn to love each other with His love. It is only then that this veil of darkness will be lifted, and peace will come into your hearts and souls, and then throughout the world." [January 23, 1993]

And, just as at Medjugorje, by 1993 in South Phoenix Mary was also calling for hearts to become consecrated:

"I come to the world to help all who will listen to return to His love. With God's grace, I come to touch hearts, to tenderize and prepare souls to receive God's love. There are many lost souls who need and want to return, yet, they do not know how. I ask all these souls to consecrate your hearts to my Immaculate Heart, that I may lead you and guide you to His love. Allow your heart to blend with mine that I may show you the beauty of God's love in your life." [January 9, 1993]

269

This consecration, the Virgin explained to Estela, will lead to the fulfillment of her promises at Fatima, the promise of the Triumph of the Immaculate Heart in the world:

"As you think of me on this feast of my Immaculate Heart, keep this ever present in your hearts: this is the reign of my Immaculate Heart, and I have come to tell the world that God loves you, and as each one understands and believes this, then I ask you to help me by preparing yourselves to go announce the good news to all whom you meet. Together we will be victorious in our battles, until each man and woman understands God's love for them and all humanity. I love you and I thank you for listening to my words." [June 19, 1993]

Thus, following the example of the Fatima children, our consecration brings us into the Alliance of the Hearts of Jesus and Mary. It is an alliance of love, but it is also an alliance of suffering. Just as the Resurrection came through the cross, it is only through the cross that the Triumph of the Immaculate Heart will come into the world.

Through our consecration, then, we are called to go to Calvary with Jesus and Mary. Our hearts become one with Theirs in God's redemptive plan for the world, which will result in peace, the true and lasting peace which will blanket the earth. It is a peace that will spring forth as a result of the love that will rule all hearts.

This is why Estela so often tells the crowds on Saturday nights before they leave, *"Focus on going home and learning to love each other. For if we can focus on the fact that love is what's going to make the peace of the world become possible, then we need to develop love within ourselves, for ourselves and for other people. Then, we can make possible the salvation of souls through the help of Our Lord and Our Lady."*

Indeed, as Estela has stressed time and time again, the essence of the Virgin's messages in South Phoenix is love. Beyond that, *Mary asks very little of us,*

CHAPTER TWENTY-EIGHT

A CELEBRATION OF FAMILY

As the Ruiz family has valiantly sought to do God's will, their heroic actions have not gone unnoticed by Heaven. Not surprisingly, the Queen of Heaven has sought to reinforce and guide their struggle toward sainthood.

Each year at Christmas, the Virgin Mary has given a special message for the entire Ruiz family. She also delivers at Christmas a personal message to each member of the family. These messages, like her public ones, are designed to continue to call the Ruizes closer to God, closer to holiness.

The following private message was given to the Ruiz family on December 23, 1995:

"My Dearest Family, Beloved of My Heart,
    "As we celebrate together these wondrous days, which are always joyous because we remember the coming of My Sacred Son into the world, I bless you with My own very special blessing and I ask our Lord in the Trinity to pour His abundant graces over each one of you.
    "As we begin this moment, when I communicate My words to you, let us begin by praising our Lord, for indeed our souls can rejoice in God our Savior. He is a great and amazing God, always ready to fill our lives with joyous moments so that during moments of sadness we can remember His love for us and have strength to overcome. Now let us thank Him for His goodness in our lives, for everything that He is for each one and for all His wonderful gifts, freely given to each one in this family, for even if the world fails you His love for you will never fail.

We thank Him for loving humanity, even when many in the world do not love Him or even acknowledge Him, for He loves all His children even in their sinfulness. We as His faithful servants however, do acknowledge Him and we proclaim His greatness and profess our own love for Him and His might. We worship Him, we glorify His Name now and forever. His strength and might continues to work through you, His chosen and my chosen and it is only through His doing that you, His weak children have accomplished what you have. My beloved family, never forget to praise Him unceasingly, to thank Him and to recognize that it is only through Him that there is success in your work, for truly it is not your work but His.

"Years have gone by since I came to call you to the work I came to do with you. At this moment I wish that each one of you take a few moments to remember where your life was at when I first came to you. If you take these few moments to mediate, you will remember that even though you believed you loved God, you were still very far from the true faith that God asks of His committed souls. You were a prideful, almost arrogant family, with much self-worship when dealing with your daily tasks. (pause to meditate).....

"Oh, how great our Lord has worked in each one of you, and all you had to do was say "yes" to Me, as I came as His ambassador to seek help from you. It was because God had prepared this family through much prayer. (before) It is through that pride and arrogance that the spirit of intensity was born in you, and it is that intensity that God needed to work His miracles. It is a perfect example of how God can turn bad things into good, for He turned this intensity of pride and self-love into intensity of love of God and love of others. All souls called to sanctity by God must possess a spirit of intensity for it is this spirit that causes the soul to persevere, to continue ahead, not to give up.

"As I bring you to the recent moment you now understand why and how God can work through you.

Everything that has been built is only to help edify the body of Christ, to bring souls out of the darkness that prevails over the world, to defeat Satan and his demons that prowl through the world destroying souls. It is the salvation of the children of god, whom He created to be with Him for all eternity but who have been lost because He gifted all men with free will which would and could have been a loving tribute to Him, but has instead been a source which satan has used to destroy humanity. Satan is having his way during these times, destroying young and old. However, his days of destruction are numbered as God works to restore His reign on earth. You, My beloved, have been chosen by God for this work He works with you and through you, not by your power, but by His power and strength.

"After all these years in which He has asked you to do His work, you have come to understand this truth, that it is through His hand that things are moved and not through you. It moves smooth and easy when you let Him, as a puppet moves when the puppeteer moves the strings. All you have to do is say yes, go along with it and not resist. I no longer tell you there are great things to happen, because you have already seen great things happen. Now you believe because your own eyes have seen, and you cannot deny God's mighty power. It is His work and not yours. Bow down to your Lord and acknowledge His greatness for He has done great things in you and Holy is His name.

[I will now direct words to each one of you, that you may find courage and strength to persevere, to continue to say "yes."]

"As I close My love letter to each one of you, My beloved family, I want you to understand how much I love you, how much each one of you is important to the work of God. I so depend on you not only to take the good news of God's love to all, but I depend that your

*actions also exemplify how much God loves all His chil-
dren in the world. I depend that you continue to say yes
to Me and the work I am doing with you. Take care of
each other, for I cannot afford to lose any of you to evil.
Pray for each other and with each other. Do not forget
that prayer is the foundation of your work. Without prayer
there can be no success. Prayer keeps you focused on
The One who makes everything possible and nothing is
impossible for our God. Love each other with mutual respect and dignity and help each other edify God in your
souls. Remember that you cannot do anything on your
own. You must always count on Jesus for your strength.
Ask the Holy Spirit of God to give you what you need to
continue this great work of saving souls. Ask Him for
strength, courage and fortitude. Ask Him to help you to
persevere in this great task, for it is not an easy one to
tackle. You have come to see God's greatness by being
involved in His work. You can no longer deny your God
because now you have seen with your own eyes the Glory
of God. It is an awesome experience to be united this
close to your Lord and Creator. As he works with you,
you have been privileged to see and feel Him in the things
that have come to pass. You will see many more things
happen as God continues to reveal Himself to you more
and more and you will have no other recourse but to praise
Him constantly. It is only when your heart and soul understand the magnitude of His greatness, that as the Angels who know Him, will sing His praises without ceas-
ing. Together let us pray; all glory, honor and praise be
to Him who created us, Who loved us in the beginning,
now and forever. Glory to Him, Who desires to be one
with us, even as undeserving of His love that we are. I
raise My arms to give you My motherly blessing, asking
that you remain faithful to your God and His work, THAT
SOMEDAY THE WHOLE WORLD MAY EXALT HIM
BECAUSE YOU MY BELOVED ONES WERE HERE
ON THIS EARTH TO DO WHAT WAS NEEDED TO
BE DONE. I love you for you are My special children on
whom I depend."*

CHAPTER TWENTY-NINE

FROM EVANGELIZATION
TO SAINTHOOD

Though the Virgin Mary's many messages to Estela Ruiz can be studied and meditated upon for months on end, one thing seems clear. Her numerous words are, in essence, a call to action, strong and aggressive action, and we must consider them seriously if we are to grow in holiness.

Indeed, Mary told Estela that her intention is to call us to repentance and conversion. But a deeper consideration of the messages reveals that the Virgin expects even more. Once firmly on the path of conversion, she calls us to evangelization, and eventually to Sainthood! Most importantly, all of this can be achieved by falling back on her main focus of love. For by loving oneself and one's neighbor, the desire to more closely imitate God - and then to spread his good news with others - will naturally spring forth.

Such and invitation to perfection is not new. Indeed, it is a call which the Church has sounded throughout the ages, which has become even more audible in recent years. In 1993, Cardinal Ratzinger defined our times and the Church's mission:

> *"We need to overcome the anathematization of the sacred and the mystification of the profane. By its nature, Christianity is a ferment and a leaven; the sacred is not something closed and completed, but something dynamic. The priest has received the mandate: 'Go, therefore, and make disciples of all nations.'"* [1] (Mt 28:19)

And Cardinal Ratzinger explained what this means in today's world:

> *"But this dynamic of mission, this inner opening out
> ampleness of the Gospel, cannot be translated by formula:
> Go into the world and become the world yourselves. Go
> into the world and conform yourselves to its 'worldliness.'
> The contrary is true. There is God's holy mystery, the gos-
> pel grain of mustard seed, which does not identify with the
> world, but is destined to be the ferment for the whole world.
> Therefore, we ought again to find the courage to return to
> the sacred. The world does not need that we agree with it,
> but that we transform it."*[2]

Cardinal Ratzinger's statement is clear. The world will change for the better only if it is confronted with Christ's call for Christians to evangelization. Each generation has faced this challenge, and today's generation is no different, no less called.

While the horrors of today's modern world leave one feeling overwhelmed by so much evil, in actuality they call us to new heights of Sainthood. For God will not let the courageous defenders of His truth enter the battle alone.

Catholic Columnist Robert Moynihan captures this sentiment in his article *"One Man Against the World"* (*Inside the Vatican*, August-September 1994):

> *"Catholics have historically believed that God raises
> up saints in each age to keep the Church from being de-
> stroyed. This belief further holds that even if the Church's
> enemies enjoy success after success, and its defenders suf-
> fer seemingly endless humiliations and torments, the
> Church will always triumph over those who would destroy
> it even to the end of time ... The greater the enemies, the
> greater the saints, and even more wondrous the victory
> granted by the Almighty."*[3]

Indeed, the Church has always awaited the emergence of its next Saints, individuals who seek to share and celebrate their victories in God's name.

Over the centuries, the Catholic Church has declared hundreds of Saints, many of whom are obscure and unknown. Yet, there can never be too many saints, as they are true friends of God. Their words and lives speak constantly of His presence, and they draw us closer to Him either by insistence or by accident.

In a sense, the saints are non-denominational a sort of "interreligious elite," so to speak. Even outside the Catholic Church, one can sense an irresistible attraction toward them, one which often engenders admiration, and even imitation.

And it is imitation which Mary seeks from her children, particularly the imitation of heaven's greatest earthly allies. The present times are greatly troubled, and thus require the assistance of greatly pious individuals. Their emergence and fervor is particularly crucial now, as they help encourage and maintain the presence of God's truth in the world. Indeed, Mary makes it clear God is seeking Saints; great Saints! For these are the times foretold to raise up such individuals.

As far back as the Fifth Century, Saint Augustine spoke of the great souls who would arise during the latter times. *"Who are we,"* exclaimed the great saint, *"compared to the saints and faithful of the latter times, who shall be called to resist the attacks of an enemy unchained, who we can feebly resist while he is yet in chains?"*[4]

Centuries later Saint Louis de Montfort prophesied:

> *"The power of Mary over all devils will be particularly outstanding in the last period of time. She will extend the Kingdom of Christ over the idolaters and Moslems, and there will come a glorious era in which Mary will be the ruler and queen of human hearts."*[5]

Saint De Montfort added:

> *"The training and education of the great saints, who will appear toward the end of the world, is reserved for the Mother of God. These great saints will surpass in holiness the majority of the other saints as the cedar of Lebanon surpasses the lowly shrub. These great saints, full of grace and zeal, will be chosen in order to oppose the enemies of God who will appear everywhere. By their word and example these saints will bring the whole world to a true*

veneration of Mary. This will bring them many enemies, but also much blessing."[6]

Approximately one hundred years after Saint de Montfort's proclamation, the elders of the Church again noted the urgency of approaching times, and issued a call for an army of saints. Catholic French theologian, Father P. Huchedé, wrote in 1884, the same year as Pope Leo XIII's famous vision of a coming war between God and Satan:

"God, who never fails to raise up men equal to the wants of the times apostles burning with zeal, martyrs endowed with courage, doctors whose learning and erudition vindicated Truth in all its beauty will raise up at the critical juncture a vast number of extraordinary people, adorned with all the noble qualities and virtues of all the saints of preceding ages."[7]

Father Huchedé concluded: *"If the Church be compared to an army drawn out in battle array, we have reason to believe that Jesus Christ, her Captain, would receive the best soldiers to withstand the most terrible shock... Not only saints, but also the angels will hasten to the standard of the cross and aid the Church in this, her great tribulation."*[8]

Saint Louis de Montfort, Saint Augustine and Father Huchedé all foresaw our times. Saint Augustine knew that a day would come when hell would be let loose, while the Reverend Huchedé saw the approach of the times of Tribulation. And according to the Virgin Mary's messages, both visions were correct. As Mary told Estela Ruiz on December 4, 1993, ***"It is during these special times that Satan has unleashed all the powers of hell so that his evil may not allow God's children to be saved."***

One year later, Mary explained to Estela in even greater detail what was happening:

"Satan has unleashed all the demons in hell, and I have come to help you, each and every one of you, to resist

this evil which is so powerful throughout the world. You, My children, are not blind, and you can see this evil that is so evident all over. You can feel him trying to destroy you and thus overtake all whom he can. Many of you do not know how to fight him. I am here to help all those who desire to be helped, but you must open your hearts and allow me to touch them, that through My guidance and love you may turn to your God who is your salvation."

"As time moves on and Satan accelerates his attacks on the world, you must know how to defend yourselves, how to be saved through our Lord, by His Mercy and goodness. If you allow Me to touch your hearts and lead you to salvation, you thus become strong of spirit and become the defenders of God's goodness and love.

"God sees Satan's attacks and does not leave you and has never left you helpless. He is also around you, wanting and desiring that you turn to Him out of love. Only He can give you the strength to overcome Satan's attacks. Never has it been harder for you, My earthly children, to resist. However, Satan cannot overpower you if you have our Lord's strength in you. for that to happen, you must allow God to rule your life for He will give you strength and courage and help you go against the evil that pervades the world. Then you will become a powerful instrument of God, and you will receive salvation through your love for Him. He loves you, and He wants each one of you to return that love. Let me help you because as your heavenly Mother, I want nothing more than to lead you to Him, Who awaits." [October 1, 1994]

The Virgin's messages to Estela, as well as her work with the Ruiz family, clearly chart what awaits the world. A great victory of good over evil is in store, for even with hell unleashed, God will now bring into the world His greatest Triumph.

This coming Triumph was promised at Fatima, and has been prophesied throughout the world in modern times. Mary repeatedly tells Estela that God calls His faithful to share in this Triumph, for He is ready to fulfill the prophecies of Saint Augustine,

Saint De Montfort, and Reverend Huchedé. And in order to do so, He is calling for Saints!

Early in her apparitions to Estela, Mary revealed this fact:

"This evening I want to remind you that if you have heard me call to you and have decided to change your lives and made a commitment to Our Lord to love Him and follow Him, you must being to understand what changes are required from you to live up to this commandment. I want to remind you that I am calling you to sanctity. Please, my children, do not let this word scare you. These are times in the world, especially in your land, that God is last and few people are, or want to be, committed to Our Lord. Our Lord has been set aside by many, trader for other priorities that belong to the world, and God has become a stranger in your land. It is precisely for this reason that those that have heard my call can truly work to become saints. By helping me in my work to bring others to God, you can become a saint. Never has there been a greater need to work to bring my lost children of the flock.

"To be a saint, you need to be living my messages as I teach you to love. First, to guide you to love God, Our Lord, above everything else, and then to love your brothers and sisters in the world. To become a saint, you must being to change your priorities from desiring the world and what it offers, to desiring God and what He offers. Our Lord offers you His Kingdom and everlasting life.

"When you being to love God over all other things, you being to free yourself from the bond that holds you to worldly things that can become your perdition. Once you are free from worldly concerns, you can begin to give yourself to the work that is waiting for you that of loving and helping others find God in their lives. Once you find the purpose for which you were brought into this world and follow it, you are on your way to your sanctification.

"The world awaits you. Begin today." [March 17, 1990]

Two years later, Mary confirmed to Estela that God's plan is to raise up Saints:

"The world is in need of the goodness and love of God. As Mother of God, Jesus our savior, I come to touch men's hearts so that out of those who hear me and answer, God can raise up great Saints, men and women of great faith, strong in their love of God, trusting God implicitly, men and women obedient to God's commandments. These holy people will become the light of God, bringing peace and joy to all, in God's name." [March 20, 1993]

"My children, I seek those who can believe this truth, even just a few. I seek those few who have opened up to this truth, those whose faith allows them to live in hope, for you are the ones whom God is seeking to raise up as great saints to lead the world to faith, hope and love. May I ask you this day where you are at, you who listen to my words? Are you the one who will lead men to faith and hope, or are you still following, seeking to find the way?" [May 8, 1993]

And nine months later, Mary spelled it out even more clearly:

"I as your Heavenly Mother, come to invite you, to encourage you to open your hearts to God's Spirit that He may change you from weak humans to great soldiers of His work. For it is during these times that god seeks to transform all who will allow Him into great Saints.

"Those who are willing to allow the Spirit of God to work in them, open your hearts that He may fill you with courage, strength and commitment. If you say yes to Him, He will fill you with His Spirit and will do great things through you.

"I call on all of you, my children, who have heard my voice and made changes but have gotten lukewarm in your zeal for God, to open your hearts to receive God's Spirit, that He may fill you to make you strong again. He can turn you into souls who are not afraid of the world,

who God can use to bring other souls to His love. These are times that God is seeking men and women of strong commitment to His great Commandment, which is to love Him above all else, and through his love, love your brothers and sisters in the world. I come to invite you, all those who love me, to this call. Who will answer this great need?" [February 5, 1994]

For Reyes Ruiz, the fulfillment of his prayer was near complete. When he first arrived in Medjugorje, Reyes begged Mary to help his family. But by the end of his week-long pilgrimage, he pleaded for their sainthood. In retrospect, and particularly in light of the Blessed Virgin's messages to Estela, Reyes' prayer was divinely inspired.

But Reyes' prayer was not confined to his own family. Through the apparitions of the Virgin Mary to Estela, God was also revealing that all families are being called to sainthood.

Undoubtedly, the Ruiz family was responding. Besides the conversions of Estela, Little Rey, Armando, Fernando, Peggy and Leticia, their other children were also firmly wrapped in Mary's arms. What Mary wanted to totally accomplish through this family was still a mystery, but by late 1996, even more of the mystery was unfolding.

As Cardinal Ratzinger elucidated the call to evangelization, the Ruiz family began to understand that their path to sainthood would involve evangelical work. Indeed, Mary had said right from the beginning that the family would evangelize, but at first, no one knew what her words meant.

As it is obvious the Virgin Mary's messages to Estela Ruiz reveal that Satan is attempting to conquer America with his evil plans, so is it no accident God desires to use America for the exact opposite to lead the world back to Him and to open a new era of Evangelization of the Gospel of Jesus Christ. The Ruiz family now understand this picture as true apostles on the road to holiness, and they soon discovered their role in heaven's great endeavor.

Ever since the beginning of his papacy, Pope John Paul II has pointed to the new times. In a prophetic manner, through numerous encyclicals, talks and prayers, the Holy Father has expressed his belief that mankind is approaching a *"New Advent"* in the Church, a new outpouring of the Holy Spirit as at Pentecost. The Holy Father has continuously emphasized that the Church must prepare for this era with a new wave of evangelization, and, he insists, our model must be Mary, the *"Star of Evangelization."*

In 1988, during the closing liturgy of the Marian Year, the Holy Father specifically defined Mary's role in the approaching third millennium:

> *"From today onward, with full confidence, let us place under the vigilant intercession of Holy Mary, Sister and Mother of the Church, the passage to the year 2000 and the prospect of the third millennium... Blessed Mary is the guide in this new exodus toward the future... Oh Holy Mary, trustingly we invoke you..."*

Likewise, the Holy Father said in 1987 that America is to help lead the Church in its mission of evangelization. According to Pope John Paul II:

> *"With the third millennium just around the corner, the Americas should feel called to unveil to the Universal Church and to the world a new zeal for evangelization that will in turn unveil the power of Christ's love toward all people, and sow Christian hope in hearts thirsting for the living God."* (Marian Helpers Bullentin, 1995)

It cannot be denied that Mary's apparitions and messages play a role in this evangelization. Theologians have noted that the Medjugorje apparitions began not long after the Church's proclamation of the New Evangelization, which was in response to Pope Paul VI's 1975 encyclical *EVANGELI NUTIANDI.*

Monsignor Dr. Kurt Knotzinger of Vienna, who is president of the Ecclesiastic Institute's *"Marian Lourdes Committee,"* wrote in 1992:

> *"In 1981, at the time of the proclamation of a New Evangelization, the events at Medjugorje began to take place.*

The messages given to the young visionaries repeat the basic Gospels. Anyone who recognizes the need for a New Evangelization and who takes seriously the events of Medjugorje, will realize that the fundamentals of the New Evangelization may be clearly seen in the messages given to the visionaries... The argument for compromising the messages of Medjugorje in relation to Evangelization lies on a completely different level: in personal experience, it lies in the fruits of Medjugorje. Wherever people live the messages, spiritual life grows, A Christian renewal takes place. This is precisely the goal of the New Evangelization."[9]

Indeed, this seems to be exactly what Mary is doing through the Ruiz family. It involves a call to *Sainthood*, achieved through a call to *Evangelization*, and ignited and spurred by the simple call to *Love*.

On April 8, 1994, the Virgin brought a unique and special message to the Ruiz family which concerned their newly-founded project of instruction for evangelization. Mary told them:

"I am with you during these times and especially today to let you know that I love you, and that being part of each one of you, I share in your pain and in your joys, for I am your Mother, your confidant and your friend. I am with you in your moments of happiness as well as your moments of tribulation.

"You live in an imperfect world because there are many who do not know God and His love for them. There are many that do not know that my Son came to the world to save men from their net of sin. Some have heard of it (the salvific act of Jesus), but do not understand it. There is chaos and turbulence in the world, and sometimes it seems to you that there is no way out of it.

"Yet, here I am with all of you in these turbulent times to call you out of this turmoil. Here I am to tell you that it is possible to live in peace. You have heard my call and believe. Know how hard it is to have total confidence in God and how hard it is to turn your life and control to

your God. It is so hard to trust Him, because you see the chaotic times and you do not believe God is at work, that His hand is in the world. In your own small world, you do not see men changing, converting in great numbers. Yet, as your heavenly Mother, who sees the hearts of all my children throughout the world, I tell you that there are many, many souls being touched by God. You must believe me and trust and have faith. I want your lives to be the examples of faith that matches the faith of those who have gone before you as saints and whose lives are written down as models for you to follow.

"How can God touch His children on earth? What is it that He does to call all His children to conversion? He touches souls such as yours, and because you have been open to His touch, He works a miracle in you. As your hearts change and you come to be His faithful children, He fills you with His Holy Spirit and makes you His servants, those who seek to win souls for Him. He depends on you!

"You have started a project that has as its goal to bring men to God. Do you believe that it is because of your greatness that it will flourish? I must warn you that you do not allow this thinking to take over. It will be because of God's greatness that it will blossom, and only when you keep your mind and eyes focused on this will it grow. It is the Holy Spirit working in you that will allow these great thing to occur, for it is the Holy Spirit who will give you courage, strength and faith because these are gifts from God to you, so that His Kingdom on earth will grow, so that those who are lost will be found and will have an opportunity to be saved.

"Never forget prayers, praying as I instructed you during my message in December. Begin by praising Our Lord and thank Him for His goodness and faithfulness to you, for He loves you and gives Himself to you through His Holy Spirit each day. After you thank Him and praise Him, begin to ask for all those who do not know God as their Savior. Ask Our Lord to touch them in His own

special way, that they may become ready for your work and your words that will come from His Holy Spirit. As that their hearts become softened and opened to Him.

"And for yourselves, ask that each day you will allow Him to reach you more intimately. Ask for humility, for that is what saints are made of. Ask for faith, to believe God's goodness and greatness and that with Him anything is possible. Ask that your faith grow bigger than the greatest tree that grows from the mustard seed. Ask to learn how to be kind and loving to one another, to have tender hearts for all men, no matter who or what they are, for remember that only God can be the judge of souls. You are called only to love and serve. I guarantee that if you can understand this and do it, you are on your way to becoming a 'saint.' Remember then, that a saint is humble, that he or she trusts and believes in the Lord and that he finds his greatest joy in loving and serving others. I ask each one of you to measure at what level you are on your love and service to others, and as you go through life, work to become better and better.

"Leave your worries and concerns of everyday life to He who knows better than you what you need. Those worries and concerns keep you away from doing God's work. Have faith that He will take care of it, even when it doesn't seem to be happening.

"Know that I am with you at each step of the way for you are my beloved ones, and I am your Mother."

Sainthood! That's what it's all about. Nothing in life, Mary repeatedly explained to Estela, should be considered a higher call. And clearly, Cardinal Ratzinger, Saint Augustine, Saint Louis de Montfort and Father Huchedé were saying the same thing. We live only one life, and that life should be dedicated to striving to do God's will. For as members of the Body of Christ, each of us is called to this end.

Pope Pius XII clearly defined our times and the call to sainthood through evangelization in his 1943 encyclical, *MYSTICI CORPORIS*. Wrote the Holy Father:

"No one, of course, can deny that the Holy Spirit of Jesus Christ is the one source of whatever supernatural powers enter into the Church and its members. For the Lord will give 'grace and glory,' as the Psalmist says. But that men should persevere constantly in their good works, that they should advance eagerly in grace and virtue, that they should strive earnestly to reach the heights of Christian perfection, and at the same time, to the best of their power should stimulate others to attain the same goal - all this the heavenly Spirit does not will to effect unless they contribute their daily share of zealous activity. For divine favors are conferred not on those who sleep, but on those who watch, as Saint Ambrose says."

Not surprisingly, by late 1994, the Virgin Mary again made this same plea for Saints at Medjugorje:

"I am with you and I rejoice today because the Most High has granted me to be with you and to teach you and to guide you on the path of perfection. Little children, I wish you to be a beautiful bouquet of flowers which I wish to present to God for the day of All Saints. I invite you to open yourselves and to live, taking the Saints as an example. Mother Church has chosen them, that they may be an impulse for your daily life." [October 25, 1994]

And indeed, this call is addressed to everyone, including the least of her children, those who believe themselves to be the most isolated and alone, or the least worthy of her motherly concern.

Just ask Little Rey...

Rosie Ruiz Cardenas with husband Ron and daughter Veronica

CHAPTER THIRTY

THE TOP OF THE MOUNTAIN

As they sit next to each other, with a handful of friends and family, a deep peace and total serenity seem to emanate from Reyes and Estela Ruiz. Though not yet saints, they have accepted the Virgin's call to holiness. They know that they have been charged with an important task. This does not escape them. But they also know that it is not up to them alone.

God and time and of course, the Blessed Virgin are on their side.

So within themselves, peace abounds and flows, as the song says, *"like a river."* And that peace within surges forth in the form of joy. Especially when the Ruizes break into their own favorite songs, like *"Bendito, Bendito"* or *"Oh, Maria,"* one can truly see how the Queen of Peace has changed their lives, and how their peace and joy are fruits of that change.

It has been a complete and permanent change.

A local newspaper, the *Phoenix New Times*, ran a story on the Ruiz family in the summer of 1992. While trying to emphasize the apparitions, the reporter, Deborah Lake, couldn't help but focus on something else. Though she affirmed all the basics – yes, Mary was appearing to Estela with serious messages, and yes, the event was supernatural and strange – Lake kept drifting to another topic. The real story, according to this article, was the Ruiz family.

According to the article, the Ruizes demonstrated amazing love, deep, true and contagious love. What's more, the love they freely offer is unconditional. It is available both to the strong and proud, as well as the weak and insecure. They have love for the elderly and for children. They even have love for the desperate. And always, they have great love among themselves as a family, which is why they are able to love so many.

The entire Ruiz family

The reporter marvelled at it all. Profiling a young street boy whom the family befriended named Ricky, Ms. Lake beautifully painted the Ruiz family portrait:

> *"It is clear that despite his [Ricky's] profession of faith, his greatest influence in these matters is the Ruizes themselves. They say, "I love you" to total strangers! he (Ricky) marvels. He remembers an evening when Estela was explaining to Ricky and some other street kids that her home is their home. She talked about how this was a haven for us – to come off the street, come away from the violence. There wasn't a dry eye in here. He adds that Reyes demonstrated his love for the teenagers that night by literally kissing all their feet.*
>
> *"This display of love is, amazingly, a technique that the former tough guy is now trying to emulate among his friends. It is easier to go up and pick a fight with some body than to tell him, "I love you," he (Ricky) observes. They think you are gay. It's not that, though. Everybody needs to be loved.*
>
> *"Later in the evening, before he'll [Reyes} allow a visitor to leave the house, he insists on throwing his arms*

around them in the symbol of acceptance he has learned to extend."[1]

While this portrayal of family love and tenderness is accurate, the Ruizes themselves take no credit for it. For this loving picture, they are quick to tell you, was totally masterminded by the Almighty.

Indeed, God put His hand on their family, a worldly American family totally mired in the problems of the present age. God put His hand on their family, and He rebuilt it, healing it with His love and mercy. And then, He sent it forth into the world as a living example of what He can do with all families, if only they say *"yes"* to Him.

Rather than accolades, this is what the Ruiz family would have the world learn from their story. Just as Estela claims no greatness in herself as a visionary, the Ruizes proclaim no greatness in their new life or work. God did it, they insist. He did it all.

For the Ruizes, it's simple. They are all weakness, God is all strength. They are nothing, God is everything. No manufactured humility can be found here. This story, the Ruiz family will tell you, could only be written in one way. They could have never saved themselves, and if their Heavenly Mother had not intervened by God's grace, this story would not have such a hopeful ending.

At Fatima, Mary warned that great suffering would come into the world if mankind did not change its ways. Clearly, almost eighty years later, this has occurred.

Yet, at the same time, God is saying that the solution to the world's problems is not terribly complicated. People must begin to love each other, not hate. And this must start, the Virgin Mary insists, in the family. Once firmly rooted in the family, this love will rapidly spread throughout the world.

The Ruiz family has avidly accepted its role as a cornerstone for this change. There can be no doubt about this. It is why the Virgin has chosen to visit them.

While some cities erect monuments to the false god Quetzalcoatl, in other cities God is erecting monuments to the family. These monuments are not made of stone, but of flesh, living monuments like the Ruizes, whose words and deeds of love will greatly outlive any human edifices Satan can inspire. For while it was the family Satan sought to destroy in the Twentieth Century in order to rule the world, so it will be that God will save the world through the family.

Indeed, Pope John Paul II declared that 1994 was the year of the family. He insisted that the many sufferings and attacks satan has waged against families and against the Holy Father himself will be the foundation for the third millennium of families, when the world will be filled with children of God. Said John Paul II:

> *"The Pope has to be attacked, the Pope has to suffer, so that every family and the world may see that there is a higher Gospel: the Gospel of suffering by which the future is prepared, the third millennium of families, of every family, and of all families."*

Likewise, in 1996, the Holy Father moved again in a special way to save the family. As Pope Benedict XV did when all his attempts to end World War I failed and he instituted the invocation, *"Mary, Queen of Peace, pray for us,"* to the Litany of Loretto, so has Pope John Paul II now moved to add to the Litany of Loretto, *"Mary, Queen of the Family, pray for us."*

Reyes Ruiz, the pillar of the Ruiz family, doesn't spend much time thinking about it all. He can't. There's too much to dwell on, and there's too much work to be done in the meantime. And besides, Reyes knows well that no one can truly understand what God is doing. God's ways are a mystery, and they always have been. And while small links of this mystery may at times seem clear, more often than not, God retains the depth of the mystery to Himself.

But one cannot help but ponder the mysteries. One cannot help but contemplate how *"The Woman Clothed in the Sun,"* Our Lady of Guadalupe, appears to have come to the *"Valley of the Sun,"* Phoenix, Arizona, in what many say are apocalyptic times. One also ponders the significance of how Pope John Paul II, the only Pope to ever visit the Basilica of Our Lady of Guadalupe in Mexico City also came to Phoenix, Arizona, in 1987, just one year before the apparitions of Our Lady of the Americas to Estela Ruiz. How these events link together no one fully knows. But they appear to connect. And God seems to want us to understand, though not completely, that they do connect.

Indeed, the heavenly thread which ties together Mary's apparitions at Guadalupe, Fatima, Medjugorje and South Phoenix will never be fully understood, but it's there. And it appears that God is completing something which He began long ago.

However, the focus of these and all apparitions should remain the messages God has sent, and how His messengers have chosen to respond. For in listening to the messages and observing their fruits, change in the world will come about.

Juan Diego, indeed, responded with zeal and love. And the children at Fatima an Medjugorje, in all their innocence, also reacted affirmatively to the Virgin's call. Without a doubt, the same positive response was given by the Ruizes, especially Reyes Ruiz, the faithful steward of Our Lady of Guadalupe and of the legacy of his forefathers.

Faith and devotion seem to be the ultimate keys here. As Reyes not only proclaimed his faith he practiced it and grew in it. He never gave up, not even when he and his family journeyed through their own valley of death.

But beyond the valley are the hills and mountains the high points in the world and in life. Numerous writers over the centuries have noted the mystical nature of the mountaintops when portraying man's relationship with God. It is not surprising, then, that Mary has frequently appeared to visionaries on the tops of mountains, as has the Lord Himself.

God's interaction with His people on mountain tops is well documented in the Bible. The events on Mt. Tabor and Mt. Sinai are two of the strongest Scriptural examples of God interacting with His people on mountainous summits. Symbolically, it has often been noted that if one can climb the mountain, whatever his mountain in life may be, he will then arrive at a special moment and place prepared for him by God. And like Moses on Sinai, a mountaintop encounter with God is sure to be a unique moment between a soul and its Maker.

After a long life of devotion to the Church, Reyes Ruiz has certainly reached one of these moments. Up until May of 1995, he still held down his job in the Hispanic Ministry Office of the Diocese of Phoenix, but he's near the top of his mountain.

No, Reyes still hasn't completely won the fight. No, he doesn't feel like a victor. Much work remains, and he is forging ahead with enthusiasm.

Indeed, the Ruizes' schedule is a busy one. Speaking invitations abound for the whole family, and their organization, *Mary's Ministries*, conducts weekly prayer meetings and a three-day retreat every December on the anniversary of the apparitions. Most incredibly, what began as a small local Montessori school in their back yard for special kids, has now grown to a 300 student, full time endeavor involving almost the whole family. Even a huge school building is expected to be soon erected.

In addition, the family has started a school of evangelization, *Project America*, which educates lay people on how to spread love and social justice throughout the community.

Project America is one of 700 evangelization schools in the world associated with Evangelization 2000 (E2000). E2000 is a 1990's worldwide evangelization movement set up by the Catholic Church. The movement promotes worldwide prayer campaigns, organized regional and worldwide retreats for priests, published information, and evangelization through the media. Reyes Ruiz is more than excited about this new challenge as he and his family continue to work for God and their "Mujer Bonita."

In fact, the Virgin indicated to Estela that the reason she came in the first place was to prepare the family for this very endeavor.

"Mark this day," Our Lady told the Ruizes, *"the work of evangelization you are now to begin is the legacy you will leave your family."*

And so, it seems obvious to the outside observer that Reyes has reached a spiritual peak. God, through His great patience and mercy, has molded a willing soul to His plan. And now the plan, like all of God's successful plans, will bear fruit, fruit borne from suffering and many years of perseverance.

Somehow, the same reporter from the *Phoenix New Times* again noted how this mystical unfolding of God's plan for Reyes Ruiz was reaching perfection:

> *"The changes for Reyes are not as marked. One gets the feeling, watching him blow leaves from in front of the Jesus statue on a Saturday afternoon, watching him energetically polish the wooden shrine and rig the speaking system, that he has only found his element. He seems to revel in, rather than resent, the sacrifices this new life demands. These socks were given to me, these pants were given to me, these shorts were given to me, these shoes were given to me! he says proudly of his unremarkable clothes. I prayed four months for the shoes! Somehow it has always worked out!*
>
> *"Where Estela needs to be drawn out a little, Reyes is always ready to testify, to pray in a deep voice, to talk at length about the family conversions that now link him to his wife and children as though they have themselves all become the beads on a rosary. He refers constantly to this one and that one: Have you heard Little Rey's story? A beautiful story! A beautiful story! Have Fernando and Leticia told you their story? A beautiful story!*
>
> *"You get the feeling that there can never be enough stories for him, that each transformation within the family is proof to him that life is at last working out."*[2]

But while the world can only reflect on what has happened in Reyes' life, Heaven sees everything with crystal clarity. The plan, the Ruizes' role in Heaven's plan, must have the entire celestial court rejoicing. And anchoring it all, by God's grace, is Reyes' life-long best friend, the Virgin Mary.

Indeed, in December of 1993, Mary brought a special Christmas gift for Reyes, her loyal friend. It was a gift of love, appreciation and celebration. Mary relayed the following message through Estela:

"My dear son Reyes, you are the light of my heart, and my heart rejoices in your devotion and love for me, your mother and friend. Thank you for all you do and are for God's glory. Thank you for your perseverance and your commitment. Thank you for your love of God and your love of the family He gave you. Thank you for everything you have done for me and for striving to be obedient to God's laws and Commandments.

"Continue to be the example of perseverance to your family because it is important that they know that it is possible to live a life dedicated to God until death. They have found out it is not easy through their own experience, but it is through your commitment and devotion that they will know that it can be done if you love God enough.

"This is a good time of year for you, all of you. You, my son, have seen God work great miracles in those you love. You have seen much healing in your family and you have seen your older son give his first step towards the truth. Your change in behavior toward him, the unconditional love I asked for, has brought him to this first step. Continue to nurture him and his family with this same love, that the process of his return be rapid yet lasting.

"You have asked me about a dream you had where you saw many souls gathered around the shrine. Indeed, God gifted you with a vision that will occur someday, but it may not be in your lifetime. It is hard for many to discern God's true gifts to the world, and for this reason the recognition of my coming to this place will take many years. Our Lord wanted you to know that your devotion to me and your prayers for the salvation of the world will bear much fruit. It is already bearing much fruit, but God's glory and greatness will be recognized much later. Do not let this concern you any longer. Continue to do the work God has given you and be prepared to be refreshed as the Holy Spirit of God becomes your refreshment and your guide. you cannot imagine the joy that lies ahead with your God and my God. Be assured of my ongoing love for you and let my blessings bring you peace."

Two years later, Reyes Ruiz, Sr., was diagnosed with cancer of the prostate gland. For Reyes, it was another cross he accepted. In fact, several years before he had asked for it by name. Again, the Virgin sent her love in a special message to him.

On December 2, 1995, the Virgin Mary told Reyes,

"My dearest son,

"Remove all fear and anxiety from your mind. I know you and everything about you. So you must know me and know that I would never abandon you in your hour of need.

"Am I not your Mother and your intimate friend? Let no fear overtake you, for I will be there with legions of angels to thwart any evil that might come against you.

"I am faithful to you as you are faithful to me. I bless you on this day with a very special blessing, asking Our Lord, My son Jesus, Who is the great healer to allow His Spirit to fall upon you, be with you now and forever until you meet with Him in glory, and I ask that all fear and anxiety be taken away from you. I ask God Our Father in heaven to hold you in His loving and powerful arms that all peace and calmness that comes from Him over-shadow you and that you feel His loving Presence. I am with you now, always and forever, with my love and sup-port. I am your Heavenly Mother and your intimate friend and I love you."

To put it mildly, Reyes Ruiz's heart danced as he read the mes-sage from his *"Beautiful One."* Nothing more profound or more special could have been given his soul. But more *was* to be given. Two weeks later, Mary again wished him to know in a special way, her great love for him.

"My dearest and most faithful son, Reyes the elder,

"You continue to be My special one, a sweetness to My heart and a joy. Your children have inherited your intensity of life in God, but as yet have not reached the level you experience. God knows your love for Him as He knew Job's faith in Him. He knows everything about

you, your strengths, your weaknesses. He knows how you strive to do away with those things that are not pleasing to Him, and how you strive to make your life be totally pleasing to Him, and that in itself is pleasing to Him. You are a strong and mighty warrior of God, which in turn makes you very pleasing to My heart. Continue to make Jesus My Son your model using your great strength with great humility. Always acknowledge to the world that God has done great things in you and that all that you are you owe to Him. Never question My love for you or doubt that I am with you every moment of your life, for you are My beloved and I am well pleased with you."

Indeed, Reyes Ruiz is today a refreshed man, a man totally renewed in his love and commitment to God. Not only has the future promise of heavenly and earthly blessings renewed him, but his present life filled with family and personal peace is his new strength. For peace has come to the Ruiz family.

Reyes prayer was heard and embraced by heaven. God's blessings continue to pour out upon them, bringing an even deeper peace and joy, a peace that can be found especially in their work.

❖❖❖

It's Saturday night, December 2, 1995, and the entire family wastes not a second preparing for the Virgin's arrival at their annual anniversary retreat. Each has a designated role to ensure a successful outcome. For Mary's work in Phoenix is not over. She is still appearing, she is still speaking. And God is perhaps still sending SIGNS to confirm her presence. Like the Yucca tree, new reports have Mary in a tortilla, on a billboard in Yuma, Arizona, and on a bathroom door in Phoenix, although the Virgin hasn't confirmed any of these curious sightings to Estela.

But in spite of the unusual claims, the greatest sign of Mary's presence is always peace, and this peace is most certainly felt in the Ruiz household in South Phoenix. As the pilgrims pour into the yard, Leticia greets them with a smile from behind a table where prints of the Virgin Mary are available. Her sister-in-law Petty is out in front helping the sick and wheelchair bound, while Peggy's husband Armando warms up the crowd by leading the Rosary.

Afterward, outgoing Little Rey ventures to the platform and grabs the mike. Reyes Sr. wraps his arms protectively around Estela, then holds his breath and listens carefully as 'Little Rey' fires off a 'little humor.' Though his stand-up comedy is all clean and fun, one can see from the look on Reyes' face that his son is testing dangerous waters with his jokes about nuns and priests. The three-day retreat is full of work and enjoyment, though, and even oldest son, Isidore and his wife Louisa, come in to put on a puppet show for the many children who are always present at the Ruizes.'

Inside, the rest of the family is quite busy. Little Rey's wife Norma and Estela arrange the chairs in the living for those who will be inside for the apparition. While youngest family member, Tony, darts in and out running errands for anyone in need. Later that night, there's a Rosary procession around the city block, and all the Ruizes can be seen at their posts, like sentinels guarding the children God has sent them.

The annual retreats come and go quickly. As the family pulls together, gets the job done and starts to wind down, the Virgin

Ruizs' Annual Retreat

Mary's message has once again been delivered, along with more love than you'll find in most places throughout the world that day. Indeed, God's peace and blessings pour out from the Ruiz family in abundance to be harvested and collected by the people of God, in His time and in His way.

Reyes Ruiz understands this. And he is pleased.

But after so much peace and joy from the weekend's work, after so many blessings have been granted and so much grace poured out, it's time to start to pray again.

So as the Virgin Mary's message of the day is circulated and faxed the world over, late that same night Reyes' hands are again busy at work... steadily moving once again over his beads.

For Reyes Ruiz, he will not reach the very top of the mountain in this lifetime, for each day he remains alive he knows he can climb a little higher.

EPILOGUE

TO THE WORKERS IN THE VINEYARD

As of the printing of this book, the Blessed Virgin Mary continues to appear to Estela Ruiz. Our Lady now comes to Estela on the first Saturday of each month. As she did on a weekly basis for over five years, Mary still brings to Estela each month a message for America and for the world.

However, in December of 1994 the Virgin Mary told Estela Ruiz that her messages were now going to be especially directed toward those who *"have responded"* to her call and to those who were *"doing God's work."* Here is the last message received by Estela Ruiz prior to the printing of this book.

MESSAGES FROM OUR LADY OF THE AMERICAS TO ESTELA RUIZ NOVEMBER 2, 1996

"My Dear Children,
"I have come into the world to be with you because I love you and because God loves you. I was sent to touch hearts for our Lord, and I came to reveal God's love to the many children whom He created. I wish to speak to you about your Creator, Whom many have failed to acknowledge because of lack of faith.

"Who is this God Whom I serve and Who calls you to be His own, not as a master over his slaves, rather as a loving Father over His loving children. In the present times, God has become such a mystery to His people. They

301

do not know Him, nor do they recognize His work among them. I have come to help you, My beloved children in the world, to clarify this mystery, to announce to you the good news that God is alive among you, that His Spirit lives and dwells within His people. It is only to those whose hearts are closed, whose souls have not opened to feel His love that God seems to be such a mystery. God is not a mystery My beloved, His is real and He works His wonders in your world and in your lives if you let Him.

"So many wait for signs, great signs to convince those who do not believe, to believe. Many desire and wait, that God move His mighty hand in power to bring about faith among the non-believers. Yet, I say to you, do not desire this from Him because our God is more merciful than just. He desires to bring souls to faith through love — His love, reflected in your eyes and in your hearts to others. That He desires to win souls through the faithful is a mystery and can only be explained and understood by those that understand His incomprehensible love for humanity. Some wait for His justice so that men may come to faith, yet justice is not what God will use to bring His children to faith at this time. Even now, His mighty power is bringing souls to His love, but that power is not destruction by His Hand, it is the mighty power of His love for His children. He has sent the Court of Heaven to rescue His children from sin and self-destruction. I have told you that I come to wage war against Satan and the power of evil, who seeks to destroy souls. Do you think My coming has been in vain? I have come accompanied by the Court of Heaven, and with the Spirit of God ever by My side. Do you believe there is no power in this force? Yes, My children, you know many souls have returned to God as I have manifested Myself throughout the world and it is not because of your power but because of God's mighty power and His love for His people on earth. As the power of God is revealed through you, His faithful, many souls will be won — many souls have been won! It is though you His faithful that God works at the present time and it

is only those, whose hearts are opened to this truth, that can see His mighty Hand at work over the world.

"Expect many other wonders through the Hand of God as He works though His faithful people to bring about the salvation of many. I repeat to you My beloved, God is love and He is merciful. He sent Me to you out of His love. He has sent the Court of Heaven out of His love. This is the truth I bring to you — His tremendous love for you!

"I love you and I thank you for listening to my words."

FOR THE SOUL OF THE FAMILY

NOTES

CHAPTER ONE - *"Medjugorje was Supposed to Take Place"*

[1] Deborah Laake, "Awe in the Family," *Phoenix New Times 15, July 1992, 25.*

CHAPTER THREE - *"Dancing with the Devil"*

[1] Quote is taken from the bi-monthly newsletter written and circulated by Sister Emmanuel Maillard, the author of the book, *Medjugorje: The War Day by Day.*

CHAPTER FIVE - *Two Sides to the Same Coin*

[1] T. Howland Sanks and John A. Coleman (Contributing Editor-Joseph P. Fitzpatrick), *Reading the Signs of the Times* (Mahwah, New Jersey: Paulist Press, 1993) 28-29.

[2] Ibid., Laake, 26.

CHAPTER SIX - *America: Good, Bad, and Very Ugly*

[1] Joe Klein, "Whose Values? from *Newsweek* (New York: Newsweek, Inc., 8 June 1992), 19.

[2] Ibid., 21.

[3] Vittorio Messori, "Mystical and Realistic" in *Inside the Vatican* (New Hope, Kentucky: St. Martin de Porres Lay Dominican Community Print Shop, October 1993), 12.

[4] Richard Ostling, "The Generation that Forgot God" in *Time* (New York: Time, Inc. 5 April 1993), 19.

[5] Michael Brown, *The Final Hour* (Milford, Ohio: Faith Publishing Company, 1992), 260.

CHAPTER SEVEN - *Power and Prestige*

[1] Ibid, Laake, 22.

[2] Kristy Lynn Nabhan, "Estela Ruiz: Portrait of a Marian Visionary" (Thesis presented to Arizona State University) May, 1994. 27.

CHAPTER EIGHT - *Let It Convert All the Americas*

1 Michael Brown, *The Final Hour* (Milford, Ohio: Faith Publishing Company, 1992). 215.

2 Ibid., 310

3 Kraljevic, Svetozar O.F.M., (Michael Scanlan, T.O.R.-editor) *The Apparitions of Our Lady at Medjugorje* (Chicago, Illinois: Franciscan Herald Press, 1981), 125-126.

4 Ibid., 126.

CHAPTER NINE - *"Good Morning: Daughter"*

1 Jayne Clark, "Praising Arizona" from *Pittsburgh Post Gazette* (Pittsburgh Pennsylvania: Pittsburgh Post Gazette 23 January 1996), Cl.

CHAPTER ELEVEN - *The Woman Clothed with the Sun*

1 Francis Johnston, *The Wonder of Guadalupe* (Rockford, Illinois: TAN Books and Publishers, 1981).

CHAPTER TWELVE - *A Decisive Battle*

1 Daniel J. Lynch, Our Lady of Guadalupe and her Missionary Image (St. Albans, Vermont: The Missionary Image of Our Lady of Guadalupe, Inc.) 19.

2 Ibid. 20.

3 Ibid. 20.

CHAPTER THIRTEEN - *The Return of Quetzalcoatl*

1 Daniel Schorr, "Violence on TV: So, what' new?" *USA Today* 13 February 1996 9A.

2 Ibid. 9A.

3 Michael H. Brown, *Prayer of the Warrior* (Milford, Ohio: Faith Publishing Company, 1993) 70-72.

4 Daniel L. Lynch, *The Call to Total Consecration to the Immaculate Heart of Mary* (St. Albans, Vermont: Missions of the Sorrowful and Immaculate Heart of Mary, 1991) 26.

5 Rev. Randall Paine, ORC, *His Time is Short: The Devil and His Agenda.* (St. Paul, Minnesota; The Leaflet Missal Company, 1989) 11.

CHAPTER FIFTEEN - *A Woman Molded to Perfection*

1 Webster's Dictionary (Twentieth Century - Unabridged Version) (no publisher or date given)

[2] Francois Abbe Trochu, *St. Bernadette Soubirous* (Rockford Illinois: TAN Books and Publishers, Inc., 1985.

[3] John M. Haffert, *Her Own Words to the Nuclear Age* (Asbury, New Jersey: 101 Foundation, Inc., 1993) 92.

[4] Ibid. 92.

CHAPTER SIXTEEN - *"I want you to learn to love each other"*

[1] Dirvin, Father Joseph., C.M. *Saint Catherine Laboure of the Miraculous Medal* (Rockford, Illinois: TAN Books and Publishers, Inc., 1984) 83.

[2] Ibid. 84.

[3] Ibid. 84.

[4] Ibid. 84.

[5] Ibid. 91.

CHAPTER SEVENTEEN - *The Diagnosis*

[1] *Associated Press - Time CNN Poll*, January, 1995.

[2] *Pittsburgh Catholic CNS Poll*, June 11, 1993.

[3] Richard Ostling, "The Church Search" from *Time*, 5 April 1993.

CHAPTER EIGHTEEN - *Our Lady of Conversion*

[1] Author's interview with Fr. Robert Faricy in San Diego, California, June 14, 1994.

[2] Ibid.

CHAPTER NINETEEN - *"Like John the Baptist"*

[1] Ibid., Nabhan, 46.

CHAPTER TWENTY - *A Gold Mine of Revelation*

[1] Ibid., Laake, 27.

CHAPTER TWENTY-ONE - *Pearl Hunting*

[1] Eddie Doherty, *Wisdom's Fool* (Bayshore, New York: Montfort Publications, 1987) 13-14.

[2] Ibid., 58-59

[3] Ibid., 60-61

[4] Ibid., 62-63.

CHAPTER TWENTY-TWO - *For the Soul of the Family*

1 Thomas W. Petrisko, *Call of the Ages* (Santa Barbara, California: Queenship Publishing Company, 1995) 100.

2 Thomas W. Petrisko (editor), Article from *Our Lady Queen of Peace - Special Edition I* (Pittsburgh, Pennsylvania: Pittsburgh Center for Peace, 1991) 3

3 Richard Langley, *Signs of the Time...Apparitions, Visions and Locutions Concerning the Last Times Before the Glorious Return of Our Lord Jesus Christ* (no publisher given, 1991) 112-122.

4 Ibid. 105-106.

5 Ibid. 161-162.

6 Scott and Kimberly Hahn, *Rome Sweet Home* (San Francisco, California: Ignatius Press, 1993) 28.

7 Kristy Nabhan, "30 East Cody Street" (Thesis proposal submitted to Arizona State University, 13 April 1993) 10.

CHAPTER TWENTY-THREE - *Armando and Fernando Come Home*

1 Ibid., Trochu, 96-97.

2 Ibid., Laake, 26.

3 Ibid., Nabhan, 10.

4 Ibid., Laake, 26.

5 Ibid.

CHAPTER TWENTY-SIX - *The Greatness of God*

1 Mary Catherine Fairborn, "An interview with Visionary Estela Ruiz" from *Signs of the Times* (Sterling Virginia: Signs of the Times, March/April 1993) 6-12.

2 Ibid.

3 Ibid.

4 Ibid.

5 Ibid.

6 Ibid.

7 Ibid.

CHAPTER TWENTY-SEVEN - *Preparing Hearts*

1 Fr. Francis Larkin, SS.Cc., *Understanding the Heart* (Orlando, Florida: Reconciliation Press), 1975.

2   *Webster's Dictionary* (20th Century - Unabridged Version - no publisher or date given) 796.

3   Ibid., Petrisko, 234.

4   Ibid., 247.

5   Ibid., 249.

6   Ibid., 249.

7   Ibid., 260.

CHAPTER TWENTY-NINE - *From Evangelization to Sainthood*

1   Cardinal Joseph Ratizinger, "Presentation of the Encyclical Veritatis Splendor" from *Inside the Vatican* (New Hope, Kentucky: St. Martin de Porres Lay Dominican Community, March, 1993) 14-17.

2   Ibid.

3   Robert Moynihan, "One Man Against the World" from *Inside the Vatican* (New Hope, Kentucky: St. Martin de Porres Lay Dominican Community, August-September) 40.

4   Rev. P. Huchede, *History of Antichrist* (Rockford, Illinois: TAN Books and Publishers, 1968) 28.

5   Article from *Our Lady Queen of Peace - Special Edition II* (Pittsburgh, Pennsylvania: Pittsburgh Center for Peace, 1992) 28

6   Ibid., 7.

7   Ibid., Huchede, 28.

8   Ibid., 28.

9   Msgr. Dr. Kurt Knotzinger, "Medjugorje and the Call to New Evangelization" from *Medjugorje Gebetsaktion Mary Queen of Peace-27* (Vienna, Austria: Gebetsaktion Maria-Konigin des Friedens - no date given), 21.

FOR THE SOUL OF THE FAMILY

SELECTED BIBLIOGRAPHY

Aqulina, Mike (editor). *Pittsburgh Catholic*. Pittsburgh, Pennsylvania: Pittsburgh Catholic, 11 June 1993.

——, "As the Third Millenium Draws Near" in *Inside the Vatican*. New Hope, Kentucky: St. Martin de Porres Lay Dominican Community Print Shop, January, 1995.

Brown, Michael H. *The Final Hour*. Milford, Ohio: Faith Publishing Company, 1992.

Brown, Michael H. *The Prayer of the Warrior*. Milford, Ohio: Faith Publishing Company, 1993.

Chandler, Russell. *Doomsday*. Ann Arbor, Michigan: Servant Publications, 1993.

Collins, Thomas and Thomas W. Petrisko (editors) *Our Lady of the Americas*. McKees Rocks, PA: Pittsburgh Center for Peace, 1994.

Conway, John. "Catholics learn to spread faith door-to-door" from *The Catholic Sun*. Phoenix, Arizona: The Catholic Sun, 7 April 1994.

Craig, Mary. *The Mystery of the Madonna of Medjugorje Spark from Heaven*. Notre Dame, Indiana: Ave Maria Press, 1988.

Davis, James D. "Marymania" from *Sun-Sentinel* 26 September 1992.

Dirvin, Father Joseph, C.M. *Saint Catherine Laboure of Sister Mary of the Holy Trinity*. Rockford, Illinois: TAN Books and Publishers, Inc. 1987.

Doherty, Eddie. *Wisdom's Fool*. Bay Shore, New York: Montfort Publications, 1987.

Fairborn, Mary Catherine. "An interview with Visionary Estela Ruiz" from *Signs of the Times*. Sterling, Virginia: Signs of the Times, March/April, 1993.

Feeney, Robert. *Mother of the Americas*. Still River, Massachusetts: The Ravengate Press, 1989.

Gobbi, Don Stefano. *Our Lady Speaks to Her Beloved Priests*. St. Francis, Maine: The National Headquarters of the Marian Movement of Priests in the United States of America, 1988.

———. "Guadalupe, 1531 Our Lady Comes to the Americas" from *Mary's People* (Supplement of *Catholic Twin Circle* and *National Catholic Register)* 26 December 1993.

Haffert, John M. *Her Own Words to the Nuclear Age*. Asbury, New Jersey: Lay Apostalate Foundation, 1993.

Haffert, John M. *You, Too!* Asbury, New Jersey: Lay Apostolate Foundation, 1995.

Hahn, Scott and Kimberly. *Rome Sweet Home*. San Francisco, California: Ignatius Press, 1993.

Huchede, Rev. P. *History of Antichrist*. Rockford, Illinois: TAN Books and Publishers, 1968.

———. Immaculate Conception Novena (prayer pamphlet - no publisher or date given).

John Paul II, Pope. *Crossing the Threshold of Hope*. New York: Alfred A. Knopf, 1994.

Johnson, Francis, *The Wonder of Guadalupe*. Rockford, Illinois: TAN Books and Publishers, Inc., 1981.

Jones, Gregg, "Urban Church is Aztec reminder" from *National Catholic Register*. Encino, California: Twin Circle Publishing Company, 1994.

Klein, Joe. "Whose Values" in *Newsweek*. New York: Newsweek, Inc., 8 June 1992.

Knotzinger, Msgr. Dr. Kurt. "Medugorje and the Call to New Evanglization" from *Medugorje Gebetsaktion Mary Queen of Peace-27*. Vienna, Austia: Gebetsaktion Maria-Konigin des Freidens (no date given), 21.

Kraljevic, Svetozar O.F.M. (Michael Scanlan T.O.R.-Editor). *The Apparitions of Our Lady at Medjugorje*. Chicago, Illinois: Franciscan Herald Press, 1981.

Laake, Deborah. "Awe in the Family" in *Phoenix New Times*. Phoenix, Arizona: Phoenix New Times, 5 July, 1992.

Langley, Richard. *Signs of the Time...Apparitions, Visions and Locutions Concerning the Last Times before the Glorious Return of Our Lord Jesus Christ*. (no publisher given), 1991.

Larkin, Fr. Francis, SS.CC. *Understanding the Heart*. Orlando, Florida: Reconciliation Press, 1975.

Lynch, Daniel J. *Our Lady of Guadalupe and her Missionary Image*. St. Albans, Vermont: The Missionary Image of Our Lady of Guadalupe, Inc., 1993.

Lynch, Daniel J. *The Call to Total Consecration to the Immaculate Heart of Mary*. St. Albans, Vermont: Missions of the Sorrowful and Immaculate Heart of Mary, 1991.

Moynihan, Robert. "One Man Against the World" from *Inside the Vatican*. New Hope Kentucky: St. Martin de Porres Lay Dominican Community, August-September, 1994.

Nabhan, Kristy Lynn. "Estela Ruiz: Portrait of a Marian Visionary" (Thesis presented to Arizona State University), May, 1994.

Nabhan, Kristy. "30 East Cody Street" (Thesis Proposal submitted to Arizona State University) 13 April 1993.

Ostling, Richard. "The Church Search" from Time. 5 April 1993.

———. "Our Lady of Ocotlan" (pamphlet) from *Fatima Family Messenger*. Steubenville, Ohio: Merciful Mother Association, 1992.

Paine, Rev. Randall, ORC. *His Time is Short: The Devil and His Agenda*. St. Paul, Minnesota: The Leaflet Missal Company, 1989.

Peers, E. Allison (editor) *Dark Night of the Soul A Classic in the Literature of Mysticism By St. John of the Cross*. New York: Bantam DoubleDay Dell Publishing Group, Inc., 1959.

Perkes, Kim Sue Lia. "Virgina Mary appearing in Valley, the faithful say" in *The Arizona Republic*. 13 November 1994.

Perkes, Kim Sue Lia. "Voices in the Desert" in *The Arizona Republic*. 16 August 1989.

Petrisko, Thomas W. *Call of the Ages*. Santa Barbara, California: Queenship Publishing Company, 1995.

Petrisko, Thomas W. *The Sorrow, the Sacrifice, and the Triumph The Apparitions, Visions and Prophecies of Christina Gallagher*. New York: Simon & Schuster, Inc., 1995.

Pius XII, Pope. *"Mystici Corporis" - Encyclical Letter of His Holiness*. Boston, Massachusetts: St. Paul Editions (no date).

Ratzinger, Cardinal Joseph. "Presentation of the Encyclical "Veritatis Splendor" from *Inside the Vatican*. New Hope, Kentucky: St. Martin de Porres lay Domincan Community, March 1993, 14-17.

Rengers, Christopher, OFM Cap. *Mary of the Americas Our Lady of Guadalupe*. New York: Alba House, 1989.

Rourke, Mary. "Seeing and Believing" in *Los Angeles Times*. Los Angeles, California: Los Angeles Times, 7 July 1994.

Sanks, T. Howland & John A. Coleman. *Reading the Signs of the Times*. Mahwah, New Jersey: Paulist Press, 1993.

Schorr, Daniel. "Violence on TV: So what's new? *USA Today* 13 February 1996.

———. "The Splendor of Truth" in *Inside the Vatican*. New Hope, Kentucky: St. Martin de Porres Lay Dominican Community Print Shop, November 1993.

Trochu, Abbe Francois. *Saint Bernadette Soubirous*. Rockford, Illinois: TAN Books and Publishers, Inc., 1985.

Webster's Dictionary (Twentieth Century - Unabridged Version - No Publisher or Date given)

White, Gayle. "Apparition followers see warning in recent events" from *The Atlanta Journal The Atlanta Constitution* 12 June 1994.

ABOUT THE COVER

After a pilgrimage to Medjugorje, cover artist and designer, Gerry Simboli, found that most of the assignments coming her way were of a spiritual nature. She has designed and illustrated video jackets for *Marian Apparitions of the 20th Century, The Father's Gift* and a new video about the effects of abortion called *Don't Cry Mary*. *The Bridge to Heaven* book jacket is also her work.

Gerry and husband Joe, a talented designer and woodworker, have created sculpted religious works in wood. One of their creations is the Mother of the Holy Eucharist monstrance where the Mother of God, with humility and in shadow, holds the luna containing the Blessed Sacrament over her heart.

For further information about this monstrance, you may write to:

Simboli Design
Box 26
Cheyney, PA 19319
(610) 399-0156

Visit your local bookstore for other great titles from:
QUEENSHIP PUBLISHING

Call of the Ages - Thomas W. Petrisko
The Apparitions and Revelations of the Virgin Mary
ISBN # 1-882972-59-7 .... $11.95

His Power is Among Us - Patricia A. Kelly, Ph.D.
The Story of a Healing Ministry
ISBN # 1-882972-39-2 .... $6.95

The Gift of the Church - Msgr. Bob Guste
*Current Questions and Objections about the Catholic Church and
Down-to-Earth Answers*
ISBN #1-882972-01-5........................... $7.95

Facts on Acts (of Apostles) - Rev. Albert Joseph Mary Shamon
ISBN #1-882972-65-1........................... $8.95

**Prepare for the Great Tribulation and the
Era of Peace, Vol. III** - John Leary
ISBN #1-882972-72-4........................... $8.95

The Coming Chastisement - Br. Craig Driscoll
ISBN #1-882972-41-X $1.95

The Light of Love - Patricia Devlin
My Angel Shall Go Before Me
ISBN #1-882972-53-8........................... $8.75

Marian Apparitions Today - Fr. Edward D. O'Connor
Why So Many?
ISBN #1-882972-71-6........................... $7.95

Lord Jesus Teach Me to Pray - Sr. Lucy Rooney and Fr. Robert Faricy
A Seven-Week Course in Personal Prayer
ISBN #1-882972-55-4........................... $5.95

A Guide to Healing the Family Tree - Dr. Kenneth McAll
ISBN #1-882972-64-3........................... $8.95

Pray, Pray, Pray
A Special Collection of Prayers, Meditations, Poems and Readings
ISBN #1-882972-21-X $6.95